A T

NEGRO BUILDERS AND HEROES

The University of North Carolina Press, Chapel Hill, N. C.; The Baker and Taylor Company, New York; Oxford University Press, London; Maruzen-Kabushiki-Kaisha, Tokyo; Edward Evans & Sons, Ltd., Shanghai; D. B. Centen's Wetenschappelijke Boekhandel, Amsterdam.

E. M. Brawley.

NEGRO

BUILDERS

AND

HEROES

By

BENJAMIN BRAWLEY

PROFESSOR OF ENGLISH, HOWARD UNIVERSITY

*

. . . the large hearts of heroes.
—WALT WHITMAN

*

CHAPEL HILL

THE UNIVERSITY OF NORTH CAROLINA PRESS

1937

To the Memory of my Father
EDWARD MacKNIGHT BRAWLEY

PREFACE

THE PRESENT work is intended as an introduction to Negro biography. Much in it naturally has also to do with history and literature. The endeavor has been to consider practically all the great spheres of achievement, and among the figures included are not only men and women prominent in the past but also a number of those who are now in mid-career.

It happens that not within recent years has there been a biographical work with the aim of this. There have been one or two books dealing with people of to-day, but nothing that thus attempted to survey the whole field or to include characters as widely different as John Jasper and Blanche K. Bruce, or Sojourner Truth and Maudelle Brown Bousfield.

While the earlier chapters are mainly devoted to individuals, the later ones have had to deal with several persons. This does not mean that people prominent to-day are less important than those of a hundred years ago; it is simply a sign of progress that in any line of work there are now so many to be considered.

I am conscious of many debts. More than once there has come back something said to me years ago by Mrs. Booker T. Washington. I was editing a little book of speeches and asked if I might include one or two selections from the addresses of her husband. "Use anything you please," she said, "and use all for the glory of God."

Several of my colleagues at Howard University have given me the benefit of their learning or experience, especially Dean Numa P. G. Adams, Dean William E. Taylor, and Professors Frank Coleman, James V. Herring, and Hilyard R. Robinson. Some friends working elsewhere have also helped on special points, among them Professor Gordon B. Hancock, of Virginia Union, and Mr. Charles H. Williams, of Hampton Institute. To one and all I extend my thanks.

To several New York publishers I am indebted for the privilege of using brief selections from books on their lists —to the Frederick A. Stokes Company for quotations from Peary's *The North Pole* and Henson's *A Negro Explorer at the North Pole;* to Dodd, Mead and Company for the quotations from Dunbar; and to Harcourt, Brace and Company for the poem by McKay and the lines from DuBois's *Black Reconstruction.*

BENJAMIN BRAWLEY

Washington, D. C.

January 1, 1937

CONTENTS

ILLUSTRATIONS

NEGRO BUILDERS AND HEROES

Mother Africa

AFRICA IS A vast continent. It contains over 11,500,000 square miles, and is between three and four times as large as the United States. From Cape Town to Cairo is a distance of 5,000 miles, and the farthest points east and west are 4,650 miles from each other. The lake system of Central Africa is equaled only by that of our own Great Lakes, and four mighty rivers—the Nile in the North, the Zambezi in the Southeast, and the Niger and the Congo on the West Coast—rival the Mississippi.

Not all of the land is equally fertile, for between the Barbary States and the Sudan is the Desert of Sahara. In the central and southern portions, however, are the most notable flora and fauna in the world. Here are the antelope, the hippopotamus, the giraffe; the ostrich, the python, and the crocodile. In the North are the olive, the date, the fig; in the South the baobab, the banana, and cotton. The gold and diamond mines are unsurpassed in richness. Neither Asia nor Europe can equal the wealth or the dreams of this lonely continent. It was the home of the Pharaohs and of Cleopatra. It has nourished the Carthaginians and the

Ethiopians. It has also seen such traffic in human lives as the world in all its history never saw before.

The population is of many different types. The natives (perhaps a hundred and fifty million in number) are anywhere from four to seven feet in height. They range all the way from the Central African Bushman to the warlike Zulu and the cultivated Egyptian. In the North are the Algerians and the Moors, people partly of Hamitic or Semitic stock. In the region of the Upper Nile are the Ethiopians, even more a mixed nation. On the West Coast are the Negroes, and in the vast region extending two thousand miles south of the Sudan are the many related Bantu tribes. On the continent also are three million Europeans—Englishmen, Germans, Frenchmen, Italians, Portuguese, Spaniards, Boers—living mainly in cities and towns near the coast. What might not be the future of Africa with such a medley of races?

When, in the fifteenth century, the first modern explorers came to the continent, they found a country by no means entirely savage. Five hundred years before, there flourished in the Sudan the Negro kingdom of Ghana. By the middle of the eleventh century this had a capital built partly of stone, and a king with an army of two hundred thousand men. Early in the thirteenth century the kingdom of Melle, five hundred miles north of the Gulf of Guinea, began to take the place of the older Ghana, and for a hundred years was the leading power in this part of the world. Three hundred years later, in the great bend of the Niger River, rose Songhay, largest of the Negro empires. Its chief ruler was Askia, a student and organizer who built up an empire nearly as large as Europe. We are told that he was obeyed in the farthest corner of his dominions as well as in his own palace. Such was Africa at its best, before the European came with his greed and his firewater.

The center of the slave-trade was the coast for two hundred miles east of the Niger River. From this region came as many slaves as from all the rest of Africa together. In 1441 Prince Henry of Portugal sent out Antam Gonsalves, who captured three Moors on the African coast. These men offered as ransom ten Negroes whom they had taken. The Negroes were brought to Lisbon the next year, and in 1444 Portugal began the regular trade from the Guinea Coast. For fifty years this country enjoyed a monopoly of the traffic, the slaves being taken first to Europe and then to the Spanish possessions in America. Spain herself joined in the trade in 1517, and as early as 1530 William Hawkins, a merchant of Plymouth in England, took from the Guinea Coast a few slaves. In 1562 Captain John Hawkins, son of William, also went to the West Coast, intending to take to the New World the persons whom he captured. From that time forth there were many such voyages. England thought the slave-trade so important that in 1713, in making the Peace of Utrecht, she insisted on having for thirty years the exclusive right to transport slaves to the Spanish colonies in America.

This traffic in human lives continued throughout the eighteenth century and for some decades into the nineteenth. As early as 1726 the three cities, London, Bristol, and Liverpool, alone had one hundred and seventy-one ships engaged in the trade. But this was not to continue indefinitely. Through the efforts of such men as William Cowper, William Wilberforce, and Thomas Clarkson, the conscience of the English people was at last awakened. Even men who had profited by the traffic were aghast at the stories unfolded. Slavery in the British dominions was abolished by an act of 1833, and in the United States by a proclamation thirty years later.

Now arose another evil. The travels of Livingstone and

Stanley revealed to Europe the riches of the so-called Dark Continent, and soon there was a mad scramble for territory. The most notable advance was that of the British in South Africa. By 1890 England had not only widened her boundaries over Bechuanaland and Zululand, and extended her influence in Rhodesia, but had also won the province of Nigeria and gained a foothold in Egypt. France came to control the whole of Northwest Africa from Tunis to the Congo and from Senegal to Lake Chad, as well as the island of Madagascar. In 1884 Bismarck declared the West Coast from Angola to Cape Colony under German protection, and thus German Southwest Africa appeared on the map. In the same year Bismarck also declared a protectorate over the little kingdom of Togoland and over Kamerun (Cameroons), a much larger territory farther east. German East Africa also took shape, and Belgium won the region of the Upper Congo. When the World War broke out in 1914, France had under control 4,400,000 square miles of the continent of Africa, Great Britain 3,700,000 square miles, Germany 931,000, Belgium 909,000, Portugal 794,-000, and Spain 593,000. While France possessed the greatest number of square miles, her portion included the Desert of Sahara. England held the richest parts of the continent.

It thus appears that Africa was, to a large extent, the prize of the war. When Germany invaded Belgium, she had as one of her aims the enhancement of her empire. Her colonies in Africa were at the points of a triangle, and in the heart of that triangle was the Belgian Congo. To win that vast territory was supremely important. One officer said: "A victorious war would give us the Belgian Congo, the French Congo, and, if Portugal continues to translate her hostile intentions toward us into actions, would also give us the Portuguese colonies on the East and West

Coasts of Africa. We should then have a colonial empire of which our fathers could never have dreamed."

That hope was not to be realized. Germany lost, and her colonies passed to England or France. Some day, she said to herself, those colonies would have to be returned.

Meanwhile the Africans themselves were restless. For a hundred years they had fought against the invaders of their country. In South Africa had risen two outstanding Zulu chieftains, Chaka and his nephew Cetewayo. Chaka, who lived from 1783 until 1828, was a strong and capable leader, ruthless in dealing with his enemies. He massed his troops in a crescent formation, with a reserve force in a parallelogram, and also used enclosures for his warriors. By his skill and prowess he became master of most of Southeastern Africa. His nephew, Cetewayo, became king of the Zulus in 1872 on the death of his father Panda, brother of Chaka. He had disputes with the Boers, and later with the English, about boundary lines. In 1878 a commission gave a decision in his favor, but the British continued to press their demands, so that war began. On January 22, 1879, the Zulus surprised an English force at Isandlhana and practically wiped out a regiment. It is said that 806 Europeans lost their lives in the event. Reënforcements came from England; on July 4 the Zulus were defeated; and on August 28 Cetewayo was captured. The chieftain was taken to London, where he excited great interest. He died in 1884.

In our own time, in the summer of 1935, the attention of the world centered on Ethiopia, Italy having determined to possess that country. Against a people that asked only to be left alone in their home, the invader rained death-dealing chemicals. For weeks the resistance of the Ethiopians was brave, even surprising, but the contest was unequal. Limited ammunition and a few old-model planes were no match for whole fleets of swiftly moving aircraft. By the first of May, 1936, the Italians were approaching the capital, and within a few days Addis Ababa had fallen.

By the covenant of the League of Nations it was the duty of the powers to act against any aggressor. The Emperor, Haile Selassie, appealed to Geneva. Weeks passed, and nothing was done. More weeks passed, and it appeared that nothing would be done. Both England and France feared to act with decision. A British fleet was massed in the Mediterranean, but the show of strength was only a gesture. The great wrong remained unredressed.

2

The Wake of the Slave-Ship

On a hot day near the end of August, 1619, there came to Jamestown in Virginia a bluff-bowed craft, with a rounded stern towering above the water. The sails, two on the fore and the main masts and one on the mizzen, were like great bags blown out before the wind. On either side was a row of black-muzzled cannon projecting through the bulwarks. This was the Dutch vessel that brought to the settlement twenty Negroes to be sold into servitude. In course of time hundreds of thousands of other victims of the slave-traffic were brought from Africa to America, and the seizure of these people became a well organized industry. New England was as guilty as old England, and a three-cornered trade developed. Molasses was taken from the West Indies to New England; there it was made into rum to be taken to Africa and exchanged for slaves; and the slaves, in turn, were brought to the West Indies or the Southern colonies.

The capturing of the people to be sold was by no means a simple matter. A captain had to use various methods to get his cargo of slaves. The commonest way was to bring a ship-load of gay cloth, muskets, powder, knives, pots, cheap ornaments, and whiskey, and to exchange these articles for the Negroes brought to him. The captain's task was most easy when a native chieftain brought him scores of prisoners of war; but usually the work was more toilsome, and kidnapping a favorite method. There was always danger, for the natives living along the coast soon became suspicious. After they had seen some of their tribesmen taken away, they learned not to go unarmed while a vessel was near, and often there were hand-to-hand encounters.

Those interested in the trade soon realized that it was not good business to make a captain responsible for getting three or four hundred slaves, and that it would be much better if his cargo could be waiting for him when he reached Africa. Thus arose the so-called factories, which were nothing more than warehouses. Along the coast were placed small settlements of Europeans whose task it was to start slave-hunting expeditions, buy the slaves brought in, and keep them until the ships arrived. Practically every nation engaging in the traffic planted factories of this kind along the West Coast from Cape Verde to the equator.

Once on board, the slaves were put in chains, two by two. When the vessel was ready to start, the hold would be crowded with moody and unhappy wretches who had to crouch so that their knees touched their chins. Sometimes the little space between floor and ceiling was made still smaller by the water-barrels. On top of the barrels were placed boards, and on these the captives had to lie as well as they could. There was generally only one entrance to the hold, and the only other provision for air was through the gratings on the sides. The food was of the poorest quality, nor was care taken to see that each received his portion. Water was always limited, a pint a day being a generous allowance; frequently no more than a gill could be had. The rule was to bring the slaves from the hold twice a day for an airing, but this plan was not always followed. On deck they were often made to dance or sing by the lash. When opportunity offered, some of the victims leaped overboard, while others refused food in order to hasten death. Throughout the night the hold resounded with the moans of those who awoke from dreams of home to find themselves in bonds. Women became hysterical, and often both men and women became insane. Fearful and contagious diseases broke out. One was smallpox. More common was ophthalmia, a frightful inflammation of the eyes. A blind and hence a worthless slave was thrown to the sharks. A captain always counted on losing a fourth of his cargo. Frequently he lost a great deal more.

The poet of freedom, John Greenleaf Whittier, in "The Slave Ships" has recorded once for all an incident of the traffic. In April, 1819, a French ship, the *Rodeur*, with a crew of twenty-two men and with one hundred and sixty Negro captives, set sail from Bonny in Africa. After a few days an epidemic of ophthalmia broke out, and this was made worse by the scarcity of water. The disease extended to the crew, and man after man became blind, until only one remained unaffected. If, on such a voyage, slaves died of illness, the loss fell on the owners, including the captain of the vessel. If, however, they had to be thrown overboard to save the ship, the loss would have to be borne by the underwriters who had insured the cargo. Accordingly, in order to save the expense of supporting unsalable slaves and to be able to claim insurance, the captain of the *Rodeur* threw thirty-six of the Negroes who were blind into the sea. While such things were taking place on this ship, a sail was discovered, that of the Spanish slaver *Leon*. On that vessel, it was learned, all the members of the crew had become blind. Unable to help each other, the ships parted. The *Leon* was never heard of again. The *Rodeur* at length reached Guadaloupe, and the one man who had escaped the disease and had thus been able to steer the vessel into port, was smitten three days after its arrival.

A case somewhat similar was that of an English slaver, the *Zong*, which in September, 1781, set sail from Africa for Jamaica with four hundred and forty Negroes. Before he reached his destination the captain threw overboard one hundred and thirty-two of those who were ill, sharks meanwhile lying all about. Granville Sharp, famous for his efforts against slavery, asked the English authorities to see that those responsible for the crime were punished. The Government refused to act, but the incident was one of those that did most to arouse sentiment against the slave-trade.

One day in the year 1767 six English vessels, the *Indian Queen*, the *Duke of York*, the *Nancy*, the *Concord*, the *Edgar*, and the *Canterbury*, were lying near the mouth of the Calabar River in Southern Nigeria. On one island was a village known as Old Calabar; on another a settlement called New Town. Between the two there was bitter feeling, especially as New Town had the favor of the slave captains. On pretense of making peace, the captains invited the Old Calabar people to come unarmed to a palaver, promising not only safety but much rum as well. The native chief, Ephraim Robin John, did not go to the banquet, but three of his brothers went, among them Amboe Robin John, the special foe of the New Town people. In the canoe with the three brothers went twenty-seven other men, and nine canoes followed. The leaders of the group went first to the *Indian Queen*, then to the *Edgar* and the *Duke of York*; and after a while the visitors were well scattered over the different ships. While Amboe Robin John and his brothers were still in the cabin of the *Duke of York*, the officers and crew dropped their rum-cups, took up their muskets and cutlasses, and attacked the unarmed Negroes. There was a dash for freedom, but when the three brothers tried to get through the window, they were pulled back and put in irons. Meanwhile the Negroes on the decks were cut down or shot and the canoes alongside were sunk, the New Town people beating back any man who made for their shore. In all, more than three hundred of the Old Calabar people were killed or enslaved. Among other rewards for their assistance the New Town folk asked as a special boon the head of Amboe Robin John. The man begged to be kept on the ship, but the captain forced him over the rail and into the hands of his enemies.

Such were but a few instances of the cruelty and sorrow, the deceit and inhumanity, bred by the system of slavery.

3

CRISPUS ATTUCKS

To UNDERSTAND THE Boston Massacre of 1770, and the feeling it aroused, one must keep in mind the previous decade in the history of Massachusetts. Some have thought that the occurrence was merely a slight encounter between a few arrogant British soldiers and some sensitive citizens of Boston. Such a view fails to take into account the deep-rooted causes of the event.

Trouble between the American colonies and England began soon after 1761, when revenue officers were granted writs of assistance. These were general search warrants giving customs collectors power to enter houses or shops to hunt for smuggled goods; but the law did not state clearly just what kinds of goods might be seized. Three years later there was a new customs act, with provisions for enforcing trade regulations. In 1765 came the Stamp Act, designed to make the colonies pay for the support of the British army in America. There was a storm of protest, and a congress representing nine colonies met in New York and declared that "it is inseparably essential to the freedom of a people, and the undoubted right of Englishmen, that no taxes be imposed upon them, but with their own consent, given personally or by their representatives." In Massachusetts there were outbursts of violence, and this example was followed elsewhere.

Two years later, in 1767, came the Townshend Acts, so named because they were promoted by Charles Townshend, Chancellor of the Exchequer in England. These acts placed taxes on tea and other articles; but the governors and judges whose salaries were to be paid by the revenue, were to be responsible to the Crown and not to colonial assemblies. This was a serious blow at self-government. Merchants in different places now pledged themselves to buy no goods until the acts were repealed, and the Massachusetts Assembly went so far as to invite the other colonies to coöperate in resisting enforcement. When George III heard of this action, he ordered that it be rescinded, but the vote in the Assembly against rescinding was 92 to 17. James Otis said, "Let Great Britain rescind her measures, or the colonies are lost to her forever."

In 1768 the British Government sent the fifty-gun frigate *Romney* to mount guard in the harbor of Boston, and some citizens were seized and forced to act as seamen. On June 10 John Hancock's sloop *Liberty* was seized without warrant by some of the crew of the *Romney* for alleged violation of the laws. Otis now addressed the people at a great gathering in Old South Meeting House, asserting that the state of the town was the same as if war had been declared. The British Government was requested to order the immediate removal of the *Romney* from the harbor, and a committee of twenty-one citizens was appointed to deliver the petition to the Governor of Massachusetts at his home. His answer was read in town meeting the next day. He declined to remove the frigate but did promise that no more citizens would be pressed into service. In October two regiments of English troops arrived. Samuel Adams now published a series of letters saying that to quarter troops on the people of Massachusetts without the consent of the Assembly was as gross a violation of the Bill of Rights as to quarter an army in London without the consent of Parliament.

Such was the situation at the beginning of 1770. Throughout the month of February there were minor clashes between the citizens and the soldiery. On Friday, March 2, occurred an incident in which several persons suffered slightly. On the evening of Monday, March 5, took place the most important incident of all, one in which the prominent figure was a tall, stalwart man of Negro and perhaps Indian descent, Crispus Attucks.

About the early life of Attucks little is known. It seems that he was born in Framingham, Massachusetts, about 1723 and that he worked on a whaling-ship. At any rate, in his mature manhood he was almost a giant in stature and had the qualities of a leader. As one who spent much time about the docks in lower Boston, he knew well the public temper and the spirit of the British soldiers.

The fifth of March had been a cold, threatening day with a light fall of snow. The early night, however, was clear and the moon shone brightly. A sentry was on duty in Dock Square. Some young men came out of a house in Cornhill; words passed between them and the sentry, and soon a crowd collected. Soldiers came up, but they were forced to take refuge in the Custom House; and meanwhile there were such cries as "Drive them out! They have no business here." Bells were rung, the tumult spread, and an even greater crowd collected. Captain Thomas Preston, in charge of one of the British detachments, received word of what was happening and set out for the Custom House with seven of his men. The soldiers came up King Street (now State) with fixed bayonets, clearing everything before them. They had almost reached the head of the street and the heart of the city when they were met by forty or fifty persons armed with clubs, sticks, and icy snowballs. Attucks was the leader of the crowd and is reported to have said, "The way to get rid of these soldiers is to attack the main guard! Strike at the root! This is the nest!" There was an order to fire. Just who gave it is uncertain; Preston later said that he did not. The first shot, from the gun of a soldier named Montgomery, killed Crispus Attucks. The second, fired by one Kilroy, slew Samuel Gray, who was just stepping toward the fallen Attucks. The third victim was James Caldwell, a sailor standing in the middle of the street. Samuel Maverick, a youth of seventeen, and Patrick Carr were mortally wounded, Maverick dying the next morning and Carr nine days later. Some other persons were injured, though not seriously.

Lieutenant-Governor Hutchinson, in his study in North Square, heard the bells and supposed there was a fire; but when there was a knock on his door, and a cry that the soldiers were firing on the people, he hastened to King Street to Captain Preston. "Are you the commanding officer?" he asked. "Yes, sir," was the reply. "What do you mean by firing on the people without an order from a civil magistrate?" To this there was a mumbled answer about saving the sentry. A few minutes later Hutchinson addressed the people from the balcony of the Town House; and while he was known to have Tory sympathies, his high character gained him a hearing.

The people of Boston, however, were furious, and they forced the withdrawal of the British regiments to Castle Island. The seven soldiers were arrested with Preston and tried for murder, but they were acquitted, though two were declared guilty of manslaughter and given light punishment.

To many this seemed unfair. The colonists in Massachusetts and elsewhere felt that their rights had been violated. The event was everywhere regarded as significant, and soon there was sentiment for a memorial. "From that moment," said Daniel Webster in later years, "we may date the severance of the British Empire. The patriotic fire kindled in the breasts of those earnest and true men, upon whose necks the British yoke never sat easily, never was quenched after that massacre, until the invader had been driven from the land and independence had been achieved."

For some decades the idea of a memorial was not carried out, but in 1888 a monument was erected on Boston Common, where it now stands facing Tremont Street. The dedication took place on November 14. After prayer, there were remarks by Governor Oliver Ames and Mayor Hugh O'Brien, a poem by John Boyle O'Reilly, and then the chief address by the historian, John Fiske, whose research was so thorough that it is unlikely that much about the Boston Massacre will ever be added to what he said. He too emphasized the significance of the event in the history of the nation, saying, "It was the sacrifice of the lives of Crispus Attucks, Samuel Gray, James Caldwell, Samuel Maverick, and Patrick Carr that brought about this preliminary victory of the American Revolution. Their death effected in a moment what seventeen months of petition and discussion had failed to accomplish."

O'Reilly in his spirited poem looked not only to the past but to the future. Said he in part:

And honor to Crispus Attucks, who was leader and voice that
day;
The first to defy, and the first to die, with Maverick, Carr, and
Gray.
Call it riot or revolution, or mob or crowd, as you may,
Such deaths have been seed of nations, such lives shall be
honored for ay.
They were lawless hinds to the lackeys, but martyrs to Paul
Revere;
And Otis and Hancock and Warren read spirit and meaning
clear.

Ye teachers, answer: what shall be done when just men stand
in the dock;
When the caitiff is robed in ermine and his sworders keep the
lock;
When law is a satrap's menace, and order the drill of a horde—
Shall the people kneel to be trampled, and bare their necks to
the sword?

Oh, we who have toiled for freedom's law, have we sought for
freedom's soul?
Have we learned at last that human right is not a part but the
whole?
That nothing is told while the clinging sin remains half-uncon-
fessed?
That the health of the nation is periled if one man be
oppressed?

Has he learned—the slave from the rice swamps, whose children
were sold—has he
With broken chains on his limbs and the cry in his blood, "I
am free!"
Has he learned through affliction's teaching what our Crispus
Attucks knew—
When Right is stricken, the white and black are counted as
one, not two?

For this shall his vengeance change to love, and his retribution
    burn

Defending the right, the weak, and the poor, when each shall
    have his turn;

For this shall he set his woful past afloat on the stream of night;

For this he forgets, as we all forget, when darkness turns to
    light;

For this he forgives, as we all forgive, when wrong has turned
    to right.

4

PHILLIS WHEATLEY

IN THE SUMMER of 1773 a young Negro woman, nineteen years of age, was in England as a guest of the Countess of Huntingdon. She was neat in appearance and bright in conversation. All who met her were impressed by her intelligence and piety. Many regarded her as a prodigy.

In 1761, when about seven years of age, she had been brought on a slave-ship from Senegal to Boston. Her bright eyes attracted the attention of Susannah Wheatley, wife of John Wheatley, a tailor, who desired to have a girl who might be trained as her personal attendant. Accordingly she was purchased, taken home, and given the name *Phillis*. From the first she received unusual care. Assisted by Mary Wheatley, the daughter of the family, ten years older than herself, she learned to read, and soon was composing verses after the manner of Alexander Pope. In time she showed special ability in the study of Latin. In 1770, when sixteen years of age, Phillis wrote her poem "On the Death of the Reverend George Whitefield," the first of her pieces to be published. She now became "a kind of poet laureate in the domestic circles of Boston." By the spring of 1773, as her health was failing, the physician advised that she have the benefit of the air of the sea. A son of the family was about to go to England on business and it was decided that she should go with him. Mrs. Wheatley, not willing to have her go as a slave, saw to it that she was manumitted before she sailed.

It happened that some years previously in England, George Whitefield had served as chaplain to the Countess of Huntingdon, formerly known as Selina Shirley, second daughter of the Earl of Ferrers. That lady, while still a young woman, married the Earl of Huntingdon, and under the influence of her husband's sisters and a severe illness, became deeply interested in religion. By the time she was forty all her children and the Earl had died; thenceforth she gave herself wholly to the life of the spirit, uniting with the Methodists. She opened her home in London for preaching services, founded a theological seminary in Wales, and built several chapels, the expense of the first, that at Brighton, being met by the sale of her jewels, which yielded seven hundred pounds. When the break occurred between John Wesley and Whitefield, she took sides with the latter, and at his death became sole trustee of his institutions in Georgia. It was to her that Phillis Wheatley addressed her poem on the famous preacher, speaking especially of his work for orphan children. The Countess was pleased, and assumed the care of the young author on her arrival in England.

Even the strange history of Phillis and her ability to write verses could hardly account for the interest she awakened. To her unassuming courtesy she added a wit tempered by gentleness. Presents were showered upon her. Among others was a copy of the 1770 Glasgow folio edition of *Paradise Lost*, given to her by the Lord Mayor of London. This was sold after her death in payment of her husband's debts and is now in the library of Harvard University. At the top of one of the first pages, in her own handwriting, are the words, "Mr. Brook Watson to Phillis Wheatley, London, July, 1773." Here as elsewhere she spelled her name with an *i* rather than a *y*.

As the young visitor from Boston had not come to England at the most fashionable season, the ladies of the circle of the Countess wished that she might remain long enough to be presented at the court of George III. Something unforeseen prevented this; Mrs. Wheatley became ill and longed for her old companion. Phillis could not be persuaded to delay her return. Before she left England, however, arrangements were made for the publication of her book, *Poems on Various Subjects, Religious and Moral.* This is the only collection of her work. Individual poems were written later and another volume was contemplated; but there were changes in the Wheatley family, the Revolutionary War came on, and the second book never saw the light.

Poems on Various Subjects was "Printed for A. Bell, Bookseller, Aldgate," London, 1773. Whoever now has a copy of this original edition possesses the greatest treasure in the literature of the Negro. As it had been suggested to the publisher that there might be some question as to the authorship of the poems, he procured proof of this from "the most respectable characters in Boston, that none might have the least ground for disputing their originality." Among those who so vouched for them were Governor Thomas Hutchinson, Lieutenant-Governor Andrew Oliver, John Hancock, John Wheatley, the Reverend Samuel Cooper, and the Reverend Samuel Mather.

Phillis Wheatley gained much from her reading of the greater Latin authors, but the writer who influenced her most was Pope. She used that poet's verse form, and the ease with which she chiseled the heroic couplet when only sixteen or eighteen years of age was amazing. The diction also—"fleecy care," "tuneful nine," "feathered vengeance" —is constantly in the eighteenth-century tradition. What one misses is the personal note. With the exception of the short juvenile piece, "On Being Brought from Africa to America," the only poem suggested by a Negro subject is "To S. M., a Young African Painter, on Seeing his Works," and even in this the only reference to race is in the title. Emphasis is mainly on abstractions; seldom is there a genuine lyric. In all this Phillis Wheatley was like most other writers of the time. If she had lived fifty years later, when the romantic writers had given a more natural tone to English poetry, she might have been considerably different; but even then, with her sense of the fitness of things, she would doubtless have exercised restraint.

Typical of the quality of the thirty-eight pieces in the book is the poem "On Imagination," in which the best lines are these:

> Imagination! who can sing thy force?
> Or who describe the swiftness of thy course?
> Soaring through air to find the bright abode,
> Th' empyreal palace of the thundering God,
> We on thy pinions can surpass the wind,
> And leave the rolling universe behind:
> From star to star the mental optics rove,
> Measure the skies, and range the realms above.
> There in one view we grasp the mighty whole,
> Or with new worlds amaze th' unbounded soul.

At least a few of the later poems of Phillis Wheatley have been preserved. In 1775, while the siege of Boston was in progress, she wrote a letter to General George Washington enclosing a complimentary poem. Washington replied graciously and later received her at his headquarters in Cambridge. This was an event not soon to be forgotten. The close of the Revolution was marked by another poem, "Liberty and Peace." In general, however, the visit to England marked the highest point in the career of the young author; after her return to America misfortunes came fast. Mrs. Wheatley died in March, 1774, and thereafter Phillis seems not to have lived regularly at the old home. John Wheatley died just four years later, in March, 1778; and his daughter, Mary, who had married, in the following September. Nathaniel, the son of the family, was living abroad. There were other changes in the home circles of Boston, and the time was one of general distress.

It was in these days of uncertainty and loneliness, just a few weeks after the death of John Wheatley, that Phillis became the wife of John Peters. She had known him for some time; four years previously she had referred to him in a letter to a friend, Obour Tanner, living in Newport, saying, "The young man by whom this is handed to you seems to be a very clever man, knows you very well, and is very complaisant and agreeable." While she could write verses, time was to prove that she was not the best judge of character. Peters is variously reported to have been a baker, a barber, a grocer, a physician, and a lawyer, but with all these occupations and professions seems not to have had the ability to earn a living. He wore a wig, sported a cane, and generally felt himself superior to labor. Once at least he was in trouble with the law. His conduct estranged the old acquaintances of his wife, while her pride kept her from informing them of her distress. At length she was forced to work in a cheap lodging-house. Her strength declined rapidly and she died December 5, 1784. Two of her children had died previously and the third was buried with her.

The book *Poems on Various Subjects* has been through

numerous editions. In the early years of the nineteenth century some of the pieces were included in school readers. If after some years the work of the author received less attention than before, interest greatly revived at the time of the anti-slavery agitation, when anything indicating ability on the part of the Negro was received with eagerness. Accordingly, when Margaretta Matilda Odell, a descendant of the Wheatley family, republished the *Poems* with a memoir in 1834, there was such a demand for the book that two more editions were called for within the next four years. In recent years there has been still further interest, with new editing and critical appraisal.

5

BENJAMIN BANNEKER: ASTRONOMER

IN THE EARLY years of the nineteenth century the Negro most frequently referred to as proof of the intellectual capacity of his people was Benjamin Banneker, of Maryland. To understand the career of this man it is necessary to go back two hundred years, to a time when Baltimore was still a village of thirty houses and white servitude a system of labor in the colonies. The Negro had yet to prove his ability in mental pursuits; on the other hand the relations between the races were not yet so fixed as they later became.

Banneker received the rudiments of his education from his grandmother, an Englishwoman by birth, who taught him his letters so that he could read the Bible to her. Molly Welsh, while a young woman working on a farm in her native country, was accused of stealing a pail of milk. Although she insisted that a cow kicked over the pail, she was sold under the system of indenture and forced to serve in Maryland for seven years. With the "freedom dues" that she received at the end of her term she bought a small farm, and by 1692 was able to purchase two men just brought from Africa. One of them, Banaky, a prince in his own land, was not as good a worker as his companion, but had a dignified manner and pleasing address. After a few years Molly Welsh liberated both men and married Banaky.

Four children came into the home before the father died. One of the daughters, Mary, was married in 1730 to Robert, an African, who had become free and preferred to use his wife's surname rather than that of his former owner. Again there were four children. The oldest, and the only son, was Benjamin, born November 9, 1731. At first the surname was given not only as *Banaky* but also as *Banneky* and *Bannaker*, but by the time it came to the most famous member of the family, it had become fixed as *Banneker*.

Robert Banneker was an industrious man. When his son was six years of age, he purchased a farm of a hundred and twenty acres ten miles from Baltimore. Within the next few years Benjamin attended a little school not far from his home. He showed interest in anything mechanical and when about twenty-two made a clock that not only kept time but also struck the hours. When he was twenty-seven his father died, leaving with him the responsibility for the farm, generally known as one of the best in the section. Thus the years passed until he was forty.

In 1772 preliminary steps were taken for the erection of the flour mills of Ellicott City. The site selected was near Banneker's home and he was intensely interested in the construction of the buildings the next year. The Ellicotts, who were Quakers, were friendly and purchased from his farm provisions for their workmen. One of the younger members of the family, George Ellicott, was interested in mathematics and astronomy, and, when not more than seventeen years of age, surveyed and laid out a road from Frederick to Baltimore. This young man visited Banneker from time to time and loaned him Ferguson's *Astronomy*, Mayer's *Tables*, and Leadbeater's *Lunar Tables*, with some astronomical instruments. So thoroughly did Banneker master the books that he was soon able to point out errors and discrepancies in them. He reversed his habits, studying the stars at night and sleeping so much in the day that the neighbors said he was growing lazy. Under his new inspiration also he overcame a fondness for strong drink. In 1789, when commissioners were appointed for the surveying of the Federal Territory now known as the District of Columbia, at the suggestion of Andrew Ellicott he became a member of the group.

In 1791 Banneker began the publication of a series of almanacs. The first was that for the year 1792 and the last that for 1802. He wrote a dissertation on bees and calculated the locust plague as recurrent in seventeen-year cycles. In order better to devote himself to his scholarly work, he sold his land to the Ellicotts for an annuity of £12 based on the market value and his expectancy of life, reserving only a residence for himself. He lived eight years longer than he calculated, but the Ellicotts faithfully kept the contract to the end.

Banneker never married. Two sisters, Minta Black and Molly Morton, lived near him and helped to care for his wants. In his later years he was described as "a large man of noble appearance, with venerable hair, wearing a coat of superfine drab broadcloth," and again as "of black complexion, medium stature, of uncommonly soft and gentlemanly manners and of pleasing colloquial powers." Though not a member of any church, he sometimes attended the meetings of the Society of Friends.

On August 19, 1791, Banneker sent a copy of his almanac with a letter to Thomas Jefferson, then Secretary of State. He pointed out to the distinguished statesman the inconsistency of slavery with the ideals of the Declaration of Independence, and said among other things: "Your knowledge of the situation of my brethren is too extensive to need a recital here; neither shall I presume to prescribe methods by which they may be relieved, otherwise than by recommending to you and all others, to wean yourselves from those narrow prejudices which you have imbibed with respect to them, and as Job proposed to his friends, 'put your soul in their soul's stead'; thus shall your hearts be enlarged with kindness and benevolence toward them; and thus shall you need neither the direction of myself or others, in what manner to proceed herein."

Another important paper, "A Plan of Peace-Office for the United States," appeared in the almanac for 1793. When Banneker began his larger work the ideas of the French Revolution were abroad in the western world, and in England Richard Price, Thomas Paine, William Godwin, and Mary Wollstonecraft were making a new declaration of the rights of man. In the latter portion of his paper Banneker became slightly fantastic, but the main thing he had to say was sound. In general he anticipated both the formation of the Department of the Interior and such an ideal as that of the League of Nations. He was strongly opposed to capital punishment, saying, "To inspire a veneration for human life, and an horror at the shedding of human blood let all those laws be repealed which authorize juries, judges, sheriffs, or hangmen to assume the resentments of individuals, and to commit murder in cold blood in any case whatever. Until this reformation in our code of penal jurisprudence takes place, it will be in vain to attempt to introduce universal and perpetual peace in our country."

Somewhat similar was the word against anything that breeds a martial or warlike spirit: "To subdue that passion for war which education, added to human depravity, has made universal, a familiarity with the instruments of death, as well as all military shows, should be carefully avoided. For which reason, militia laws should everywhere be repealed and military dresses and military titles should be laid aside: reviews tend to lessen the horrors of a battle by connecting them with the charms of order; militia laws generate idleness and vice, and thereby produce the wars they are said to prevent; military dresses fascinate the mind of young men, and lead them from serious and useful occupations; were there no uniforms, there would probably be no armies; lastly, military titles feed vanity, and keep up ideas in the mind which lessen a sense of the folly and miseries of war."

Benjamin Banneker was thus not only an original thinker but also an enlightened spirit deeply concerned for the welfare of mankind. While he had to work with scanty materials, he achieved results of which a university man might have been proud, and in his social vision was years beyond his time.

In his later life, when he was not as active as formerly, prominent visitors more than once came to his home. To one he apologized for not having any fruit worthy of acceptance to present him, saying, "I have no influence with the rising generation; all my arguments have failed to induce them to set bounds to their wants." After 1802 he suffered the political disability imposed upon his people in the state.

On Sunday morning, October 9, 1806, Banneker strolled forth as usual to enjoy the air and the sunshine. Meeting an acquaintance, he conversed pleasantly for a while and then, feeling ill, returned to his cottage. He lay upon his couch and within a few minutes was gone. His personal effects he had said were to be given to his sisters, but most of these were destroyed in a fire that consumed the house two days later even while the service for him was being held. Some papers ordered to be sent to George Ellicott were fortunately removed at once and thus preserved.

6

Richard Allen and Absalom Jones

In the year 1793 a fearful epidemic of yellow fever swept over the city of Philadelphia. The catastrophe left its mark upon every activity in the growing city. One matter that came up in connection with it is of special significance in the history of the Negro.

Philadelphia at that time was by no means the great city it is to-day. It was of course important in the life of the young republic, but the development of vast commercial enterprises was the work of later years. The situation of the Negro was that of a struggling people still groping for freedom and an economic foothold. Many questions of fugitive slaves arose, and unemployment abounded. In 1796 the Pennsylvania Society for Promoting the Abolition of Slavery deemed it advisable to address a special circular to the Free Africans and other Free People of Color in order to urge them at all times to behave in such manner as to avoid contention and remove every just cause of complaint.

In September, 1793, when the epidemic was nearing its height, the Negro citizens were asked to come forward, attend the sick and bury the dead, as they were supposed to be immune from the disease. The unheard-of request naturally appalled them at first, and in their dilemma they turned to their leaders, Richard Allen, later the first bishop of the African Methodist Episcopal Church, and Absalom Jones, later the rector of St. Thomas's, the African Episcopal Church.

Richard Allen was born a slave in Philadelphia in 1760. While still young he was sold to a farmer near Dover, Delaware. Later he was converted under Methodist influence and while still a young man began to preach. His master permitted services to be conducted in his home, was himself converted, and in general showed a helpful spirit. By cutting wood, working in a brickyard, and serving as a wagoner during the Revolution, Allen was at length able to purchase his freedom. He traveled through the eastern part of Pennsylvania, also the neighboring states, and after a while began to receive appointments from Bishop Francis Asbury of the Methodist Episcopal Church. Removing to Philadelphia in 1786, he occasionally preached at St. George's, an outstanding church of the denomination, and conducted prayer-meetings with the Negroes. In 1787, when there was trouble about the seating in St. George's, he and his friends withdrew and organized the Free African Society, which became the nucleus of formal effort by Negroes in both the Methodist and the Episcopal denominations. He was a man of strict integrity and indomitable perseverance.

Absalom Jones, thirteen years older than Allen, was born a slave in Sussex, Delaware. While still young, he was taken by his master from the field to work in the house, and even in those years had the good sense to save the pennies given him by visitors from time to time. He bought a primer, a spelling-book, and a Testament in the endeavor to use his leisure hours to advantage. When he was sixteen years of age, his immediate relatives were sold, and he was taken by his new master to Philadelphia, where his work was to help in a store and carry out goods. He got permission to attend night school and was so thrifty that he was finally able, with some assistance from the Friends, to purchase the freedom first of his wife and then of himself. Thenceforth his progress was rapid, and he figured prominently in the incident that caused Richard Allen and other Negroes to leave St. George's, as it was he whom an usher sought to pull from his knees during prayer.

These were the men who had to reply to the request made of the Negroes of Philadelphia. It was easy for them to say that the request should not have been made; that did not alter the fact that it had come or that upon the answer hung very largely the future of the Negro in the city. They thought prayerfully about the situation, about their own people and the public distress, and finally decided that it was their duty to help their fellow men.

As the epidemic advanced, the city was seized by panic. Many of the people fled. Hardly anyone was willing to go near the sick; and when someone died, so great was the difficulty of removing the body that few were willing to undertake the work even when offered great rewards.

Such was the situation when Allen and his associates set forth to see what they could do. They went first to an alley where a man was dying. His wife was already dead and in the house were two helpless children. As many as twenty families were visited the first day, and some of the scenes were full of woe. However, as Allen and Jones said, the Lord was pleased to strengthen them, to remove all fear, and to dispose their hearts to be as useful as possible.

In order the better to regulate their conduct, the Negroes called on the mayor the next day, to consult with him about the method of procedure. He recommended strict attention to the sick and the procuring of nurses. The men then gave notice in the papers that they would remove the dead and provide nurses for the sick. "Our services," they said later, "were the production of real sensibility; we sought no fee nor reward until the increase of the disorder rendered our labor so arduous that we were not adequate to the service we had assumed."

When the sickness became general, several of the physicians died and most of the survivors were exhausted by their labors. Dr. Benjamin Rush, knowing that Allen and Jones could bleed, informed them where to procure medicine duly prepared and at what stages of the disorder to act. In the weeks that followed, when no physician was available, they were constantly on call and helped to save the lives of hundreds of those who were stricken.

Their best effort, however, did not save them from misrepresentation. When all was over, Mathew Carey published *A Short Account of the Malignant Fever*, asserting that the Negroes should have done much more and charged much less than they did, though he praised the work of the leaders. Allen and Jones were not to be moved by any compliment to themselves when the efforts of their associates were thus unfairly dealt with; accordingly they replied in a pamphlet, *A Narrative of the Proceedings of the Black People during the Late Awful Calamity in Philadelphia*. They gave a detailed statement of receipts and expenditures to show that all the cash they had received had not been sufficient to pay for the coffins purchased and the labor employed; and further showed that they had buried hundreds of poor persons and strangers without either asking or receiving compensation. That some extravagant prices were paid, they admitted; the situation was not one they could fully control. Applications for nurses became more and more numerous, and sometimes when a person had been engaged to serve at six dollars a week, it was found that he or she had been lured away by the prospect of higher wages, in some cases three or four dollars a day. It was natural, thought Allen and Jones, for people in humble circumstances to accept a voluntary and generous reward, especially when many of the sickrooms were loathsome and when the difficulty of the work was aggravated by lunacy. They wondered what Mr. Carey would have demanded in such a situation. He, it appeared, although a member of the committee on public welfare, had soon hurried away, leaving his associates to struggle with the epidemic as well as they could.

Fortunately most of the citizens of Philadelphia were better disposed than Mathew Carey. When conditions were again normal, the Mayor and the City Council formally thanked Allen and his associates for the service they had rendered. Thus in a time of need men only recently in bondage thought first not of themselves but of the public interest. Thus they climbed another rung on the ladder of American citizenship.

7

Paul Cuffe: Seaman and Philanthropist

Paul Cuffe was born January 17, 1759, on Cuttyhunk, the southernmost of the Elizabeth Islands not far from New Bedford, Massachusetts. His parents were Cuffe Slocum, an African who had purchased his freedom, and Ruth (Moses) Slocum, who was of Indian descent. Paul was the seventh of the ten children and the youngest of the sons in the family. Of his early years we are told by one who knew him: "His father died when he was about fourteen years of age, at which time he had learnt but little more than his alphabet; and having from thence, with his brothers, the care of his mother and sisters devolving upon him, he had but little opportunity for the acquisitions of literature. Indeed, he never had any schooling, but obtained what learning he had by his own indefatigable exertions, and the scanty aids which he occasionally received from persons who were friendly towards him. By these means, however, he advanced to a considerable proficiency in arithmetic, and skill in navigation." When he was still a youth he persuaded his brothers to drop their father's slave name and to use his Christian name as their surname.

At the age of sixteen Cuffe became a sailor on a whaling

vessel. On one of his early trips to sea, after the Revolutionary War had begun, he was captured by the British and held in New York for three months. Released, he went to Westport, a town on the coast of Massachusetts a few miles west of New Bedford, where he engaged in agriculture and the study of navigation. When twenty years of age, he commenced business for himself, using a small open boat. He had unhappy experiences at first, these including the capture of his goods by pirates, but at length, by dint of perseverance and industry, succeeded in his efforts and was able to purchase a good-sized schooner. In 1795 he launched a sixty-nine-ton vessel, the *Ranger*, and by 1806 was the owner of one ship, two brigs, and several smaller vessels, besides considerable property in houses and lands. More and more he enlarged his sphere of action, going with his Negro crew to points in the South and the West Indies, then crossing the Atlantic to England.

As early as 1780 Paul Cuffe and his brother John had raised question about paying taxes in Massachusetts, inasmuch as Negroes were denied the right of suffrage, and taxation without representation was one cause of the war. They were at first unsuccessful in their protest, but presented a petition to the legislature, and in 1783 Massachusetts extended to the Negro people the rights and privileges of citizens. On February 25, 1783, Paul Cuffe was married to a young Indian woman, Alice Pequit. In 1797 he bought for $3,500 a farm on the Westport River. Realizing that there was no place in the vicinity for the instruction of youth, and desiring that his children should have the advantages of education, he proposed to his neighbors that they unite with him in building a schoolhouse. The suggestion led to so much contention (largely, it is thought, on account of his color) that he abandoned the effort at coöperation and built the schoolhouse on his own land. Then, having secured a teacher, he gave the use of the facilities to all in the neighborhood. In 1808 he was received into the Society of Friends, and he assisted these people in the building of a new meetinghouse.

It is, however, by reason of his efforts for the Negro in Africa that Cuffe is best remembered. As early as 1788 he had thought of colonization, and he read with eagerness anything he could find about Sierra Leone, the English colony founded in 1787. On January 1, 1811, with his crew of nine Negro seamen, he sailed in his brig, the *Traveller*, from Westport for Sierra Leone. Arriving without mishap, he made himself acquainted with the condition of the colony and held a number of conferences with the governor and other prominent men. Among other things he suggested the organization of a society looking toward general improvement. The idea was readily approved, and thus came into existence "The Friendly Society of Sierra Leone." Cuffe then sailed for England, where he was cordially received by such men as William Wilberforce and Zachary Macaulay. Given opportunity to present his views to the Board of Managers of the African Institution, he interested these men in his plans and secured from them authority to take over from the United States a few Negroes of good character to instruct the colonists in agriculture and mechanical arts. He then went back to Sierra Leone with a consignment of goods for the Friendly Society, and after this second visit returned to America. Thus closed his first mission to Africa, an effort prompted by the purest spirit of benevolence, undertaken at his own risk, and happily brought to a successful termination.

Burdened by the needs of his people on both sides of the Atlantic, Cuffe now conceived the idea of an annual trip to Sierra Leone. Of his effort at this time Peter Williams, an Episcopal minister of New York, said: "In the hope of finding persons of the description given by the African Institution, he visited most of the large cities in the Union, held frequent conferences with the most reputable men of color, and also with those among the whites who had distinguished themselves as the friends of the Africans; and recommended to the colored people to form associations for the furtherance of the benevolent work in which he was engaged. The results were the formation of two societies, one in Philadelphia and the other in New York, and the discovery of a number of proper persons who were willing to go with him and settle in Africa. But unfortunately, before he found himself in readiness for the voyage, the war [of 1812] commenced between this country and Great Britain. This put a bar in the way of his operations, which he was so anxious to remove that he traveled from his home at Westport to the city of Washington, to solicit the Government to favor his views, and to let him depart and carry with him those persons and their effects whom he had engaged to go and settle in Sierra Leone. He was, however, unsuccessful in the attempt. His general plan was highly and universally approbated, but the policy of the Government would not admit of such an intercourse with an enemy's colony."

Cuffe had no alternative but to remain at home and await the close of the war; but there was no dampening of his enthusiasm. He matured his plans and extended his correspondence with persons in both England and America. As soon as the war was over, he hastened preparations for his departure. On December 10, 1815, he sailed with a total of nine families and thirty-eight persons, and after a voyage of fifty-five days landed them safely in Sierra Leone. In taking over so large a company he had exceeded his instructions. The African Institution had approved his taking six or eight men, and he had no claim on the board for expenses incurred by more than this number. However, rather than disappoint any who expected to go, he assumed responsibility for their passage, and when all were landed in Sierra Leone, made such provision for the destitute as would supply their needs until they were able to provide for themselves. The total expense to him was nearly four thousand dollars, a sum much greater in those days than it is with us to-day.

Cuffe had no sooner returned to America than he began to think of still another voyage. By this time, however, his health had begun to fail; meanwhile something else happened. In December, 1816, there was organized in Washington The American Society for Colonizing the Free People of Color of the United States, commonly known as the American Colonization Society. The president was a Southern man, twelve of the seventeen vice-presidents were Southerners, and all of the twelve managers were slave-holders. Consternation spread among the Negro people of the country, North as well as South. They were convinced that the real purpose of the organization was to get rid of all the free people of color in order that the slaves might be more securely bound. There were meetings of protest, the most important being that in Philadelphia, where the presiding officer was James Forten, a prominent man of business, and one of the leading spirits was Richard Allen, now bishop of the African Methodist Episcopal Church. In view of this new development any personal effort for colonization was naturally overwhelmed.

Paul Cuffe was tall, well formed, and athletic. He had tact and discretion, and soon impressed people by his dignity of manner and his piety. When he died September 9, 1817, he left an estate of twenty thousand dollars. It was largely due to his character that there was founded in New Bedford early in the century a tradition of justice for all.

8

Negro Insurrectionists

THE NEGROES BROUGHT to America from Africa, or recently imported from the West Indies, did not always submit readily to enslavement. In the colonial period there were not less than sixteen insurrections, and in the early decades of the nineteenth century there was a series of revolutionary outbreaks. More than once there was coöperation with the Indians, as in Louisiana in 1730; and the protection given by the Indians to fugitive slaves was one of the chief causes of the Seminole Wars. Sometimes the outbreak was sudden and sporadic, and hence not fully planned; but in several instances the plot was deeply laid and the whole design carefully matured. Insurrections most frequently took place on Sunday, because on that day the Negroes were more free than usual. In the vicinity of Charleston, South Carolina, some from the country districts might even spend the week end in the city.

As early as 1687 there was a conspiracy in Virginia that was detected just in time to prevent slaughter. In New York in 1712 occurred a revolt that created intense excitement. On the morning of April 7 some slaves of the Carmantee and Pappa tribes who had suffered harsh treatment, set on fire the house of Peter van Tilburgh and killed or wounded any who came to extinguish the flames. When the Governor gave the alarm they fled to the woods, and there some committed suicide. Those who were captured were speedily sentenced. All told, eight or ten white persons lost their lives in the event, and twice as many Negroes. This was generally the proportion of fatalities in such occurrences.

In South Carolina the great plantations along the coast were a fertile field for unrest. The first rebellion in this colony in which Negroes were "actually armed and embodied" took place in 1730. Within the one year 1739 there were three insurrections, and in one of these six houses were burned and twenty-five white persons killed. The Negroes were pursued and fourteen were shot at once; and within the next two days twenty more were killed and twice as many captured. This "exemplary punishment," as Governor Gibbes called it, was not as effective as it was thought it might be, for in the very next year, 1740, there occurred the most formidable insurrection in the South in the whole colonial period. A number of Negroes, having assembled at Stono, surprised and killed two young men in a warehouse, from which they then took guns and ammunition. Having elected as captain one of their number named Cato, they proceeded to march toward the southwest and they burned or plundered each house to which they came, killing the white people and compelling the slaves to join them. After spreading desolation for twelve miles, they stopped in an open field and too soon began to rejoice with drinking and dancing. The militia surrounded them, and all of the first insurgents were ultimately put to death. The whole of Carolina, we are told, was struck with terror by this uprising, in which more than twenty white persons lost their lives. It was followed immediately by legislation imposing prohibitive duties on Negroes brought into the colony, but the provisions of the act were soon disregarded.

Three attempts were especially notable, by reason either of the character of the leaders or the nature of the plan for the outbreak.

The first was Gabriel's insurrection in Virginia in 1800. This ended in failure, but, coming soon after the revolution in Hayti, and giving evidence of young and unselfish leadership, was regarded as of extraordinary significance. Gabriel Prosser was an intelligent slave only twenty-four years of age, and his chief assistants were his brother Martin and a friend, Jack Bowler, who was twenty-eight. Throughout the summer there were meetings at which Martin interpreted passages of Scripture as bearing on the situation of the Negroes. The insurrection was finally set for the first of September, and the plan was that the force of eleven hundred men should assemble at a brook six miles from Richmond and march under cover of night in three columns on the city. The right wing was to seize the arsenal and the left the powder-house; and while these columns were doing their work, the central force, armed with muskets, knives, and pikes, was to begin the carnage. On the day appointed, however, there was such a storm as Virginia had not seen for years. Bridges were carried away, and roads and plantations submerged. The country Negroes could not get into the city, nor could those in the city get out to the meeting-place. Meanwhile a slave who did not wish to see his master killed, divulged the plot, and all Richmond was soon in arms. A troop of United States cavalry was ordered to the city, and arrests followed quickly. Bowler surrendered, but it was weeks before Gabriel was found. He was finally captured at Norfolk on

September 24, on a vessel that had come from Richmond; was convicted on October 3, and executed four days later. He showed no disposition to dissemble as to his plan, but said nothing to incriminate anyone else. Eleven of his followers met death before him, and twenty-four were executed later.

Even more carefully planned was the effort of Denmark Vesey in Charleston in 1822. The Christian name of this man was originally Télémaque, but this was corrupted to *Telmak* and then to *Denmark*. Vesey was the slave and personal attendant of a sea-captain of the same name who commanded a trading vessel going chiefly between Charleston and the West Indies. In 1800, at the age of thirty-three, he won $1,500 in a lottery, and with $600 of this amount he purchased his freedom. Meanwhile he worked diligently at his trade, that of a carpenter. Of striking appearance, handsome, alert, magnetic, he came to·have unbounded influence over the slaves, understanding well their superstitious nature and having just the domineering temper needed to make his conquest complete.

Vesey conceived an insurrection that aimed at the annihilation of the white population of Charleston. His assistants he selected with the utmost care. Peter Poyas was intrepid and resolute, cautious, and not easily deterred by obstacles. Rolla Bennett was plausible in address and had uncommon self-possession. Gullah Jack was feared as a sorcerer and was thought to bear a charmed life. Others were hardly less capable. "Take care," said Poyas, in speaking to a recruit about the plan, "and don't mention it to those waiting men who receive presents of old coats from their masters, or they'll betray us." In course of time Negroes within a radius of seventy or eighty miles about Charleston were brought into the plot, and the date set was the second Sunday in July. The plan was for Poyas to lead in the seizure of the Arsenal in Meeting Street opposite St. Michael's Church, and the other leaders, coming from six different directions, were to converge upon this center. Meanwhile a body of horse was to keep the streets clear. "Eat only dry food," advised Gullah Jack as the day approached, "parched corn and ground nuts, and when you join us as we pass, put this crab claw in your mouth and you can't be wounded."

Late in May a slave spoke to his master about some things he had heard, and the arrest of some of the men followed. Poyas and Mingo Harth, a leader of one of the companies of horse, were cool and collected; they ridiculed the whole idea and were discharged. Ned Bennett, brother of Rolla, hearing that his name had been mentioned, voluntarily went before the officials and succeeded in baffling them further. By Friday, June 14, however, another informant had spoken to his master, and this man had the facts well in hand. He said that the original plan had been changed and that the night of Sunday, June 16, was the time now set for the insurrection. A messenger moving about on Saturday night found sentinels on guard, and arrests soon followed. As a result of this effort for freedom thirty-five Negroes were executed and forty-three banished. Vesey was hanged on July 2 with five of his chief associates. He made no confession, and Poyas was similarly resolute. "Do not open your lips," he said; "die silent as you shall see me do."

Not quite of the same character was the insurrection in Southampton County, Virginia, nine years later. In general the difference between the leader, Nat Turner, and Denmark Vesey was that between the emotional and the intellectual insurgent. Turner was a religious enthusiast, and the first sense of his mission had come to him six years before. Born October 2, 1800, just the day before Gabriel was convicted in Richmond, he had on his head and breast marks which the Negroes interpreted as signs of a high calling. In his mature years he had also on his right arm a knot from a blow he had received. He experimented in paper and gunpowder, and it is said that he was never known to swear an oath, to drink a drop of liquor, or to commit a theft. Instead he lived in a mystical world, fasting and praying, reading the Bible, and communing with the voices that he heard. Once he ran away for a month, but was commanded by the Spirit to return. About 1825 a realization of the purpose of his life came to him, and thenceforth he labored to be more worthy. From time to time as he worked in the field, he saw drops on the corn, and white and black spirits contending in the skies. In May, 1828, he was relieved of all doubt or misgiving. A great voice said to him that the Serpent was loosed, that the time was coming when the last should be first, and that he, Nat, was to take up the yoke which Christ laid down. An eclipse of the sun in February, 1831, he interpreted as the sign to go forward; yet he waited for a few months to be sure of his chief associates.

About noon on Sunday, August 21, on the plantation of Joseph Travis at Cross Keys in Southampton County, four of Turner's friends, Hark Travis, Henry Porter, Nelson Williams, and Sam Francis, were assembled as if for a barbecue. Soon two other men came, one being a gigantic Negro, Will Francis. Two hours later Turner, a short, thickset man, joined the group, and he raised some question about the presence of Will and his companion. The giant hastened to say that life was worth no more to him than the others and that liberty was as dear to him as to them. This answer was satisfactory, and Nat Turner now went into conference with his colleagues. All through the summer afternoon and evening they remained together, and when near midnight the low whispering ceased, the doom of nearly threescore white persons—and, it might be added, of twice as many Negroes—was sealed.

It was understood that Turner himself was to spill the first blood, and that he would begin with his own master, Joseph Travis. Going to the house, Hark placed a ladder against the chimney. On this Nat ascended; then, when within the house, he unbarred the doors and removed the guns from their places. He and Will then entered Travis's chamber, and the first blow was given to the master of the house. The wife and three children were also killed immediately. Through the late hours of the night, at one home or another, the slaughter continued, and meanwhile Turner's company increased. Sometimes the band would divide; fifteen or twenty of the mounted men would be put in front to prevent escape, and Will especially wrought havoc wherever he went. Prominent among the events of the morning was the killing of one Mrs. Waller and ten children who were gathering at her home for school. More and more, however, the Negroes were getting drunk and noisy. The alarm was given, and by ten o'clock on Monday morning one Captain Harris and his family had escaped. The tide now turned, and within the next twenty-four hours the insurrection was over. Turner himself eluded his pursuers for more than two months, but was finally captured on October 30, sentenced on November 5, and hanged on Friday, November 11.

A list prepared soon after the event gives the number of white persons killed as fifty-five, but from other sources it appears that the correct number is fifty-seven. Of fifty-three Negroes arraigned seventeen were executed and twelve transported. These figures, however, give no conception of the number of those who lost their lives in connection with the outbreak. The period was one of terror, with voluntary patrols, frequently drunk, going in all directions. A party went from Richmond with the intention of killing every Negro in Southampton County. One man boasted that he alone had killed between ten and fifteen.

The panic created throughout the South could hardly be exaggerated. The wildest rumors were abroad. One was that Wilmington, North Carolina, had been burned. In Fayetteville scores of white women and children fled to the swamps, coming out two days later muddy, chilled, and half-starved. In Macon, Georgia, there was a report that an armed band of Negroes was only five miles away, and within an hour the women and children were assembled in the largest building in the town, with a military force in front for protection.

The effects on legislation were immediate, slave codes everywhere being made more harsh. Thus, as in similar uprisings, the Negro for the moment lost. In the long run, however, he gained, for the insurrections increased the agitation against slavery and thus led on to the Civil War and emancipation.

9

John Chavis: Early Schoolmaster

John Chavis was a Negro school-teacher in North Carolina in the early years of the nineteenth century, long before the state had entered upon its era of industrial development, and when, for most of the time at least, the relations between the races had not yet been strained by the insurrection led by Nat Turner. He taught both white and Negro students, and among the former were several later prominent in the public life of the state.

The facts of the early life of Chavis have been much disputed. He himself once said in a letter that he was "a free born American and a revolutionary soldier." There is no direct evidence as to either the date or the place of his birth, but it seems likely that he was born near Oxford, in Granville County, North Carolina, about the year 1763. It is definitely known that about the close of the century he pursued the regular course of study at Washington Academy, now Washington and Lee University, and it appears probable that he also studied at Princeton. Some have said that he was sent to the latter institution on a wager to see if a Negro could take college training. It is perhaps more important to remember that among the Scotch-Irish settlers of the mountain section of Virginia there was a tradition of liberality, that they cultivated missionary enterprise, and that their interest extended to the Negro. To these stalwart Presbyterians Chavis seemed to be a man of promise and they gave him their support accordingly.

The records of the Presbytery of Lexington, Virginia, show that at the meeting in Lexington in October, 1799, "John Chavis, a black man, personally known to most members of Presbytery and of unquestionably good fame, and a communicant in the Presbyterian church, was introduced and conversed with relative to his practical acquaintance with living religion and his call to preach the ever lasting Gospel. Presbytery considering that they, like their Heavenly Father, should be no respecter of persons, being satisfied with his narrative, agreed, notwithstanding his colour, to take him under their care, for further trials in the usual form." Accordingly an exegesis in Latin on the theme *In quo consistat salvatio ab peccato* and a homily on the decree of Election were appointed him as trial pieces at the next meeting, which was to take place at Tinkling-Springs on the second Wednesday in the following June. For some reason satisfactory to the body, Chavis did not appear at the Tinkling-Springs meeting, but he presented himself at Timber-Ridge November 18-19, 1800; and on the second day it was duly recorded that he met all the trials to the satisfaction of the Presbytery and was licensed, he himself being given a copy of the minutes.

Meanwhile, in May of the same year, the General Assembly of the Presbyterian Church of the United States, meeting in Philadelphia, had had as one of the subjects for consideration the "instruction of the Negroes, the poor and those who are destitute of the means of grace in various parts of this extensive country." The following year that body passed the resolution that "Mr. John Chavis, a black man of prudence and piety, who has been educated and licensed to preach by the Presbytery of Lexington in Virginia, be employed as a missionary among people of his own colour, until the meeting of the next General Assembly"; and a committee of three was appointed to give advice and instructions. One year still later the record reported that "the journal of Mr. John Chavis, a black man, licensed by the Presbytery of Lexington, in Virginia, was read in the Assembly. He appears to have executed his mission with great diligence, fidelity, and prudence."

Chavis asked for transfer from the Lexington to the Hanover Presbytery, and for the next three years was engaged in missionary work, chiefly in southern Virginia. In 1805 he returned to North Carolina; some time thereafter he joined the Orange Presbytery; and for twenty years or more preached in Granville, Orange, and Wake counties, though he did not have a regular pastorate. Meanwhile he began his work as a teacher.

In the *Raleigh Register* for August 26, 1808, appeared the announcement: "John Chavis takes this method of informing his employers, and the citizens of Raleigh in general, that the present quarter of his school will end the 15th of September, and the next will commence on the 19th. He will, at the same time, open an evening school for the purpose of instructing children of color." The statement went on to give further details. The terms for teaching the white children were two and a half dollars per quarter; those for the Negro children were one dollar and three-quarters.

Year by year the young people went forth, and Chavis followed their careers with solicitude. The chief letters of his that have been preserved are those that he wrote to Willie P. Mangum, later United States senator for several terms. From the correspondence one might suppose that

Mangum was at some time his pupil, but there is no proof of this. At any rate the future senator was his best friend. On December 18, 1827, Chavis wrote to Mangum: "I would thank you to attend my next examination in Wake. It will be at Revises Cross roads where you were once on the last Thursday in July. I shall tell the people that you will be there. I know it will be pleasing and give dignity to my prospects." A few months later there was a similar request. In the issue of the *Raleigh Register* for April 22, 1830, the editor, Joseph Gales, said that he had recently attended an examination "of the free children of color, attached to the school conducted by John Chavis, also colored, but a regularly educated Presbyterian minister," and had "seldom received more gratification from any exhibition of a similar character."

Chavis discussed political matters with Mangum and sometimes spoke very frankly. Under date September 3, 1831, he wrote: "I must plainly and honestly tell you that I have ever been grieved that you were the professed political friend of Gen. Jackson, because I ever believed him to be expressly what he has proved himself to be . . . and you as an honest statesman (as I believe you to be) can not keep sides with him any longer; therefore put on again your full coat of Federalism, and not only support the election of Clay, but go forth to Congress with a full determination to support the renewal of the United States Bank, to trample under foot the doctrine of Nullification, to support the tariff in its main bulwarks, and to support Internal improvements—in a word, to prove that you are an American in the full sense of the word."

Already, and even while Chavis was writing this letter, the country was in the throes of the aftermath of the Southampton Insurrection. In North Carolina as elsewhere it now became unlawful for any free Negro, slave, or free person of color to preach or exhort in public under any pretense, or in any manner to officiate as a preacher or teacher in any prayer meeting or other association for worship where slaves of different families were brought together. The new statute silenced Chavis as a preacher and closed his school. Moreover he was getting to be an old man. He presented to the Orange Presbytery the difficulties of his situation and was advised to acquiesce in the decision of the legislature until such time as God should again open to him the path of duty in regard to the exercise of his ministry. At the same time the Presbytery took steps to supply his immediate needs, and at successive meetings there were collections for his benefit.

It may have been his straitened circumstances as well as his interest in theology that led Chavis in 1837 to print and circulate a pamphlet on the theory of the Atonement. The price of this was fifteen cents, and it seems to have had a good sale. Although a Presbyterian, the author took a position opposed to that of the Calvinists and closer to that of the Arminians, maintaining that the Atonement was "commensurate to the spiritual needs of the whole human family."

This liberal spirit in religion did not extend to matters political. The most remarkable thing about Chavis and his opinions was his attitude toward the Negro in bondage. He was opposed to immediate emancipation and to all such effort as that of the abolitionists. This was not due to any lack of interest in his people or any pressure incident to the situation in which he was placed. The explanation is rather to be found in the conservatism that so often characterizes men of scholarly temper. Chavis was a teacher and he believed in the processes of education. He had no sympathy with violent or revolutionary changes.

He must have been very lonely. In no account do we

find any reference to marriage or home-life. He lived with dignity until he died in 1838, and his friend, Senator Willie P. Mangum, was faithful until the end.

Forty-five years later, in 1883, George Wortham, a lawyer of Granville County, testified that in his youth he several times heard Chavis read and explain the Scriptures to his father's family and the slaves on the estate. He recalled the pure English of the teacher, his clear and concise exposition, and his common-sense views and happy illustrations, all given without effort at oratory or sensational appeal.

In the same year Paul C. Cameron, son of a well known judge in the state, said: "In my boyhood life at my father's home I often saw John Chavis, a venerable old Negro man, recognized as a free man and as a preacher or clergyman of the Presbyterian church. As such he was received by my father and treated with kindness and consideration, and respected as a man of education, good sense, and most estimable character. He seemed familiar with the proprieties of social life, yet modest and unassuming, and sober in his language and opinions. He was polite, yes, courtly, but it was from the heart and not affectation. I remember him as a man without guile. His conversation indicated that he lived free from all evil or suspicion, seeking the good opinion of the public by the simplicity of his life and the integrity of his conduct. If he had any vanity, he most successfully concealed it. He conversed with ease on the topics that interested him, seeking to make no sort of display. . . . I write of him as I remember him, and he was appreciated by my superiors, whose respect he enjoyed."

10

The Sailing of the *Amistad*

To the Negro who was in bondage before the Civil War escape was possible only by one of three methods: regular manumission, running away, and open revolt. In course of time there were thousands of persons who secured their liberty by legal means, and the children of such parents were of course free. In some places, especially such cities as New Orleans, Charleston, and Baltimore, there developed considerable groups of free people of color, many of whom maintained a high standard of living. A number of other people who were not so fortunate chose to run away. In spite of the harsh laws against fugitives and the almost certain pursuit of bloodhounds, they preferred to risk death in the woods rather than spend all their years in servitude. Many escaped, making their way to the North, some even to Canada. Others, like Denmark Vesey and Nat Turner, as we have seen, attempted the method of open revolt. One of the most romantic of the outbreaks was that of some Africans who were being transported to America on the Spanish schooner *Amistad*.

On June 28, 1839, the *Amistad* sailed from Havana for

Guanaja, in the vicinity of Puerto Principe. She was commanded by her owner, Don Ramon Ferrer, was laden with merchandise, and had on board fifty-three Africans. Forty-nine of these persons supposedly belonged to Don José Ruiz and the other four to Don Pedro Montes. During the night of June 30 the Africans, led by one of their number, Joseph Cinque, struck for freedom. Having overwhelmed the crew, they killed the captain, a slave of his, and two sailors. They permitted most of the crew to escape, but took into close custody the two owners, Ruiz and Montes; and they ordered Montes, who had some knowledge of nautical affairs, to steer the vessel back to Africa. So he did by day, when the Negroes would watch him, but at night he would try to make for some land that was nearer. Other vessels passed from time to time, and from these the Negroes bought provisions, but Montes and Ruiz were so closely watched that they could not make known their plight. At length, on August 26, the schooner reached Long Island Sound, where it was detained by the American brig-of-war *Washington*, in command of Captain Gedney, who secured the Africans and transported them to New London, Connecticut. It took a year and a half to dispose of the issue thus raised. The case passed from court to court, attracted the greatest amount of attention, led to international complications, and was not finally disposed of until a former President, John Quincy Adams, had exhaustively argued the case for the Negroes before the Supreme Court of the United States.

On September 6, 1839, in a letter to John Forsyth, Secretary of State, Calderon, the Spanish minister to the United States, formally made four demands: 1. That the *Amistad* be immediately delivered to her owner, together with every article on board at the time of her capture; 2. That it be declared that no tribunal in the United States had the right to institute proceedings against, or to impose penalties upon, the subjects of Spain, for crimes committed on board a Spanish vessel, or in the waters of Spanish territory; 3. That the Negroes be conveyed to Havana or otherwise placed at the disposal of Spain; and 4. That if, in consequence of the intervention of the authorities in Connecticut, there should be any delay in the desired delivery of the vessel and the slaves, the owners be indemnified for any loss that might accrue to them. In support of his demands Calderon said that he desired to invoke "the law of nations, the stipulations of existing treaties, and those good feelings so necessary in the maintenance of the friendly relations that subsist between the two countries, and are so interesting to both." Forsyth asked for any papers bearing on the question, and Calderon replied that he had none except the declaration on oath of Montes and Ruiz.

Meanwhile the abolitionists in New England were insisting that due protection had not been afforded the African strangers cast on American soil, and that in no case did the executive arm of the Government have authority to interfere with the regular administration of justice. "These Africans," they said, "are detained in jail, under process of the United States courts, in a free state, after it has been decided by the District Judge, on sufficient proof, that they are recently from Africa, were never the lawful slaves of Ruiz and Montes," and "when it is as clear as noonday that there is no law or treaty stipulation that requires the further detention of these Africans or their delivery to Spain or its subjects."

Writing on October 24 to the Spanish minister, Forsyth informed him that the two Spanish subjects, Ruiz and Montes, had been arrested on a writ issuing from the Superior Court of the City of New York upon affidavits of

certain men, natives of Africa, "for the purpose of securing their appearance before the proper tribunal, to answer
for wrongs alleged to have been inflicted upon the persons
of said Africans," that, consequently, the occurrence con-
stituted simply a "case of resort by individuals against
others to the judicial courts of the country, which are
equally open to all without distinction," and that the
agency of the government to obtain the release of Messrs.
Ruiz and Montes could not be afforded in the manner requested. Further pressure was brought to bear by Calderon,
and a previous case was cited that seemed to be in his favor.
The whole matter was next muddled by the Attorney
General of the United States, Felix Grundy, of Tennessee,
in the following opinion: "These Negroes deny that they
are slaves; if they should be delivered to the claimants, no
opportunity may be afforded for the assertion of their right
to freedom. For these reasons it seems to me that a delivery to the Spanish minister is the only safe course for
this Government to pursue." The fallacy of this was shown
in a letter from B. F. Butler, United States District Attorney in New York, to Aaron Vail, acting Secretary of State.
Said he: "It does not appear to me that any question has yet
arisen under the treaty with Spain; because, although it is
an admitted principle, that neither the courts of this state,
nor those of the United States, can take jurisdiction of
criminal offenses committed by foreigners within the territory of a foreign state, yet it is equally settled in this
country that our courts will take cognizance of *civil* actions
between foreigners transiently within our jurisdiction,
founded upon contracts or other transactions made or had
in a foreign state." Pro-slavery influence was strong, however, and a few weeks later an order was given from the
Department of State for a vessel to anchor off New Haven,
Connecticut, receive the Negroes from the United States

marshal, and take them to Cuba. On Janury 7, 1840, the President, Martin Van Buren, issued the necessary warrant.

This executive order was stayed, and the case went further on its way to the highest court in the land. Meanwhile the anti-slavery people were in touch with the Africans and were teaching them the rudiments of English in order that they might better tell their story. From the first a committee had been appointed to look out for the Negroes' interests, and while they were awaiting the final decision in their case, they cultivated a garden of fifteen acres.

The appearance of John Quincy Adams before the Supreme Court of the United States in behalf of these Negroes was one of the most notable incidents in his long career. In the fullness of years, with his own administration as President twelve years behind him, the "Old Man Eloquent" came once more to the tribunal that he knew so well to make a last plea for the needy and oppressed. To the task he brought all his talents—his profound knowledge of law, his unrivaled experience, and his dignified personal presence; and the argument he made covers one hundred and thirty-five octavo pages. He gave an extended analysis of the demand of the Spanish minister, who asked the President to do what he had no constitutional right to do. "The President," said Adams, "has no power to arrest either citizens or foreigners. But even that power is almost insignificant compared with that of sending men beyond seas to deliver them up to a foreign government." The Secretary of State had "degraded the country in the face of the whole civilized world, not only by allowing these demands to remain unanswered, but by proceeding, throughout the whole transaction, as if the Executive were earnestly desirous to comply with every one of the demands." The Spanish minister felt encouraged to press his demands because they had not been properly met at first. The slave-trade was illegal by international agreement, and the only thing to do under the circumstances was to release the Negroes. Adams closed his plea with an impressive review of his career and of the labors of the jurists he had known in the court, and he won his case.

Lewis Tappan, a prominent abolitionist, now accompanied the Africans on a tour through the states to raise money for their passage home. The first meeting was in Boston. Members of the group interested the audience by their readings from the New Testament or by their descriptions of their country and the horrors of the voyage. Cinque gave the impression of extraordinary ability; and Kali, a boy eleven years of age, was very bright. Near the close of 1841, accompanied by five missionaries, the Africans set sail from New York, to make their way first to Sierra Leone and then to their homes as well as they could.

In the autumn of this same year, 1841, there occurred on another vessel an uprising somewhat similar to that on the *Amistad*. Near the close of October the brig *Creole* sailed from Richmond and Hampton Roads for New Orleans with a cargo of tobacco and one hundred and thirty slaves. On the second Sunday night out, nineteen of the slaves revolted, cowed the others, wounded the captain, and generally took charge of the vessel. The leader was Madison Washington, and one of his most aggressive assistants was a man of powerful physique, Ben Blacksmith. These men and their associates seized the arms of the ship, demanded and obtained the manifests of slaves, permitted no conversation between members of the crew except in their hearing, and threatened that if they were not taken to some British port they would throw both officers and crew overboard. Two days later the *Creole* reached Nassau, on New

Providence, one of the Bahama Islands. The first mate went ashore to report the matter, and the American consul contended to the British authorities that the slaves on board the brig were as much a part of the cargo as the tobacco; but the governor, Sir Francis Cockburn, saw no need to interfere. He liberated the slaves not concerned in the uprising, spoke of all the Negroes as "passengers," and guaranteed to the nineteen insurgents all the rights of prisoners before an English court. He further told them that the British government would be communicated with before their case was finally passed upon. Daniel Webster, Secretary of State, aroused the anti-slavery element in the United States by making a strong demand for the return of the slaves, basing his argument on the sacredness of vessels flying the American flag; but the English authorities at Nassau never returned any of them.

The *Amistad* and *Creole* cases were both important not only for the attention they attracted at the moment, but also for the assistance they gave in crystallizing sentiment against slavery. When men were as intelligent and courageous as Joseph Cinque and Madison Washington, many could not help feeling that they should never be held in bondage.

Frederick Douglass as an Orator

Twenty years before the Civil War, at an anti-slavery convention in Nantucket, Massachusetts, there was present a young Negro of powerful physique. Just three years previously he had made his way from slavery in Maryland to freedom in New England. He had acquired only the rudiments of an education but had a voice of remarkable compass. An abolitionist, William C. Coffin, who had heard him speak to the Negro people, sought him out in the crowd and asked him to say a few words to the convention. He afterward said that he could hardly stand erect or utter two words without stammering. The next speaker was William Lloyd Garrison, who took him as a theme and delivered an address of tremendous power. That occasion marked the introduction of Frederick Douglass to the people of America.

Douglass was born at Tuckahoe, Talbot County, Maryland, probably in February, 1817. His father was an unknown white man and his mother, Harriet Bailey, a slave. In his early years he was taken to Baltimore as a servant, but he learned his letters and became eager for an education. When about thirteen years of age, he secured a book of speeches, *The Columbian Orator*, and the stirring appeals for liberty in it thrilled him with inspiration. At sixteen he was sent to work on a farm where the lash was freely applied to the slaves. One day the stalwart youth resisted the attempt to whip him and never again was he thus punished. In 1836 he planned with some others to escape, but was thrown into jail when the plot was divulged. His master then arranged for his return to Baltimore, where he learned the trade of a calker and was permitted to hire his time. In September, 1838, he escaped to New York, being then twenty-one years of age. There he was given a letter to Nathan Johnson, a public-spirited Negro of New Bedford, Massachusetts, where it was thought he might be able to work at his trade. Johnson was helpful in innumerable ways. From a reading of Scott's *The Lady of the Lake*, he suggested the name *Douglas* instead of *Bailey*, though this was later spelled with a double *s*. For the next three years the young man from Maryland worked around the docks of the city, and before long he began to look forward each week to the coming of Garrison's paper, *The Liberator*. He was still at work in New Bedford in the summer of 1841 when he decided to take a few days to attend the convention in Nantucket. Thenceforth his time was not his own; he belonged to his people and the country.

For four years, under the tutelage of Garrison, Douglass lectured in the North and East. Soon some people were led to doubt that he had ever been a slave. In 1845 he went to England, where he remained two years, meeting distinguished liberals, speaking to large audiences, and rapidly growing intellectually. He began to conceive of emancipation not only as physical freedom but also as economic and spiritual opportunity. In order that there might be no legal claim to him when he returned, English friends raised £150 to enable him to purchase his freedom. On his return to the United States he began to issue in Rochester a weekly paper, *The North Star,* the name later being *Frederick Douglass' Paper.* The establishment of this periodical marked a break with Garrison, who was aloof from politics. Thenceforth Douglass stood with Gerrit Smith and others who sought abolition by constitutional means. He was friendly with John Brown, so much so that the Governor of Virginia sought to have him arrested after the raid; but he went abroad again and for six months lectured in England and Scotland.

In the course of the Civil War Douglass often conferred with President Lincoln and assisted with enlistments for the Fifty-fourth and Fifty-fifth Massachusetts regiments, his own sons being among the first recruits. After the war he spoke strongly for civil rights; from 1869 to 1872 he conducted in Washington another weekly, *The New National Era,* and later was United States marshal, recorder of deeds for the District of Columbia, and minister to Hayti. At the World's Columbian Exposition in 1893 he was in charge of the exhibit from Hayti. In 1884, his first wife having died, he married Helen Pitts, a white woman, thus incurring much criticism. He died February 20, 1895.

Douglass was essentially an orator, not a debater, and was at his best in exposing the evils of slavery. He was not a man of great faith, and sometimes, as when he opposed the Negro exodus from the South in 1879, did not fully fathom the yearning of his people. After all, it was not the work of his later years that made him great, but that of his young manhood, when he had a story to tell, and when none who heard him could fail to be moved. In him the cause of freedom found a voice, a voice that spoke for thousands; and greater than anything he might say was himself, the supreme exhibit from the house of bondage. He had irony and he could be harsh, but he had little humor and could not be witty. Charles W. Chesnutt in a brief but valuable biography says: "Douglass possessed, in large measure, the physical equipment most impressive in an orator. He was a man of magnificent figure, tall, strong, his head crowned with a mass of hair which made a striking element of his appearance. He had deep-set and flashing eyes, a firm, well moulded chin, a countenance somewhat severe in repose, but capable of a wide range of expression. His voice was rich and melodious, and of carrying power."

Perhaps the greatest speech of Douglass was that which he delivered at Rochester July 5, 1852. With withering scorn he asked, "What to the slave is the Fourth of July?" In a superb passage he showed his aptness in quoting the Bible and likening the sorrows of his people to those of the children of Israel. "By the waters of Babylon, there we sat down. Yea! we wept when we remembered Zion. We hanged our harps upon the willows in the midst thereof, for there they that carried us away captive required of us a song; and they who wasted us required of us mirth, saying, Sing us one of the songs of Zion. How can we sing the Lord's song in a strange land? If I forget thee, O Jerusalem, let my right hand forget her cunning. If I do not remember thee, let my tongue cleave to the roof of my mouth."

An address not more powerful but of more abiding significance was "What the Black Man Wants," delivered in 1865, at a time of hesitation, to the Massachusetts Anti-Slavery Society. As the objectives of the war had been realized, and as Negro soldiers had assisted in the fight, Douglass could not understand how some people, even in New England, seemed disposed to give the black man a special status rather than the full measure of American

FREDERICK DOUGLASS

citizenship. "What I ask for the Negro," he said, "is not benevolence, not pity, not sympathy, but simple justice. The American people have always been anxious to know what they shall do with us. . . . I have had but one answer from the beginning. Do nothing with us! Your doing with us has already played the mischief with us. . . . If the Negro can not stand on his own legs, let him fall. All I ask is, give him a chance to stand on his own legs! Let him alone! If you see him on his way to school, let him alone,—don't disturb him. If you see him going to the dinner table at a hotel, let him go! If you see him going to the ballot-box, let him alone,—don't disturb him! If you see him going into a workshop, just let him alone,—your interference is doing him a positive injury. . . . If the Negro can not live by the line of eternal justice, . . . the fault will not be yours; it will be his who made the Negro and established that line for his government. Let him live or die by that. If you will only untie his hands, and give him a chance, I think he will live."

Frederick Douglass was one of the famous orators of the nineteenth century and as such invites comparison with some of his contemporaries. His speeches were generally well organized. At certain moments, in the dignity of his manner, he suggests the English humanitarian, John Bright; but he made more use of invective and scorn than Bright did. In the sharpness of his irony he recalls Wendell Phillips, but, eloquent though he was, he could hardly surpass that speaker in the liquid quality of his utterance; no one in the world could. Perhaps he is closest to the Irish orator, Daniel O'Connell; but his instrument had not as many keys as that of O'Connell, nor did he equal that speaker in human appeal. His effects were those of earnestness and massiveness; he aroused the respect and admiration if not always the affectionate regard of his hearers. All told, he gave to the western world a new sense of the Negro's possibilities.

As a leader Douglass was different from such a man as Richard Allen. When Allen and his friends found that in some churches they were not treated with courtesy, they said, We shall have our own church; we shall have our own bishop; we shall build up our own racial enterprises. As early as 1848, in a speech at Rochester, Douglass said: "I am well aware of the anti-Christian prejudices which have excluded many colored persons from white churches, and the consequent necessity for erecting their own places of worship. But such a necessity does not now exist to the extent of former years. There are societies where color is not regarded as a test of membership, and such places I deem more appropriate for colored persons than exclusive or isolated organizations." There is more difference between these two positions than can be accounted for by a mere lapse of time. Allen certainly did not approve segregation under the law; no one worked harder than he to relieve his people from proscription. Douglass, who did not formally approve organizations distinctively racial, often presided over gatherings of Negro men. In the last analysis, however, it was Allen who laid the basis of racial enterprise, and Douglass who favored assimilation in the body politic. The position of one was realistic, that of the other idealistic.

12

Harriet Tubman and Her "Underground Railroad"

Outstanding among the heroines of anti-slavery was Harriet Tubman. This brave woman not only escaped from bondage herself, but afterwards made nineteen trips to the South, especially to Maryland, helping more than three hundred slaves to make their way to freedom.

Araminta Ross, better known by the Christian name *Harriet*, which she adopted, was born about 1823 in Dorchester County, on the eastern shore of Maryland. She was the daughter of Benjamin Ross and Harriet Greene, slaves who fortunately were never separated. Of ten brothers and sisters she rescued three from slavery, and in 1857, at great risk to herself, she also took to the North her father and mother.

While still a young girl, Harriet suffered a misfortune that embarrassed her for the rest of her life. She had been hired out as a field hand. It was the fall of the year, and the slaves were husking corn and reaping wheat. One who had tried to run away was caught. The overseer swore that he would be whipped and called on Harriet with some

others near to help tie him. She refused and as the slave
made his escape placed herself in a door to keep him from
being pursued. The overseer picked up a weight and
hurled it at the fugitive. It missed its mark but gave Harriet
a blow on the head that was almost fatal. Henceforth
there was a pressure on her brain which left her subject to
fits of somnolency. Sometimes these would come on her in
the midst of a conversation; then after a while the spell
would pass and she would go on as before.

After Harriet had recovered sufficiently from the blow,
she lived for five or six years in the home of one John
Stewart. Then, being permitted to hire her time, she drove
oxen, cut wood, and plowed in order to get the fifty or
sixty dollars a year required by her master. In her later
years she had no regrets about the arduous labor, as it gave
her the constitution necessary for the trials and hardships
she had to undergo.

About 1844 she was married to a free man named John
Tubman. Not long thereafter she began to consider seriously the matter of escape from slavery. Already in her
mind her people were the Israelites in the land of Egypt,
and somewhere in the North was the land of Canaan. In
1849 the master of the plantation died, and word was
passed around that at any moment she and two of her
brothers would be sold to the far South. She decided to
start for the North at once. As she could not go away
without giving some intimation of her purpose to the
friends she was leaving, and as it was not advisable for
slaves to be seen talking together too much, she went among
her old associates, singing,

> When dat ar ol' chariot comes
> I'm gwine to leabe you;
> I'm boun' for de Promised Lan';
> Frien's, I'm gwine to leabe you.

I'm sorry, frien's, to leabe you;
 Farewell! Oh, farewell!
But I'll meet you in de mornin';
 Farewell! Oh, farewell!

The brothers started with her; but the way was un-known, the North was far away, and they were constantly in terror of recapture. They turned back, and Harriet, after watching their retreating forms, again fixed her eyes on the north star. "I had reasoned dis out in my min'," she said; "there was one of two things I had a right to, liberty or death. If I could not have one, I would have de other, for no man should take me alive. I would fight for my liberty as long as my strength lasted, and when de time came for me to go, de Lord would let them take me."

"And so without money, and without friends," says Mrs. Sarah H. Bradford in the book, *Harriet, the Moses of her People*, "she started on through unknown regions, walking by night, hiding by day, but always conscious of an in-visible pillar of cloud by day, and of fire by night, under the guidance of which she journeyed or rested. Without knowing whom to trust, or how near the pursuers might be, she carefully felt her way, and by her native cunning, or by God-given wisdom, she managed to apply to the right people for food, and sometimes for shelter; though often her bed was only the cold ground, and her watchers the stars of night. After many long and weary days of travel, she found that she had passed the magic line which then divided the land of bondage from the land of free-dom." At length she arrived in Philadelphia, where she was able to earn a little money.

Two years later she made her way back to Maryland for her husband, only to find him married to another woman. The blow was a hard one, but she did not despair, and now turned as never before to the work of her life.

Already, in December, 1850, Harriet had visited Balti-more and taken away a sister and two children. A few months later she took away a brother and two other men. In December, 1851, she led out a party of eleven, including another brother and his wife. With these people she jour-neyed to Canada. The refugees had to chop wood in the forests, but as they were poorly clad and not used to the bitter cold, they found the winter hard. Harriet cooked for them, begged for them, prayed for them until the spring came. Then she returned to the States, and to Mary-land, this time bringing away nine fugitives.

It must not be supposed that those who started on the journey northward were always strong characters. The road was rough and the dangers innumerable. Sometimes those who were escaping became faint-hearted and wanted to turn back. Then Harriet would bring into play the pistol she always carried. "You go on or die," she said, pointing it at them. They generally chose to go on.

Unfailing was Harriet Tubman's trust in God. A form of prayer customary with her was, "Lord, you've been with me in six troubles; be with me in the seventh." On one of her journeys she came to the home of a Negro who had more than once assisted her. Leaving her people a little dis-tance away, she went to the door and gave the peculiar rap that was her signal. Not meeting with a ready response, she knocked several times. At length a window was raised and a white man asked roughly what she wanted. When Harriet asked for her friend, she was informed that he had been obliged to leave for assisting Negroes. The situation was dangerous; day was breaking and something had to be done at once. Outside the town, Harriet remembered, was a little island in a swamp with much tall grass upon it. Thither she hastened with her party, carrying in a basket two babies that had been drugged to keep them from cry-ing. All were cold and hungry in the wet grass; still Harriet prayed and waited for deliverance. At dusk there came slowly along the pathway on the edge of the swamp a man clad in the garb of a Quaker. He seemed to be talking to himself, but Harriet's sharp ears caught the words: "My wagon stands in the barnyard of the next farm across the way. The horse is in the stable; the harness hangs on a nail." In a moment the man was gone. When night was fully come, Harriet stole forth to the place designated and there found not only the wagon but abundant provisions in it. Soon the whole party was on its way rejoicing. In the next town dwelt a Quaker whom Harriet knew and who readily took charge of the horse and wagon for her.

Naturally the work of such a woman could not escape the attention of the abolitionists. Harriet became known to Thomas Garrett, Wendell Phillips, Gerrit Smith, William H. Seward, F. B. Sanborn, and others interested in the emancipation of the Negro. From time to time she was supplied with money, but this she never spent for her own wants, setting it aside in case of need on her next journey.

Between 1852 and 1857 she made but one or two trips, because of the Fugitive Slave Law and the increasing vigilance of officials. Rewards were offered for her capture and she was several times on the point of being taken, but always escaped by her shrewd wit and what she considered warnings from heaven. In 1857 she made her most venturesome journey, this time taking to the North her old parents. As they were not able to walk great distances, she had to hire a wagon for them, and it took all her ingenuity to get them through Maryland and Delaware. At length, however, she reached Canada. As the climate was too rigorous for the old people, she afterwards brought them to the state of New York and settled them in a home in Auburn which she had purchased on very reasonable terms from Secretary Seward. Later a mortgage on the place had to be lifted. Harriet made a visit to Boston, returning with a sum sufficient for the payment. She met John Brown more than once, knew something of his plans, and later glorified him as a hero. Her last visit to Maryland was made in December, 1860, when, in spite of the agitated condition of the country and the watchfulness of slaveholders, she brought away with her five fugitives (by some accounts seven), an infant being in the group.

After the war Harriet Tubman made Auburn her home, establishing there a refuge for aged Negroes. She married again, so that she is sometimes referred to as Harriet Tubman Davis. She died at a very advanced age on March 10, 1913. On Friday, June 12, 1914, a tablet in memory of her work was unveiled in the Auditorium in Auburn. It was provided by the Cayuga County Historical Association, and Booker T. Washington was the chief speaker of the occasion.

The tributes to this stout-hearted woman were remarkable. F. B. Sanborn said that what she did "could scarcely be credited on the best authority." William H. Seward, who labored, though unsuccessfully, to get a pension for her granted by Congress, consistently praised her fearless spirit. Abraham Lincoln lent an ear to what she had to say. The tablet dedicated to her says in part: "With implicit trust in God, she braved every danger and overcame every obstacle. Withal she possessed extraordinary foresight and judgment, so that she truthfully said, 'On my underground railroad I nebber run my train off de track and I nebber los' a passenger.' "

13

SOJOURNER TRUTH

OF THE NEGROES who were on the scene in the United States in the years leading up to the Civil War, one of the most notable and certainly the most singular was the anti-slavery speaker, Sojourner Truth. In appearance this woman was tall and striking; her insight into men and motives was astonishing; and her faith was infinite. She seemed to have endless resources of wit and wisdom.

Her early life was one of hardship. She was born in or about the year 1797, being next to the youngest of the children of James and Betsey, two slaves on an estate in Hurley, Ulster County, New York. These parents were familiarly known as Bomefree and Mau-mau Bett, and their daughter who became famous was first named Isabella. Sojourner later said that the estate was that of Colonel Ardinburgh. A recent investigator, Arthur Huff Fauset, has shown that she doubtless had reference to Colonel Johannes Hardenbergh, a Dutch landowner well known at the time, who was succeeded by his son, Charles.

The earliest home Isabella knew was the cellar of a hotel built by Charles Hardenbergh and used by him as his dwelling. There were only loose boards on the ground, and in winter the water that settled in places turned to ice. Here all the slaves of the estate had to stay, sleeping on the damp boards, each with only a little straw on which to rest, and a blanket for covering. The old people naturally suffered from rheumatism. As Bomefree was very feeble, it was thought that he might die before his wife, and at a sale of the slaves Mau-mau Bett was given her freedom in order that she might care for him. The two had nothing on which to subsist; Mau-mau Bett died, and after some time in the care of two other aged persons, Bomefree also died of hunger and cold. Isabella was sold and sold again; then, when she was twelve or fourteen years of age and already growing tall, she came in 1810 to the home of John J. Dumont, where she remained until about thirty years of age.

Dumont was more considerate than most masters, but his wife was not kind and the work was hard. While still a young woman, Isabella married a fellow slave named Thomas and in course of time had five children. In 1827 she was legally free under the emancipating act in New York. When Dumont showed a disposition to retain her services for at least a year, she left early one morning with only her youngest child, Peter, and a little bundle. After walking some miles she applied at the home of Isaac S. Van Wagener, and this man and his wife gave her shelter. When Dumont turned up she refused to go back with him, and the matter was not settled until Van Wagener agreed to buy her services for the rest of the year, paying twenty dollars for the labor of the mother and five dollars for that of the child. Some time later, when the boy Peter was illegally seized and sold down in Alabama, Isabella besieged the offices in the court house and the home of the judge, and at length her son was restored to her.

After a little more than a year with the Van Wageners, Isabella went with Peter to the city of New York. There she remained several years and passed through the most curious episode of her life. Intensely religious, she entered the service of a fanatic named Pierson, who fasted much and intended to save the world in his own way. One day while Pierson was out, another man, an impostor named Matthias, came to the house and engaged Isabella in conversation. She was much moved, and later listened eagerly to the talk of the two men. As for them, each recognized in the other a kindred spirit, Matthias claiming to be the reincarnation of God the Father and Pierson feeling that he had to do the work of John the Baptist. Other people were drawn into the cult, among them a man named Benjamin Folger and his wife. Before Isabella awoke from her dream, the money she had taken from the savings bank to invest in the common fund was lost; Matthias was forced into exile in the West; Pierson died under mysterious circumstances; and Isabella was charged by Folger with having something to do with the murder. The one redeeming feature of the whole matter from her standpoint was that when she brought suit for slander against Folger, she was given judgment for a hundred and twenty-five dollars.

Isabella was disillusioned. New York had proved a disappointment and the years spent there seemed wasted. Further, in spite of her best efforts, Peter did not do well. He went to sea at last and, after a few letters had come, was never heard of again. Undoubtedly it was time for her to go. One morning she suddenly announced to her employer, Mrs. Whiting, that she was leaving. Her name, she said, was no longer Isabella but Sojourner, and she was going East. "What are you going East for?" she was asked. "The Spirit," she said, "calls me there and I must go."

Thus it was that on June 1, 1843, the woman reborn departed, with a bundle in one hand, a little basket of provisions in the other, and two shillings in her purse. Thenceforth she was a pilgrim on the earth. As to her name she said: "An' the Lord gave me *Sojourner* because I was to travel up an' down the land showin' the people their sins an' bein' a sign unto them. Afterwards I told the Lord I wanted another name, 'cause everybody else had two names; an' the Lord gave me *Truth*, because I was to declare the truth to the people."

She spoke whenever the Spirit moved her or opportunity offered. Sometimes lodging for a night was uncertain; again there would be comfort in a well-to-do home. She was likely to appear anywhere at any time. One week she would be in New England, and the next in the Middle West. She joined the Friends in Philadelphia, and a few days later the Adventists in Connecticut. Her retorts were not always gentle or refined, but they seldom failed to hit their mark. Once after a meeting in Ohio a man came up and said, "Old woman, do you think your talk about slavery does any good? I don't care any more for your talk than I do for the bite of a flea." "Perhaps not," she replied, "but, the Lord willing, I'll keep you scratching."

One night there was a great meeting at Faneuil Hall in Boston. Douglass was one of the chief speakers, and while he was eloquent as ever, in his words was a note of pessimism. No justice, he said, was to be found in America; the only salvation for the Negro was in his own right arm. At the close of the address, in the hush of deep feeling, Sojourner rose and with her peculiar voice, heard all over the house, asked, "Frederick, is God dead?" The effect was electrical. In a moment the sentiment of the gathering changed from doubt to hope and assurance.

To the second National Woman's Suffrage Convention, held in Akron, Ohio, in 1852, and presided over by Mrs.

Frances D. Gage, came this woman of many cares. On the second day of the meeting she sat in a corner, crouched against the wall, her elbows resting on her knees and her chin upon her broad, hard palms. In the intermission she had been selling the narrative of her life, recently published. Some of the delegates feared that her presence might lead to the confusing of their cause with that of the abolitionists. More than once to the presiding officer came the word, "Don't let her speak; it will ruin us." Gradually the meeting waxed warm. Visiting ministers discussed the resolutions presented and lauded the male intellect. The women, few of whom "spoke in meeting," were becoming filled with dismay. Then slowly from her seat rose Sojourner. Slowly and solemnly she moved to the front. She laid her old bonnet at her feet and turned her great speaking eyes upon the chair. Mrs. Gage stepped forward and announced "Sojourner Truth," begging the audience to be quiet a few minutes. The tumult subsided, and every eye was fixed on the tall figure with head erect and gaze piercing the upper air.

At the first word there was a profound hush. Sojourner spoke in deep tones that reached every corner of the house. One man had ridiculed the helplessness of women, who had to be assisted into carriages and given the best place everywhere. To him she said, "Nobody eber helped me into carriages, or ober mud puddles, or gibs me any best place," and raising herself to her full height, with a voice pitched like rolling thunder, she asked, "And a'n't I a woman? Look at me. Look at my arm." And she bared her right arm to the shoulder, displaying her great muscular power. "I have plowed, and planted, and gathered into barns, and no man could head me—and a'n't I a woman? I could work as much an' eat as much as a man, when I could get it, an' bear de lash as well—an' a'n't I a woman? I have had five chilern an' seen 'em mos' all sold off into slavery, an' when I cried out with a mother's grief, none but Jesus heard— an' a'n't I a woman? . . . Dey talks 'bout dis t'ing in de head—what dey call it?" "Intellect," said someone near. "Dats it, honey. What's dat got to do with women's rights? If my cup won't hold but a pint an' yourn holds a quart, wouldn't ye be mean not to let me have my little half-measure full?" She glanced at the minister who had made the argument, and the cheering was prolonged. She was pointed and witty, solemn and serious at will, and ended by asserting, "If de fust woman God made was strong enough to turn the world upside down, all alone, dese togedder,"— and her gesture took in the audience—"ought to be able to turn it back an' get it right side up again; an' now dey is askin' to do it, de men better let 'em."

"Amid roars of applause," said Mrs. Gage in her *Reminiscences*, "she returned to her corner, leaving more than one of us with streaming eyes and hearts beating with gratitude." Thus, as so frequently happened, Sojourner Truth turned a difficult situation into splendid victory. She not only made an eloquent plea for the slave, but, placing herself upon the broadest principles of humanity, saved the day for woman suffrage as well.

When the Civil War began, she went to Washington to help care for the wounded soldiers and to find lodging and employment for the recently emancipated slaves who flocked to the capital, half-starved and homeless. She was given audience by President Lincoln, and was among the first to urge upon him the arming of the free Negroes of the North for the defense of the Union.

When the war was over, Sojourner perceived what many able men could not see, that the ultimate welfare of the Negro was to be found not only in the ballot but also in ownership of land and education in agriculture and the trades. Realizing that the thronging of men to the cities, with the consequent overcrowding of the labor market, would in time increase the criminal element and undermine the physical stamina of the race, she advocated the placing of many of the freedmen on the public lands in the West. To this theme she frequently recurred in her lectures, and she circulated petitions to Congress and in other ways enlisted sentiment to this end.

But her real work was done; it belonged to the period of the anti-slavery movement. The time had come for her to rest. Her last years were spent in the little home that friends had helped her to acquire in Battle Creek, Michigan. "People ask me," she once said, "how I come to live so long an' keep my mind; an' I tell them it is because I think of the great things of God, not the little things."

Her life closed in Battle Creek on November 26, 1883. She was buried in Oak Hill Cemetery.

"I isn't goin' to die, honey," she said; "I's goin' home like a shootin' star."

14

JOHN JASPER: "DE SUN DO MOVE"

JOHN JASPER STAMPED himself so indelibly on those among whom he moved in his later years that there are still many who have memories of his presence. In temper and outlook, however, he was of the period before the Civil War. He grew up in slavery, had lived more than half of his long life when the war came, and was as crude in his old age as in his youth; but in one sphere at least, that of imaginative and pictorial expression, he has seldom been equaled. In this his ability amounted to genius.

He was born on a plantation in Fluvanna County, Virginia, in July, 1812, the youngest of the several children of Philip Jasper, a slave preacher, and his wife, Nina. The mother was the head of the force of working women on the farm and later became the chief servant in a rich family. As Philip Jasper had died, she took full charge of the training of her son John, and endeavored to lead him into righteous paths. As the youth grew into manhood, he was a tall ungainly figure, with a small body and long swinging limbs; but he had a dashing and self-confident manner, was full of life and humor, and was quite a beau in his neighborhood. While still a young man he went to Richmond and worked in the tobacco factory of Samuel Hargrove.

On the Fourth of July, 1837, which seems to have been his twenty-fifth birthday, Jasper passed by Capitol Square in Richmond and witnessed a holiday demonstration. Something in the scene awoke his deeper self. He realized as never before the vanity of the world, and for weeks thereafter his spirit was heavy. On the morning of July 25 the tobacco was harder to stem than usual; his sins seemed piled on him like mountains, and he felt that of all who had broken the law of God he was the worst. He thought he would die, and sent to heaven a cry for mercy. Before he knew it, the clouds vanished and he felt light as a feather. As he later said, his feet were on the mountain, salvation rolled like a flood through his soul, and he thought he could blow the factory roof off with his shouts.

He thought it best to restrain himself until the noon hour; so he cried and laughed and tore up the tobacco. Then he saw not far away an old man who had tried to lead him from darkness to light. Jasper stepped over to him and said, "Hallelujah! my soul is redeemed." Then he saw a good old woman who knew of his striving and had been praying for him. He had to speak to her too; but what was intended as a whisper became a great shout, and soon the whole room was in commotion. The overseer came to see the cause of the disturbance and was told that Jasper had "got religion." His word was short and to the effect that the new convert had better get back to work. Then Mr. Hargrove himself stepped from the office to make inquiry. He was a man of benevolent spirit, a member of the First Baptist Church. In a few minutes he sent for Jasper. "His voice," said the preacher later, "was sof' like, an' it seemed to have a little song in it that played into my soul like an angel's harp." When he learned that Jasper had told his story with such power, he said: "Go back in there and go up and down the tables, and tell all of them. You needn't work any more to-day. After you get through here at the factory, go up to the house and tell your folks; go around to your neighbors and tell them; go anywhere you want to, and tell the good news. It'll do you good, do them good, and help to honor your Lord and Savior."

Jasper joined the church and immediately began to preach. Realizing the need of acquaintance with the Scriptures, he studied hard for seven months with another slave, William Jackson, in order to learn how to read. Thenceforth he was a man of one book. He read the Bible again and again, comparing passages and lingering upon the noble diction of the King James version. In a moment he grasped the essential elements of a story, and his ability to visualize some scenes was overpowering. Without the slightest regard for grammar, he would sometimes use dialogue, and he would make a scene like that of the coming forth of Lazarus from the grave so vivid that the congregation was transfixed with terror. Again, in a funeral sermon, he would give such a picture of the great white throne and the King in his beauty that all would be sent into the wildest enthusiasm.

Preaching thus, Jasper was not long in becoming known; his fame soon spread to other cities and the country districts. One day he had to be in Farmville to officiate on an occasion when a number of the dead were to have their virtues celebrated. A great throng assembled to hear him. As was usual at the time, a white minister was present to see that the proprieties were observed. This man as master of ceremonies thought to dispose of the visitor by asking him to lead in prayer. That was all Jasper needed; he had proved to be as capable in talking to heaven as to men on earth. The congregation was carried away with his eloquence and, when the white minister had concluded his

rather tame address, cried out for Jasper. The visitor, now
on fire and emboldened by the disposition of the presiding
officer to shut him out, responded to the call and gave an
address so brilliant that all who heard it remembered it to
the end of their lives.

In the course of the Civil War Jasper often preached to
the Confederate soldiers in hospitals. The fall of Richmond
found him with seventy-three cents in his pocket and forty-
two dollars in debt. Undaunted, he began to preach to a
little group on an island in the James River, and baptized
scores of converts in the river. The crowds increased and
it was soon necessary to move to a deserted building not far
away. Then, as conditions improved, a number of the people went to live in the northern part of the city. Their
preacher went with them and led in the purchase of an old
brick building formerly used by a Presbyterian mission.
The cost was $2,025, but it was not long before $6,000 had
to be spent to remodel the edifice. At length Jasper came to
the church home that he knew and loved best, the Sixth
Mount Zion, and there he was working at the height of his
fame, about 1880. Multitudes came to hear him preach "De
Sun Do Move," a sermon he is said to have delivered two
hundred and fifty times.

One of Jasper's church members said that the sermon was
called forth by an argument between Woodson, the sexton
of the church, and another man as to whether or not the
sun went around the earth. As was usual with the pa-
rishioners, the dispute was referred to the pastor. Jasper
studied and used many texts, but the one upon which he
chiefly rested was Exodus xv. 3: "The Lord is a man of
war; the Lord is his name." It took him half an hour to
roam over the Old Testament for examples of the power of
God, and even longer to develop his theory. Naturally he
gave much attention to Joshua's commanding the sun to

stand still. At the height of his discourse he spoke somewhat as follows:

"But I ain't done wid yer yit. As de song says, dere's mo'
to foller. I invite yer to hear de fus' verse in de sev'nth
chapter of de book of Reverlations. What do John, under
de power of de Spirit say? He say he saw fo' angels standin'
on de fo' corners of de earth, holdin' de fo' corners of de
earth, an' so fo'h. 'Low me to ax ef de earth is roun', whar
do it keep its corners? Er flat, squar thing has corners, but
tell me whar is de corner of a apple, er a marble, er a cannon ball, er a silver dollar. Ef dere is any of dem pher-
loserphers whar's been takin' so many cracks at my ol'
haid 'bout here, he is corjully invited to step for'ard an'
squar up dis vexin' business. I here tell yer dat yer carn't
squar a circle, but it looks lak dese great scholers done
learn how to circle de squar. Ef dey kin do it, let 'em step
to de front an' do de trick. But, mer brutherin, in my po'
judgment, dey carn't do it; tain't in 'em to do it. Dey is
on de wrong side of de Bible; dat's on de outside of de
Bible, an' dere's whar de trouble comes in wid 'em. Dey
done got out of de bres'wuks of de truf, an' ez long ez dey
stay dere, de light of de Lord will not shine on deir path.
I ain't keerin' so much 'bout de sun, tho' it's mighty convenient to have it, but my trus' is in de Word of de Lord.
Long ez my feet is flat on de solid rock, no man kin move
me. I's gettin' my orders f'om de Gawd of my salvation."

One of the white ministers of Richmond well known at
the time was the Reverend Dr. William E. Hatcher, pastor
of Grace Street Baptist Church. To him we are indebted
for the fullest account yet given of the life and work of
Jasper. He has told how legislators, ladies of fashion, visitors from out of town, all flocked to hear the famous
preacher. One day as he was still some blocks from the
church, he was met by the returning tide. "No use of

going," he was told; "house already packed, streets full, men fighting and women fainting."

Even with such success Jasper was not a sensationalist. He was ever simple and unaffected, an earnest minister of the gospel, rightly dividing the word of truth. He loved little children and was a comfort to those in sorrow. At the height of his career, when the gifts of visitors multiplied the sums in the collection plates, his officers pressed upon him to increase his salary. He finally agreed to accept $62.50 a month and no more.

It is not to be supposed that he escaped slander and calumny. Tongues wagged especially in connection with his matrimonial ventures. While still a slave, he lived for a time in Williamsburg and married a young woman named Elvy Weaden; but he was rudely snatched away immediately after the ceremony and forced to go to Richmond. Some time later his wife wrote that if he was never coming to see her, she would have to feel free to marry another husband. Jasper sorrowfully wrote that he saw no hope of an early return to Williamsburg. Later, five years after his conversion in Richmond, he thought again of marriage. He then took the letter his wife had written, presented it to the First African Baptist Church, of which he was a member, and asked what was his duty in the situation. His brethren, weighing the matter and recalling that he was a slave, gave it as their opinion that he was free to marry again. He then became joined to Candus Jordan. There were children of the union, but in course of time Jasper had reason to believe his wife unfaithful. He secured a divorce, in which action he was fully vindicated by his brethren. Years later he married a widow, Mrs. Mary Anne Cole, who was his companion just after the war but died in 1874. This wife had a daughter who took the name of Jasper and found a place in his heart as his own. When he was advanced in years, he heard her plotting with her husband to get rid of him. In self-protection then, and in order to have someone to look out for his needs, he married a godly woman of maturity and discretion. This wife survived him.

There was one group against which Jasper especially directed the shafts of his wit and humor, all the more as it adopted toward him and his ignorance an air of condescension and disparagement. That was the group of young ministers fresh from the theological seminaries. Jasper looked upon these men as book-made rather than God-made preachers. Happily in later years they were among those who appreciated his worth and joined in doing him honor.

Jasper knew nothing of homiletics. His sermons were all delivered extemporaneously, though this does not mean that he did not meditate long upon their content. He was chiefly drawn to subjects that gave scope for imagery, such as "Joseph and his Brethren," "Daniel in the Lion's Den," "The Stone Cut out of the Mountain," and "The Raising of Lazarus"; and he had no hesitation about using a theme more than once. He was meticulously careful about the faith of those received into the church; yet, beginning on the island in the James River with nine persons, he closed his ministry with a membership of two thousand. One Sunday he baptized three hundred persons in two hours.

He died at his home in Richmond, 1112 St. James Street, Saturday morning, March 30, 1901, and was buried the following Thursday. On Wednesday the body lay in state in the church. All day long and far into the night a steady line passed in silence. Those who thus did him honor were estimated at about eight thousand. To-day a magnificent monument with a tall shaft is over his grave.

On the day that John Jasper died, one of the landmarks of Richmond, the Jefferson Hotel, was destroyed by fire.

The next morning the *Times*, the daily paper of the city, said in an editorial: "It is a sad coincidence that the destruction of the Jefferson Hotel and the death of the Rev. John Jasper should have fallen upon the same day. John Jasper was a Richmond institution, as surely as was Major Ginter's fine hotel. He was a national character, and he and his philosophy were known from one end of the land to the other. Some people have the impression that John Jasper was famous simply because he flew in the face of the scientists and declared that the sun moved. In one sense that is true, but it is also true that his fame was due, in great measure, to a strong personality, to a deep, earnest conviction, as well as to a devout Christian character. Some preachers might have made this assertion about the sun's motion without having attracted any special attention. The people would have laughed over it, and the incident would have passed by as a summer breeze. But John Jasper made an impression on his generation because he was sincerely and deeply in earnest in all that he said. No man could talk with him in private, or listen to him from the pulpit, without being thoroughly convinced of that fact. His implicit trust in the Bible and everything in it, was beautiful and impressive. He had no other lamp by which his feet were guided. He had no other science, no other philosophy. He took the Bible in its literal significance; he accepted it as the inspired word of God; he trusted it with all his heart and soul and mind; he believed nothing that was in conflict with the teachings of the Bible—scientists and philosophers and theologians to the contrary notwithstanding. . . . He followed his divine calling with faithfulness, with a determination, as far as he could, to make the ways of God known unto men, his saving health among all nations. And the Lord poured upon his servant, Jasper, 'the continual dew of his blessing.'"

15

Early Effort for Practical Training: Martin R. Delany

THE VALUE OF training Negroes in the trades and handicrafts as well as along more strictly classical lines was recognized long before Hampton and Tuskegee developed the idea of industrial education. As early as 1773 the Quakers had in Philadelphia a brick schoolhouse for Negroes, and emphasis was upon sewing and other simple arts. In 1782 the philanthropist, Anthony Benezet, assumed charge of the school, and at his death he left money for the continuance of the work. In 1796 the American Convention of Abolition Societies gave to the free people of color the following advice: "Teach your children useful trades, or to labor with their hands in cultivating the earth. These employments are favorable to health and virtue. In the choice of masters who are to instruct them in the above branches of business, prefer those who will work with them; by this means they will acquire habits of industry, and be better preserved from vice than if they worked alone, or under the eyes of persons less interested in their welfare."

The solicitude thus manifested reflected a situation already developing in the country. It was increasingly evident that in the history of the Negro in America slavery was only an incident; the ultimate question was that of the place of the black man in the body politic. In the South, in the larger cities, free men of color prospered, and individual masons or carpenters were very efficient; but in the North opportunity was more restricted. In Ohio about 1820 Mechanics' Societies, corresponding to our present trade unions, combined against Negroes, and a master mechanic was tried for assisting a man of color to learn a trade. A Negro cabinet-maker who purchased his freedom in Kentucky and went to Cincinnati had great difficulty in finding employment. When an Englishman finally gave him work, the other employees struck. Such was the tendency throughout the North and the growing Central West.

Among the Negro people themselves was a temper that did not encourage industrial training. There was still question as to the intellectual capacity of the Negro student, and earnest spirits sought to measure themselves by the highest standards. These standards were those of the classical college. The dignity of labor was not yet fully recognized, and modern methods of agriculture had a long way to go. The hard facts of the situation forced attention, however, and for three decades before the Civil War there was effort for education in the trades as well as for more liberal culture.

Definite steps were taken in a convention of Negro men assembled in Philadelphia in June, 1831. Delegates came from five states, and some prominent abolitionists were also present. The visitors addressed the convention on the subject of a proposed manual training college for Negro youth in New Haven. The site selected, it was said, was healthy

and beautiful, the inhabitants were friendly, pious, generous, and humane, the laws were salutary and protecting to
all; and as the town carried on an extensive trade with the
West Indies, many of the wealthy colored residents of the
Islands would doubtless send their sons to be educated, thus
forming a new tie of friendship. The advocates of the proposed college were destined to be undeceived. The inhabitants of New Haven may have been pious, but they
were certainly neither generous nor friendly. The citizens
expressed themselves as absolutely opposed to the project
and forced it to be abandoned. When an academy was
built in Canaan, New Hampshire, the townspeople destroyed the house that was erected.

All the while, however, in the conventions of Negro men,
the idea persisted. In 1847 the Committee on Education reported in favor of "a collegiate institution, on the manual
labor plan," and a committee of twenty-five on ways and
means was appointed. In 1853, in Rochester, there was re-
newed interest in the idea of an industrial college, and
steps were taken for the registry of Negro mechanics and
artisans and of persons willing to give them work. Frederick
Douglass, James W. C. Pennington, James McCune Smith,
Alexander Crummell, Martin R. Delany, William C. Nell,
and other representative Negroes of the period were prov-
ing that they were not impractical theorists but men scien-
tifically approaching the problems of their people.

Soon after the appearance of *Uncle Tom's Cabin* in 1852,
Mrs. Harriet Beecher Stowe conferred with Douglass about
a school of which she was thinking. Douglass advised
against any training that was merely theoretical, insisting
upon actual workshops. In a letter written from Rochester
under date March 8, 1853, he said: "We must become
mechanics; we must build as well as live in houses; we must
make as well as use furniture; we must construct bridges as

well as pass over them, before we can properly live or be respected by our fellow men. We need mechanics as well as ministers. We need workers in iron, clay, and leather. We have orators, authors, and other professional men, but these reach only a certain class, and get respect for our race in certain select circles. To live here as we ought we must fasten ourselves to our countrymen through their every day cardinal wants. We must not only be able to *black* boots but to *make* them. At present we are unknown in the Northern states as mechanics. We give no proof of genius or skill at the county, state, or national fairs. We are unknown at any of the great exhibitions of the industry of our fellow citizens, and being unknown we are unconsidered."

Even more fervent was Martin R. Delany. This eager and restless spirit was born in Charles Town, Virginia (now in West Virginia), May 6, 1812, the son of free Negroes, Samuel and Pati Delany. Persecution forced his parents to move to Chambersburgh, Pennsylvania, in 1822, and there for the first time he had opportunity to go to school. In 1831 he went to Pittsburgh, where he soon became concerned about the welfare of his people. He began the study of medicine and in 1843 started the publication of a newspaper, *The Mystery*. On March 15 of the same year he married Katherine A. Richards. To the several children born into the family he gave the names of Negroes prominent in history.

From 1847 to 1849 Delany was associated with Frederick Douglass in the publishing of *The North Star* in Rochester. In July, 1848, he was attacked by a mob in northern Ohio. In 1849 he entered the Harvard Medical School and in 1854 rendered valiant service in the cholera epidemic in Pittsburgh. Two years later he went to Chatham, Ontario, where he practiced medicine. About this time such enactments as the Fugitive Slave Law and the Kansas-Nebraska Bill forced thoughtful Negro men to reconsider the whole matter of colonization. After a series of conventions, in which he played a leading part, Delany was chosen "chief commissioner" of a party to explore the Valley of the Niger "for the purpose of science and for general information." His organization made it clear that his going in no way committed it to actual colonization. He sailed in May, 1859, and the next year visited Liverpool and London. In 1861 he published his *Official Report of the Niger Valley Exploring Party*.

While in London Delany figured in an incident that received wide publicity in the American press. It was on July 16, 1860, that he attended the International Statistical Congress, having been given a royal commission on the basis of individual claim. It was a time of tense feeling in America, as the country was drifting into the Civil War. Prince Albert presided, and by him sat on one side Lord Brougham, the first vice-president, and on the other George M. Dallas, the American minister. Henry Brougham had had a distinguished career in statesmanship. Eccentric at times, he also had amazing capacity for work, and in Parliament in the earlier years of the century had been equaled only by Wilberforce in his efforts against slavery. The presence of Delany at the Congress elicited his kindly interest. After the opening address of Prince Albert, he made some remarks referring to the visitors and, turning to Dallas, called attention to the fact that a Negro was among those present. Delany, not knowing just what the effect of this might be on the assemblage, rose and said, "I rise, your Royal Highness, to thank his lordship, the unflinching friend of the Negro, for the remarks he has made in reference to myself, and to assure your Royal Highness and his lordship that *I am a man*." This statement was greeted with applause. The American delegates, however, took umbrage at the incident and withdrew, all except one man from Boston who was a state and not a national delegate.

Before leaving London Delany read before the Royal Geographical Society, by request, a paper on his studies in Africa. Back in the United States, he assisted in recruiting Negro soldiers for the Civil War, and for some time served in Chicago as an examining surgeon. On February 8, 1865, he was commissioned major, and on April 5 ordered to Charleston. For three years he served in the Freedmen's Bureau. For some time also he was a custom-house inspector, and for four years a trial justice in the city. In 1874 he was nominated for lieutenant-governor of South Carolina on the Independent Republican ticket, but was defeated. He died in Xenia, Ohio, January 24, 1885.

Delany tried his hand at many things, including more than one form of writing, but he is chiefly to be remembered by reason of a little book published in 1852, *The Condition, Elevation, Emigration, and Destiny of the Colored People of the United States, Politically Considered.* This is a mine of information about the social and economic status of the Negro ten years before the Civil War. Delany said in his preface that he wrote the book in his spare time while in New York for a month on business. Its chief purpose seems to have been to encourage emigration to the West Indies. It was attacked by the abolitionists as advocating the idea of colonization and hence as impeding immediate emancipation. The author, whose own ideas had not yet fully crystallized, realized the force of the objection and with his usual honesty ordered that the sale be stopped. In the work itself, however, he opposed the American Colonization Society as the agency of slaveholders, and then considered the claims of the Negro upon the nation. He reviewed the effort of the black man in the wars in which the country had engaged, and devoted several chapters to the achievements of representative men and women. He then took up the whole matter of colonization, opposing Liberia and considering in turn the Canadas, Central America, South America, and the West Indies. Throughout the book he was practical, with his facts well in hand.

Delany was most convincing when advocating practical education. Said he: "Let our young men and women prepare themselves for usefulness and business; that the men may enter into merchandise, trading, and other things of importance; the young women may become teachers of various kinds, and otherwise fill places of usefulness. Parents must turn their attention more to the education of their children. We mean, to educate them for useful practical business purposes. Educate them for the store and counting-house—to do everyday practical business. Consult the children's propensities, and direct their education according to their inclinations. It may be that there is too great a desire on the part of parents to give their children a professional education, before the body of the people are ready for it. A people must be a business people and have more to depend upon than mere help in people's houses and hotels, before they are either able to support or capable of properly appreciating the services of professional men among them. This has been one of our great mistakes—we have gone in advance of ourselves. We have commenced at the superstructure of the building instead of the foundation—at the top instead of the bottom. We should first be mechanics and common tradesmen, and professions as a matter of course would grow out of the wealth made thereby."

16

Daniel A. Payne: Idealist

Daniel A. Payne was one of those men whose achievement, however distinguished, is somehow surpassed by their character. As a teacher and minister in the last century, and for four decades a bishop of the African Methodist Episcopal Church, he was on the scene in some of the most stirring years in the history of the Negro and the nation. He was interested in education and missions, in science and industry, and in literature and art; yet, when all is said, one remembers what he was even more than what he did. This is one of the tests of greatness.

The special task to which Payne addressed himself was that of the improvement of the character of the Christian ministry. This end he sought to achieve not only by emphasis on mental training, but also by consideration of the moral worth of those who entered upon the calling. He did more: wherever he went he labored for the cultural advancement of those with whom his lot was cast. Entering the African Methodist Episcopal Church when that was still a young and struggling organization, he found all the foes of enlightenment against him; but, working without

95

any advantage of voice or stature, he lived to triumph gloriously. He himself had much to overcome: he was not tactful at first and it took him long to learn the secret of sympathetic approach; but so exalted was his vision and so unquestioned his integrity that he was able at last to work mightily for righteousness.

Daniel Alexander Payne was born of free parents, London and Martha Payne, in Charleston, South Carolina, February 24, 1811. Losing both parents before he was ten, he was left to the care of a grand-aunt. When he was eight he began to attend a school conducted by a society of some free men of color. At thirteen he began to work with a relative at the carpenter's trade. At this he remained for four and a half years, and then for nine months at that of a tailor. At eighteen he was converted; meanwhile he was advancing in literature and science.

About the middle of 1829 Payne began to instruct three children in their home, but so many came to him that he had to seek larger quarters. After three or four years he had as many as sixty pupils. In 1834, however, South Carolina passed a law against the teaching of colored children. The effects of the enactment on the mind of the young teacher were terrible; whole nights would pass without his being able to sleep. The law became effective on April 1, 1835, and on May 9 Payne turned his face northward. He was leaving old moorings and launching forth into the unknown. The spiritual crisis through which he passed at this time is to be seen in his poem, "The Mournful Lute, or the Preceptor's Farewell." Two of the stanzas are as follows:

Pupils, attend my last departing sounds;
Ye are my hopes, and ye my mental crowns,
My monuments of intellectual might,
My robes of honor and my armor bright.

Like Solomon, entreat the throne of God;
Light shall descend in lucid columns broad,
And all that man has learned or man can know
In streams prolific shall your minds o'erflow.

Hate sin; love God; religion be your prize;
Her laws obeyed will surely make you wise,
Secure you from the ruin of the vain,
And save your souls from everlasting pain.
O fare you well for whom my bosom glows
With ardent love, which Christ my Saviour knows!
'Twas for your good I labored night and day;
For you I wept, and now for you I pray.

In New York Payne called on Peter Williams, rector of
St. Philip's Protestant Episcopal Church, and he met young
Alexander Crummell, also Lewis Tappan, the well known
abolitionist. Tappan asked him about slavery in the South
and his opinion of immediate emancipation. Payne, with
his conservative and aristocratic temper, said that he thought
the slaves should be educated before they were emancipated,
that they might better know how to enjoy freedom when
it came. Tappan replied, "Don't you know that men can't
be educated in a state of slavery?" The lesson was one that
the young teacher never forgot.

Having been advised that he might find his best field of
service in the ministry, Payne entered the Lutheran seminary at Gettysburg, Pennsylvania. There he studied Greek,
German, and Hebrew as well as theology and church history, meanwhile working hard to support himself. From
time to time he assisted in the work at an African Methodist
church in Carlisle, twenty-five miles away. Having become
concerned about the Negro children in the neighborhood
of the Seminary, he secured permission to use an old building belonging to the institution for a Sunday School. No

mere record of activities, however, can fully indicate the
soul struggle that Daniel A. Payne went through at this
time in his effort to .realize his best self. In his longing for
perfection, his severe judgment of himself, and his contri-
tion, he was like John Henry Newman. On his twenty-fifth
birthday he prayed for complete consecration, for for-
giveness for his "proud and disobedient heart," and that he
might be useful among his "oppressed and ignorant
brethren."

It was in this spirit that, after two years at the Seminary,
he accepted the call to a Presbyterian church in East Troy,
New York. There he labored with so little thought of
himself that one night he injured his throat. For nearly a
year he was not able to speak, and this period of enforced
quiet was for him a season of testing. As he could not know
when he would be able to preach again, he resigned his
pastorate and went to stay with old friends in Carlisle.
There, by following strictly the advice of his physicians,
he improved at length. He then decided to devote himself
to teaching in Philadelphia until the way should again be
opened for him to enter a pastorate. In that city he was
daily brought in contact with Bishop Morris Brown and
other representatives of the African Methodist Episcopal
Church, and the president of the Seminary had advised that
he might find with this connection his greatest opportunity
for service. Accordingly he joined Bethel A. M. E. Church
in 1841, was received by the Philadelphia Conference as a
local preacher in 1843, and the next year was fully accepted.

At Bethel, Payne helped with the organization of a choir,
and by the innovation aroused the opposition of some of
the old people, who were not doing well with the congregational singing but objected to the use of notes. A few
left the church never to return. To help the situation the
leader of the choir and some other prominent members

asked Payne to preach a sermon on sacred music. This he did, being much assisted by a monograph on the subject by John Wesley. A choir, he showed the people, with instruments as an accompaniment, could be a powerful aid to the preacher, provided the members had scientific training and earnest Christian spirit. These things were emphasized at Bethel and thus was the way paved for the later introduction of an organ.

It happened that just at this time Israel A. M. E. Church in Washington, D. C., was at low ebb in its spiritual life, and Bishop Brown urgently requested that Payne go there for at least a year. The teacher was in love with his work; his school numbered sixty scholars; and its leisure and pleasing duties appealed to him far more than the work of an itinerant preacher. Moreover he had promised himself never again to work in a slaveholding community. He recalled, however, that the Lord Jesus Christ "humbled himself, and became obedient unto death, even the death of the cross" that he might save sinners. The path of duty was plain. He reported to Bishop Brown and turned over his school to Alexander Crummell, then a deacon and missionary of the Protestant Episcopal Church. It was his intention to return at the close of the year. Even yet he had not fully read God's purpose for his life.

As the membership at Israel was too poor to purchase seats for its building, the pastor, recalling what he knew about carpentry, bought a jack-plane, a smoothing-plane, a saw, a hammer, and a rule, and within a few weeks had made ample provision for the congregation. He also assisted in organizing an association of the Negro ministers in Washington. He did more. As early as at the Philadelphia Annual Conference in 1842 he had offered a resolution requiring that candidates for the ministry in the Church be required to pursue a regular course of study;

and soon afterward he had offered the same resolution at the conference in New York. He now began to issue a series of "Epistles on the Education of the Ministry," contributing these to a magazine that at the time was published as the organ of the African Methodist Episcopal Church. The articles were widely read and created intense excitement. Some said that they were the work of an infidel, and that the series was a slander on the work of the Connection. Unfortunately Payne himself at this time did not always in his manner and attitude show the greatest consideration and charity. As the General Conference of 1844 approached, so great was the abuse heaped upon the author of the articles that he tendered his resignation. Bishop Brown refused to accept it. "That is the very thing they want," he said. "They don't want you to be at the General Conference; so you must go." Payne not only went to Pittsburgh, where the meetings were to be held, but also served as leader of the delegation from his section.

At the Conference, as chairman of the Committee on Education, he secured the adoption of a course of study for young ministers, though not without opposition. The entire course of the action was significant, and it showed how Payne, with a slightly dogmatic air, sometimes failed to win support for a good cause. On the fifth day of the meeting he introduced a resolution for the appointment of a committee to draft a course of studies for the education of prospective preachers. He made in this connection no speech, as the need seemed to be obvious. When the presiding bishop put the question, however, it was overwhelmingly voted down, and the foes of progress were jubilant. The next day the Reverend Abraham D. Lewis, described as "an aged father in Israel," made a powerful plea for light and learning, and then the resolution received general acceptance.

In 1845 Payne was appointed to Bethel A. M. E. Church in Baltimore, and there he spent five years in a ministry rich in fruitage and also beset by storms. As in Philadelphia he had worked in general for the cultural life of the community, so he continued to work when he went to Baltimore; and it was at Bethel in the latter city that instrumental music was first countenanced by any church of the African Methodist Episcopal denomination. Once more also it seemed necessary to conduct a school. At this time it was Payne's habit to rise at five in the morning, take a walk, study from six to nine, be in school from nine to two, then make from five to ten pastoral visits, and retire at ten o'clock. It was also from Baltimore that he sent forth a series of letters that denoted him more than ever as the opponent of ignorance in the pulpit. At the same time he discouraged in every way possible the use of "cornfield ditties" in worship, and the actions of "praying and singing bands," reminiscent of old voodoo dances.

Under the auspices of Bethel at the time were three societies—Bethel, Ebenezer, and Union Bethel; and Ebenezer was using property belonging to Bethel. Payne suggested the purchase of this. The Bethel trustees insisted on $4,000; but the pastor felt that such a nominal sum as ten dollars would be sufficient, inasmuch as the congregation at Ebenezer was poor and struggling. His point of view prevailed, though not without much opposition and strong feeling. In 1850 Payne himself was appointed by Bishop William Paul Quinn to the pastorate at Ebenezer. By this time he was well known for his dignified manner, his refusal to cater to vulgarity, and his opposition to noisy modes of worship; and the congregation that he had befriended refused to accept him. A controversy resulted from the fundamental question of polity thus raised, and the situation was not relieved until the appointee was commissioned to

write a history of the denomination. In the conduct of his
task he traveled in the East and West, visiting practically
every African Methodist church in the country, meanwhile
supporting himself by lectures on education.

Already, in 1848, Payne had been asked by Bishop Quinn
to consider candidacy for the bishopric, but had declined.
In 1852, still over his protest, the General Conference
elected him. "The announcement," he said, "fell like the
weight of a mountain upon me. I trembled from head to
foot, and wept. I knew that I was unworthy of the office,
because I had neither the physical strength, and the learning, nor the sanctity which makes one fit for such a high,
holy and responsible position." It happened also that at the
time his home life was unsettled. His first wife, Mrs. Julia
A. Farris, whom he had married in 1847, had died within
a year, and it was not until 1854 that he married Mrs.
Eliza J. Clark, of Cincinnati.

The election of Daniel A. Payne to the bishopric
proved to be the most important event in the history of
the African Methodist Episcopal Church since the election
of Richard Allen to similar office in 1816. There were two
other bishops at the time, but Payne especially traveled far
and wide, from New Orleans to Canada, consulting as to
the welfare of congregations, visiting the homes of fugitive
Negroes, and organizing historical and literary societies and
mothers' clubs. On the night of April 14, 1862, at the
White House in Washington, he and Carl Schurz together
urged upon President Lincoln the signing of the bill for
emancipation in the District of Columbia. In 1863 he led
in the purchase by his church of Wilberforce University,
an institution that had been established by the Methodist
Episcopal Church in 1856 for the education of Negro
youth; and he himself later served as president for sixteen
years. It was characteristic of him to require that all candi-

dates for the ministry should give themselves to a definite course of study and that they should lead irreproachable lives.

The close of the Civil War signalized a new era in the religious life of the Negro, for it was then that the African Methodist Episcopal Church and other distinctively Negro organizations began to make such advance in the South as had been impossible before. In 1865, thirty years after he left Charleston, to the very day, Bishop Payne returned to the city, and on May 15 he organized the South Carolina Conference, from which in course of time the influence of the church extended into Georgia, Florida, and Alabama. He made two trips to England; in 1881 he was a delegate to the First Ecumenical Conference of the Methodist Church and on September 17 presided over that body. He died on November 20, 1893. Those who knew him describe him as very thin and not above the average in height, with sharp features and a shrill voice, but also with penetrating eyes and a forehead suggesting mental power.

Daniel A. Payne was one of those rare souls whose sense of duty is so stern that they amaze and even frighten people. Most people think in the concrete. They look at men rather than ideals, at things rather than principles. Their decisions are prompted by their likes and dislikes rather than their sense of right or wrong. Payne was different. He sought the eternal verities. To him it was unthinkable that one should become a minister simply for personal gain. He opposed every deceptive and degrading tendency. No one in the church did more to encourage younger men, but to the deliberate wrongdoer, the charlatan, he was a veritable Scourge of God. Naturally he could not have accomplished so much if he had not been assisted by his own sterling character.

17

The Fifty-fourth Massachusetts

At the outbreak of the Civil War two great questions affecting the Negro overshadowed all others, those of his freedom and his employment as a soldier. There was a demand from anti-slavery sources that President Lincoln dispose of the first immediately. He, however, did not feel that he should act hastily. Sentiment in the North was not united; moreover, in 1862, the Confederates, with brilliant generalship, were winning some of their greatest victories. The repulse of Lee at Antietam at length gave the President the opportunity for which he had been waiting, and he now felt that he could act with grace to the Union arms. Accordingly on September 22 he issued a preliminary declaration giving notice that one hundred days thereafter he would free all slaves in the states still in rebellion. The Emancipation Proclamation duly followed on January 1, 1863. With the first of their objectives gained, the abolitionists now addressed themselves to the second; and the leader in the effort to employ the Negro as a soldier was John A. Andrew, the great-hearted governor of Massachusetts. His idea was for a "sample regiment" of Negroes that would be of such high quality and spirit as to lead to the formation of others. In Washington he conferred at length with Edwin M. Stanton, Secretary of War, and at last persuaded him as to the advisability of the plan. He agreed with Stanton that the commissioned officers should be white men, but suggested that some of the lower places be open to Negroes so as to give opportunity for promotion from the ranks. As to this the Secretary was firmly negative in his attitude, though in all other respects, including pay, the status of the proposed regiment was to be that of other volunteer organizations.

Thus it was that on January 26, 1863, Governor Andrew received from the Secretary of War an order to raise such number of volunteer companies as he might find convenient, "volunteers to enlist for three years, or until sooner discharged," it being stated that the companies might "include persons of African descent, organized into separate corps." The first task was to secure the proper officers. It was desired that these be young men of military experience who were above any considerations of color, and who had full faith in the capacity of Negro men for military service. They would have to be men of the highest tone and honor, and it was naturally expected that they would be found in those circles of anti-slavery society which, next to the Negro race itself, had the greatest interest in the experiment.

Reviewing the young men of the character he had in mind, Governor Andrew decided to offer the colonelcy of the proposed regiment to Robert Gould Shaw, then serving as a captain in the Second Massachusetts Infantry, and the lieutenant-colonelcy to Captain Norwood Penrose Hallowell, of the Twentieth Massachusetts Infantry. Shaw was the only son in a family well known in New England not only for its wealth but also for its public spirit; and

Hallowell was of a Quaker family of Philadelphia, one with a heritage of unselfish service. The important commission was taken to Shaw, who was then in Virginia, by his father, Francis George Shaw. The young officer hesitated at first, wondering if he was equal to the responsibility of the position; and his father, realizing the tremendous issues involved, and not feeling disposed to bring undue pressure upon him, returned to New York. On the morning after his arrival he received from his son a telegram asking that word be sent to Governor Andrew that he would accept. When he arrived in Boston, Robert Gould Shaw found that Hallowell was already there. In order that army regulations might be satisfied as nearly as possible, he was commissioned major on March 31 and colonel on April 17, and on the latter date his associate was commissioned lieutenant colonel. An older brother of Hallowell's, Edward N., also reported for duty, and in course of time succeeded his brother. Other officers who represented families similarly outstanding were John W. M. Appleton, Francis L. Higginson, Henry N. Hooper, Edward B. Emerson, and Garth W. James, the brother of William and Henry James. Luis F. Emilio, a captain, became the historian of the regiment. Several of these men were from Harvard University, and the average age was twenty-three. Shaw was twenty-five years old, and Hallowell two years younger.

No tribute can be too great for these young Americans. In the step that they now took they faced the adverse sentiment of both the army and the country. In Boston as elsewhere there were those who hoped that the Governor's experiment might fail. The Confederate Congress moreover passed an act outlawing any white person who led Negroes in arms, either slave or free. All the more then were courage, faith, and a high sense of sportsmanship required of those who rested their future on the integrity of the black man.

There was, however, one moral question that had to be met by those who were responsible for the regiment. It was to be a separate organization and one formed on racial lines, but all the commissioned officers were to be white: was that fair? As to that the general position of Governor Andrew was that while the situation was not exactly what he regarded as ideal, the terms were the best he had been able to secure from the Government and at least gave the Negro an opportunity under favorable auspices to prove his worth. If this regiment succeeded, anything whatsoever might be possible in the future. History has vindicated him in the position that he took.

The Fifty-fourth Massachusetts was not the very first organization of Negro men in the Federal armies. In the previous autumn, in the South or West, escaped slaves had been taken into the service and drilled in companies. Such organizations were the result of immediate expediency, and about them there was something more or less irregular. The significance of the Fifty-fourth was that it was the first regiment of Negro men in a Northern state east of the Mississippi, and the first that had full official approval. Its formation meant the inauguration of a new policy in the conduct of the war; if this regiment succeeded, others like it would be called into action. Moreover, the new policy meant the turning of the tide in the conflict. The North was war-weary and realized that recruiting had almost ceased. In its dilemma it turned to the black man and asked if he would not help to save the country; and it did not ask in vain.

Early in February enlistment began, not only in Massachusetts but in other Northern states, announcement being made that men in the regiment would receive the regular pay of Union soldiers, $13 a month, with state aid for their families and $100 bounty at the expiration of service. Impetus was given when Governor Andrew appointed a committee of leading citizens to superintend the work, and stations were now opened from Boston to St. Louis and as far South as Fortress Monroe. On February 21 Edward N. Hallowell was ordered to Readville, a few miles from Boston on the road to Providence; and there, at Camp Meigs, with twenty-seven men, he took charge of the buildings assigned to the new regiment. Companies A and B were filled by March 15; Company D was then formed, as C had come from New Bedford. Others followed, Company K completing the regiment. As more men came than were needed, those who were above the required number formed the nucleus of the Fifty-fifth Massachusetts. The physical examination to which the men were subjected was rigid, and nearly a third of those who applied were rejected. Very few of the recruits had been slaves, and many had some degree of education.

Colonel Shaw proved to be a strict disciplinarian. In his attitude toward the Negro there was no semblance of patronizing, nor any special favor. If men were disorderly, he saw to it that they were handled with as much severity as those in the regiment from which he had come. Yet no one of them misunderstood him. They realized that all were engaged in serious business and that severe training was necessary. When the uniforms for the regiment came, they proved to be the dark blue suits used by the contrabands in the South. The Colonel promptly sent them back, insisting upon the lighter blue used by regular soldiers. After that the men knew that their leader would accept no compromise in anything affecting their integrity. He had given up everything for them and, if need be, would die for them.

On May 18, a fine cloudless day, took place the formal presentation of the colors. Extra cars had to be placed on the trains running from Boston, and at length between two and three thousand persons were present, drawn by their deep interest in the regiment and their sense of the significance of the occasion. Among those who came were Josiah Quincy, Louis Agassiz, Wendell Phillips, William Lloyd Garrison, and Frederick Douglass. The regiment formed in a hollow square, and within this the Governor, his staff and guests took their place. Prayer was offered by the Reverend Leonard A. Grimes, pastor of the Twelfth Baptist Church of Boston, who had taken a leading part in arousing interest in the regiment among the Negro people of the vicinity.

Governor Andrew delivered what was perhaps the most fervent address of his life. "This regiment," he said, "which for many months has been the desire of my heart, is present before this vast assembly of friendly citizens of Massachusetts, prepared to vindicate by its future, as it has already begun to do in its brief history of camp life here—vindicate in its own person, and in the presence, I trust, of all who belong to it, the character, the manly character, the zeal, the manly zeal of the colored citizens of Massachusetts, and of those other states which have cast their lot with ours." In fine words he expressed to Colonel Shaw and his associates his cordial thanks. "I know not, Mr. Commander," he said, "where in all history to any given thousand men in arms there has been committed a work at once so proud, so precious, so full of hope and glory as the work committed to you. I shall follow you, your officers and your men with a friendly and personal solicitude, to say nothing of official care, which can hardly be said of any other corps which has marched from Massachusetts. My personal honor, if I have any, is identified with yours. I stand or fall, as a man and a magistrate, with the rise or fall in the history of the Fifty-Fourth Massachusetts Regiment."

The flags presented by the Governor were four in number, and all were of the finest texture and workmanship. First was the national flag given by young Negro women of the city of Boston, who had been assisted in their effort by a contribution of fifty dollars from the young men of the flagship *Minnesota*. Next was the state flag, given by the Colored Ladies' Relief Society. Andrew reminded his hearers that this had already been borne by fifty-three regiments of Massachusetts soldiers, white men, and was now to be borne by the Fifty-fourth, "not less of Massachusetts than the others." "I have the pride and honor," he said, "to be able to declare before you, your regiment and these witnesses, that from the beginning until now, the State colors of Massachusetts have never been surrendered to any foe. The Fifty-fourth now holds in possession this sacred charge in the performance of their duties as citizen soldiers. You will never part with that flag so long as a splinter of the staff or a thread of its web remains within your grasp." Third was an emblematic banner given by some citizens of Boston to whose coöperation the success of the regiment had been largely due. This showed the Goddess of Liberty in beautiful guise, and bore the words *Liberty, Loyalty, and Unity*. Finally there was a flag that represented the passion and heroism of Christianity, a cross on a blue field surmounted by the motto, *In hoc signo vinces*. This, the Governor said, had connected with it the most touching and sacred memories, coming to the regiment

from the mother, relatives, and friends of one of the dearest
and noblest sons of Massachusetts, Lieutenant William
Lowell Putnam, a name that excited in every heart the
tenderest emotions of fond regard, or the strongest feeling
of patriotic fire.

To this charge, which could never be forgotten by himself or his men, Colonel Shaw replied briefly, but with feelings of deep gratitude, with a keen sense of the cause for
which they were fighting, and with appreciation of the
work of the officers and men from the beginning. Meanwhile General David Hunter, commanding the Department
of the South, asked that the regiment be sent to South
Carolina; and this seemed the logical thing to do. The days
of training, of eager preparation, of good fellowship in
camp were over. The time for action had come.

On May 28 the regiment passed through Boston on its
way to its ship. Never did the sun shine more brightly than
that day on the Common and Beacon Hill. The early trains
from all directions were filled to overflowing, and thousands of visitors surged through the streets. On every hand
were flags to greet them, and in the air was eager expectancy. The Fifty-fourth Massachusetts was leaving for
the war.

The officers had been warned that it would not be wise
to have the regiment pass through New York; hence it
was decided to travel by sea, and in the harbor the transport
De Molay was waiting. It was also not known how even
Boston, the home of liberty, would receive the dark regiment; and a hundred extra policemen were on duty. There
was, however, no disorder.

Arms had been packed in chests and all luggage shipped
the night before, the men being given a month's rations.
Early in the morning they broke camp at Readville. Their

train was slow in starting, but at nine o'clock they reached what was then called the Providence depot in Boston, and immediately formed for a march to the Common.

Preceded by Gilmore's Band and its own standard bearers, the regiment marched through Pemberton Square and on to Beacon Street and the State House, where Colonel Shaw received his papers from the Governor. Then it was joined by the Governor, his staff, and distinguished men from all parts of the state for the march to the Common, which was reached at ten-thirty. There it was formally reviewed in the presence of a vast concourse of people. The wheeling of the different companies and the general precision of their work evoked loud and prolonged applause.

The review over, a little before noon the regiment left the Common for Battery Wharf. At a post on Beacon Street the Colonel saw his father and mother, his four sisters, and the young wife he had married less than a month before. He raised his sword and saluted in recognition and farewell.

As for the regiment itself, it was generally agreed that its appearance was soldierlike and satisfactory, equal to that of the best regiments that had gone from the state. It received an ovation over the entire route. There were cheers and the waving of handkerchiefs, and in many eyes were tears. Among those along the way was one who for the first and the last time left his home to gaze upon armed men, the good Quaker poet, John Greenleaf Whittier.

One officer who had followed with devotion the progress of the regiment from the beginning, had other service required of him on this day of days and was not destined to sail with the Fifty-fourth. By reason of his good record Lieutenant Colonel N. P. Hallowell was called back even from the wharf by an order from Governor Andrew to be colonel of the Fifty-fifth Regiment of Massachusetts Volunteers and to prepare it also for service. He was succeeded in the Fifty-fourth by his brother, Edward N. Hallowell.

Steadily as the sun went down the *De Molay* sped onward. The next day the sea was smooth all the way, and at night a fine moon came up. On May 30 it was foggy and there was an increasing ground-swell; and the next day the steamer struggled against a strong head-wind, at night barely escaping grounding on the shoals of Point Lookout. On June 1 there was fine weather, but by the evening of the next day there was a squall, with lightning and some rain. Then on the morning of June 3 a warm wind was blowing, the vessel was near the islands in Charleston harbor, and the men made ready to leave.

Not far from Hilton Head a pilot came alongside the *De Molay* in a boat rowed by contrabands, and black men from the South clasped hands with brothers from the North in the cause of freedom. As Mrs. Martha N. McKay later said, the country showed many contrasts at the time, but hardly any more dramatic than that of rescued slaves rowing out to meet the Fifty-fourth.

A month later, while he was at St. Helena off the Carolina coast, Colonel Shaw received word from Washington that his men were to receive $10 rather than the usual $13 a month. He was amazed, for this was against every assurance that had been given him and them, and he refused to have them paid. He frankly said to them that both as soldiers and as men it was their duty to protest. Several times the smaller amount was offered, but the men were a unit in their stand against the insult, even though they knew that their families were suffering at home. Now that they had enlisted, they would give their best to their country, serving without pay if need be; but they could not accept less than other soldiers received, not even $12.99. In the following November the legislature of Massachusetts passed an act providing that any difference in pay would be made up by the state, and agents besought the men to accept this disposition of the matter. They still refused; while they appreciated the solicitude of their state, they were now soldiers of the United States and were to be paid accordingly. Thus it was that for eighteen months after the first companies enlisted, they received nothing. Finally, in September, 1864, the United States Government acceded to their demands, and each man received full pay from the time of his enlistment. Of such quality was the character of the officers and men of the Fifty-fourth Massachusetts Regiment.

18

Fort Wagner

On Morris Island in the harbor of Charleston were two strong forts or batteries forming the outer defense of the city. Battery Wagner, at the north end, was the one nearest the Union lines. It was an enclosed work of huge timbers and rafters covered with earth and sand, about twenty feet thick. It afforded a bomb-proof shelter, and two hundred yards in front of it the Confederates had dug a line of rifle trenches. The fort was protected by eighteen guns; fifteen of these covered the approach by land, which was along the beach. This approach was also exposed to gunfire from Sumter and the batteries on James and Sullivan islands.

The capture of the fort was deemed important to the Union cause. It was, however, not only almost impregnable but gallantly defended. With trifling loss the garrison had withstood bombardment for fifty days. Just the week before, a battalion from Pennsylvania had tried to storm it and failed, the men falling on their faces. The Union commanders now deemed it necessary to take it at any cost, and the Fifty-fourth Massachusetts was to figure in the engagement.

Two days previously the regiment had been in a skirmish on James Island. At night the men were exposed to a driving rain, and they had to make their way through a swamp. The next day they were in a blistering sun on Cole's Island, with just a little water, and only a few crackers to eat. The following night they were again in a drenching rain as they went in a boat in groups of thirty to the *General Hunter*, which was to take them to Morris Island. They arrived at length about five o'clock in the afternoon of July 18, 1863.

Colonel Shaw and Adjutant James immediately walked to the front to report to General George C. Strong, and they were informed that Fort Wagner was to be stormed that evening. "You may lead the column if you say *Yes*," said the General. "Your men, I know, are worn out, but do as you choose." Shaw accepted and asked James to return and have the lieutenant colonel, Edward N. Hallowell, bring up the regiment. A little later he said to Hallowell, "I shall go in advance with the national flag. You keep the state flag with you; it will give the men something to rally around. We shall take the fort or die there. Good-bye."

And now for once at least the heart of the young Colonel rose above army routine. As the men were relaxing a few minutes before the attack, he walked up and down the line, telling them of his faith in their courage. "Now," he said, "I want you to prove yourselves men. The eyes of thousands are on you." General Strong also spoke to similar purpose.

Meanwhile the twilight deepened fast. The officers brought their revolvers around to the front, tightened their sword-belts, and silently grasped one another's hand. Emilio has described the scene once for all. "Away over the sea to the eastward the heavy sea-fog was gathering, the western sky bright with the reflected light, for the sun had set. Far away thunder mingled with the occasional boom of cannon. The gathering host all about, the silent lines stretching away to the rear, the passing of a horseman now and then carrying orders,—all was ominous of the impending onslaught. Far and indistinct in front was the now silent earthwork, seamed, scarred, and ploughed with shot, its flag still waving in defiance."

Darkness was fast gathering as the regiment formed six hundred yards from the fort. Among its supports were the Sixth Connecticut and the Ninth Maine. At last came the word to advance. The regiment moved in quick time, changing to double-quick. When it was within two hundred yards of the fort, the Confederate garrison swarmed from the bomb-proof to the parapet, and to the artillery was suddenly added the fire of hundreds of rifles. For an instant the regiment hesitated, but only for an instant, for Colonel Shaw, springing to the front, commanded, "Forward, Fifty-fourth." With a shout the men rushed through the ditch and gained the parapet on the right; and the Colonel himself was one of the first to scale the walls. He stood erect to urge his men on; then, while calling to them, was shot through the chest and fell into the fort.

Meanwhile before the terrific fire the men melted away, some falling down the slope and others within the fort. The bearer of the state flag leaped to the parapet and was instantly killed; but, though the flag itself was torn away, the staff was saved. The bearer of the national flag was also killed, but the standard was seized by Sergeant William H. Carney. He, though severely wounded in the chest, still held the flag aloft, and, having groped his way back to his comrades, gave them the word now famous, "The old flag never touched the ground." Fourteen of the officers were either killed or wounded. Among the latter was Lieutenant Colonel Hallowell, who was so severely injured that he could barely crawl back to the Union lines.

After an hour the attack had to be abandoned, and the men who were still not hurt formed a line seven hundred yards away under Luis F. Emilio, the ninth captain in line, all the officers above him in rank having been either killed or wounded. On the morning after the attack the Confederates dug a trench in front of the works, and in this they buried the men who had fallen over the parapet. The Colonel was thrust into it along with those whom he commanded.

From the military standpoint the storming of Fort Wagner was hardly a success. In fact, there was about the exploit much that was debatable. Never was precaution more disregarded by commanding generals. There was no provision for spiking the guns; there was no line of skirmishers; and the plain over which the regiment advanced was without shelter and swept by fire. If, however, there was question as to the technical phase of the matter, there was none as to the moral. What the North wanted to know was whether the Negro would stand up under fire. To that the answer was a strong affirmative. As a result of the work of the Fifty-fourth at Fort Wagner, and that of other Negro troops at Fort Pillow and Port Hudson, not less than 167 organizations, with 186,097 men of African descent, were mustered into the Union service.

That the larger significance of what happened at Fort Wagner was not lost upon the world may be seen not only from the tributes that poured in but also from the early demand for a permanent memorial. Shaw had come to typify all that was finest in the young manhood of the North, and the failure of the enemy to extend him courtesy at the last not only made the loss more poignant but girded anew the spirit for the fight. Thomas Hughes, of England, the author of *Tom Brown's School Days,* said that the sepulchre of the young Colonel was the grandest won by any soldier of the nineteenth century.

Years afterward, on May 31, 1897, there was formally dedicated in Boston a monument, the tribute of the hero's own state. This stands at the head of the Common, facing the State House, and was the work of the famous sculptor, Augustus St. Gaudens. On the front of the monument, in bronze, is a representation of Colonel Shaw, mounted, and surrounded by his men. On the back, facing the reader as he comes up from the Common, is an inscription composed by Charles W. Eliot, then president of Harvard University. Below this are the names of five other officers of the Fifty-fourth who were killed in battle or who died in service. In the formal exercises there were brief addresses by Governor Roger Wolcott, Mayor Josiah Quincy, and Booker T. Washington; and the chief address was given by the distinguished philosopher, Professor William James, brother of Adjutant Garth W. James. On the day before, in Sanders Theatre in Cambridge, there had been in connection with Memorial Day an address by Major Henry Lee Higginson, and on the night after the dedication there was in Faneuil Hall a meeting of the survivors of the Fifty-fourth and the Fifty-fifth, addressed by one who had been in unique relation to all, Colonel Norwood Penrose Hallowell. It was a sacred occasion, one hallowed by many memories. Over the years came the word in the tribute of Emerson,

> So nigh is grandeur to our dust,
>   So near is God to man,
> When Duty whispers low, *Thou must,*
>   The youth replies, *I can.*

19

The Negro in Congress

The period of Reconstruction is still the most discussed in American history, and the one discussed with the most heat. Emancipation meant more than the liberation of four million slaves; it involved the overturning of the whole economic system of the South. The planter who saw all his wealth swept away in a moment, not unnaturally felt aggrieved; it might have been better if he could have received from the Government at least partial compensation, as in the colonies of England a generation before. The former slaves, moreover, were placed technically in opposition to those upon whom they had once depended. They were free to go where they pleased; but they knew not where to go, and they saw thousands of their brethren in the same situation. They faced the future with hope, but also with something of bewilderment. On the whole they exerted remarkable restraint.

Even before the close of the war the National Government had been forced to take official notice of the thousands of Negroes who crowded to the Federal lines. By an act of March 3, 1865, there was created the Bureau of

Refugee Freedmen and Abandoned Lands, commonly known as the Freedmen's Bureau. This was to have "the supervision and management of all abandoned lands, and the control of all subjects relating to refugees and freedmen." The Bureau was to remain in existence throughout the war and for one year thereafter, but its powers were enlarged by an act of July 16, 1866, and its chief work did not end until January 1, 1869, its educational work continuing for a year and a half longer. Of special importance in the creating act was the provision that gave the freedmen to understand that each male refugee would be given forty acres with the guarantee of possession for three years, a promise that was never fulfilled. Throughout the existence of the Bureau its chief commissioner was General Oliver Otis Howard, who in connection with this work became the first president of Howard University. Other prominent officials were similarly men of noble purpose, but just as undoubtedly were many of the minor officials corrupt and self-seeking. Thus it happened that the Bureau did not accomplish all that it was hoped it might. Moreover, morally and practically though not technically connected with it was the Freedmen's Savings and Trust Company, commonly known as the Freedmen's Bank, which made a remarkable start in the development of thrift on the part of the Negroes, and the ultimate failure of which had the most disastrous consequences.

To the Freedmen's Bureau the South objected because of the political activity of some of its officials. To meet this, and also to guarantee for the South a stable labor supply, the provisional governments of 1865 ordained the so-called Black Codes. The theory of these ordinances—most harsh in Mississippi, South Carolina, and Louisiana—was that even if the Negro was nominally free, he was not able to take care of himself and needed the tutelage and oversight of the white man. Thus developed what was to be known as a system of "apprenticeship," by which, in South Carolina, Negro males were to be bound from the age of twelve until they were twenty-one, and females from the age of ten until they were eighteen, the "master" meanwhile receiving and using the profits of the labor of the apprentice. The Mississippi ordinance added a very sharp provision against the escape of an apprentice. From all such legislation the result was that the Negro could not serve on a jury or in the militia, nor could he vote or hold office. He was virtually forbidden to assemble, and his freedom of movement was restricted.

To the North it seemed that the South was really endeavoring to thrust the freedman back into slavery. In order to protect him and to guarantee to the country the fruits of the war, Congress, led by Charles Sumner in the Senate and Thaddeus Stevens in the House of Representatives, proceeded to pass the Thirteenth, Fourteenth, and Fifteenth Amendments to the Constitution. The Thirteenth Amendment (December 18, 1865) formally abolished slavery. The Fourteenth (July 28, 1868) denied to the states the power to abridge the privileges or immunities of citizens of the United States. The Fifteenth (March 30, 1870) sought to protect the Negro by giving him the right of suffrage rather than military protection.

The consequence of this legislation was that the situation in the South was radically altered. Negroes were placed in positions of responsibility; and within the next few years the race sent two senators and several representatives to Congress, while in some state legislatures, as in South Carolina, men of color were especially prominent. P. B. S. Pinchback served as lieutenant-governor and then as acting governor in Louisiana; Oscar J. Dunn and C. C. Antoine served for three and four years respectively as lieutenant-governor in the same state; Alonzo J. Ransier and Richard H. Gleaves held this position in South Carolina; and Alexander K. Davis in Mississippi.

The first Negro to serve as United States senator, and the first man of the race to appear in either house of Congress, was Hiram R. Revels, of Mississippi, who was called upon to complete an unexpired term and actually served from February 25, 1870, to March 3, 1871. The second senator, and the first to serve a full term, was Blanche K. Bruce, of Mississippi, who was in office from March 4, 1875, to March 3, 1881. The representatives, with their actual periods of service, were as follows: Joseph H. Rainey, of South Carolina, December 12, 1870-March 3, 1879; Jefferson Long, of Georgia, December 22, 1870-March 3, 1871; Robert C. De Large, of South Carolina, March 4, 1871-January 24, 1873; Robert B. Elliott, of South Carolina, March 4, 1871-November 1, 1874; Benjamin S. Turner, of Alabama, March 4, 1871-March 3, 1873; Josiah T. Walls, of Florida, March 4, 1871-January 29, 1873; Richard H. Cain, of South Carolina, March 4, 1873-March 3, 1875, and March 4, 1877-March 3, 1879; John R. Lynch, of Mississippi, March 4, 1873-March 3, 1877, and April 29, 1882-March 3, 1883; Alonzo J. Ransier, of South Carolina, March 4, 1873-March 3, 1875; James T. Rapier, of Alabama, March 4, 1873-March 3, 1875; Jeremiah Haralson, of Alabama, March 4, 1875-March 3, 1877; John A. Hyman, of North Carolina, March 4, 1875-March 3, 1877; Charles E. Nash, of Louisiana, March 4, 1875-March 3, 1877; Robert Smalls, of South Carolina, March 4, 1875-March 3, 1879, and July 19, 1882-March 3, 1883, and March 18, 1884-March 3, 1887; James E. O'Hara, of North Carolina, March 4, 1883-March 3, 1887; Henry P. Cheatham, of North Carolina, March 4, 1889-March 3, 1893; John M. Langston, of Virginia, September 23, 1890-March

3, 1891; Thomas E. Miller, of South Carolina, September 24, 1890-March 3, 1891; George W. Murray, of South Carolina, March 4, 1893-March 3, 1895, and June 4, 1896-March 3, 1897; and George H. White, of North Carolina, March 4, 1897-March 3, 1901. To this roll of those who served in the generation after the Civil War there would be added for more recent years, if the list of Negro congressmen was to be complete, Oscar De Priest, a Republican, representative from the first congressional district of Illinois, March 4, 1929-March 3, 1935, and Arthur H. Mitchell, a Democrat, who was elected from the same district to the Seventy-fourth Congress, March 4, 1935-January 20, 1937. In the earlier years some other men had titles to seats, among them Governor Pinchback, of Louisiana, a candidate for the Senate; but the claims were not allowed by Congress. On the other hand, the irregular dates after some names are to be accounted for by the fact that some men were seated only after a contest, though on at least one occasion a representative (Smalls) succeeded a member who had died.

Historians have endeavored to belittle the achievement of these men, but many times people were surprised by the ability they exhibited. More than one had some degree of college training. Three—Senator Bruce and Representatives Elliott and Langston—were men of such unusual calibre that they are given separate chapters in the present volume. Joseph H. Rainey, the first Negro to represent South Carolina in Washington, was elected in 1870 to the Forty-first Congress when the seat of a member was declared vacant, and then was reëlected for four consecutive terms. A man who did not go to Congress but who became prominent was Francis L. Cardozo, who was born of free parents, was of mixed Negro, Indian, and Jewish descent, and was educated, in part at least, at the University of Glasgow. He

was a man of fine appearance, well-groomed, who served as
Secretary of State in South Carolina from 1868 to 1872,
and then as Treasurer of the state until 1876. He was more
than once accused of malfeasance in office, and once at
least was thrust into jail for a few days, but from all the
attacks he emerged with his integrity inviolate.

Hiram Rhoades Revels (1822-1901), the first Negro to
sit in the United States Senate, was born of free parents in
Fayetteville, North Carolina. When still a young man he
went to Indiana; for some time he attended a Quaker seminary at Liberty and then he studied at Knox College. Ordained in 1845 as a minister in the African Methodist
Episcopal Church, he worked in several states in the Central West, then served in Baltimore as a pastor and principal of a school, and helped with the recruiting of two
Negro regiments in Maryland. In 1863 he went to St.
Louis to open a school, and for the next three years was in
various states in connection with the work of his church.
In 1866 Revels settled at Natchez, Mississippi. He went
over to the Methodist Episcopal Church, and somewhat
against his will was drawn into politics. After election to
the State Senate from Adams County, he was early in 1870
sent to Washington to take the seat in the Senate once
held by Jefferson Davis. He served for just a little more
than a year, until the completion of the term, and adopted a
conciliatory attitude toward the white South, offending
Charles Sumner in so doing. Later he was president of
Alcorn University and editor of the *Southwestern Christian
Advocate;* he was also for a brief term Secretary of State
in Mississippi. He worked with the Democrats to overthrow the "carpet-bag" government in Mississippi, defending his conduct in a letter to President Grant. He died while
attending a church conference. Revels was a man of intelligence and integrity, but by reason of his conservatism

did not awaken the enthusiasm of the Negro people, and they naturally turned to such leaders as Bruce and Elliott, who more nearly fulfilled their aspiration.

One of the large questions with which Congress was wrestling at the time was that of amnesty for the men recently in arms against the Government. As to this Revels said that he believed in manhood suffrage and could not proscribe any group or class whatever; hence it was his feeling that Southern men should be restored to a place in the Union as speedily as possible. In view of the activities of the KuKlux Klan, however, Jefferson Long took the position that disabilities should remain in full force, and this was generally the point of view of the Negro congressmen. Beyond this issue, they were interested in education and internal improvements, but naturally much of their energy had to be given to the settling of election disputes in the South.

20

BLANCHE K. BRUCE: UNITED STATES SENATOR

BLANCHE KELSO BRUCE, probably the most astute political
leader the Negro ever had, became the first man of the
race to serve a full term in the Senate of the United States.

He was born a slave in Farmville, Virginia, March 1,
1841. Even in his youth his ability to earn the good will
of people was to be seen from the fact that he was given
instruction by his master's son. While still a very young
man, in the unsettled years of the Civil War, he went to
Missouri. There he made rapid progress, reading books
and newspapers, working in a printing-office, then serving
as a teacher in Hannibal. In 1866 he went to Oberlin,
where he was given special training, but the next year he
was on a boat plying between St. Louis and Council Bluffs.
In 1868 he went to Mississippi, to Floreyville in Bolivar
County, where he became a planter. At the age of twenty-
seven he now entered upon his larger career.

Bolivar County is one of the richest in the state, but in
1868 even more than to-day it was also one of those most
in danger from floods, as it fronts on the Mississippi at the
point where the Arkansas flows into the larger river. Bruce

immediately became interested in the problems of the section, not the least of these being those affecting the levees. His broad shoulders, erect bearing, and shrewdness in judgment forced respect, while his upright dealing raised him in the esteem of those with whom he came in contact.

Soon after he reached Mississippi Bruce received from the military governor, General Adelbert Ames, an appointment as conductor of elections for Tallahatchie County. In 1870 he became sergeant-at-arms in the State Senate, and in this position broadened his acquaintance with men in the state. Within the next two years he was successively assessor, sheriff, and tax collector of Bolivar County, and also served as county superintendent of schools and on the Board of Levee Commissioners. For the office of tax collector the law required that he be heavily bonded. Such was the regard in which he was held that, although he was a Republican, some prominent Democrats went on his bond. Thus the years passed until 1875.

The story goes that after attending the National Republican Convention in 1872, Bruce visited Washington before returning home, in the company of James Hill, at the moment the most powerful Negro leader in Mississippi. The two strolled into the Senate chamber and found the seats used by the members from their state. Pointing to one of these, Hill asked suddenly, "How would you like to occupy that seat?" "What do you mean?" said Bruce. "Occupy it as Senator from the State of Mississippi," was the reply. "It is out of the question." "I can and will put you there," said Hill; "no one can defeat you."

Within the next three years there was a quiet but diligent campaign, the *Floreyville Star*, a weekly, making sentiment for the election of a Negro senator and suggesting Blanche K. Bruce, though no one could be sure that that gentleman would be willing to serve. When the legislature met,

BLANCHE K. BRUCE

the white and black Republicans held separate, then joint caucuses; the Negroes were firm in their stand for Bruce; and in due time he was elected.

When on March 4, 1875, the new senator was to take his seat, the member from his state who was already serving was James L. Alcorn, a man who had had an uncertain political career, being first a Whig, later a brigadier general in the Confederate army, then the first governor of Mississippi under the plan of reconstruction. It was customary, when a new senator was to be sworn in, for the member from his state who was older in service to accompany him to the desk. When the name of Bruce was called, Alcorn, though ostensibly a Republican, was very busy with a newspaper, and the new member started to the desk alone. Just then, however, one of the most prominent men in the Senate, Roscoe Conkling, of New York, stepped forward and said, "Excuse me, Mr. Bruce; I did not until this moment see that you were without an escort. Permit me; my name is Conkling." Later in the day this same helper asked the new senator if anyone was looking out for his interests, and saw to it that he was placed on several committees.

Bruce was soon very busy with the regular work of the Senate. He was a member of the Committees on Manufactures, Education and Labor, Pensions, and the Improvement of the Mississippi River and its Tributaries. On the last committee there was no one to surpass him in expert knowledge, and in general he impressed his colleagues by his industry and sagacity. Occasionally he even presided over the Senate. On April 7, 1879, desiring to protect the rights of depositors of the defunct Freedmen's Savings and Trust Company, he introduced a resolution for the appointment of a committee of five to consider all matters pertaining to that institution. The motion passed by unanimous consent; he himself was appointed chairman, and associated with him were such well known men as Senators Cameron, Gordon, Withers, and Garland. He was unable to bring it about, as he had hoped, that depositors would be reimbursed; but he and his co-workers did at least put an end to the salaries of so-called commissioners that were rapidly depleting the cash on hand after the wreck.

In general the course of Bruce in the Senate was one of enlightened liberalism. He was opposed to the exclusion of the Chinese, was also opposed to the harsh attitude of the Government toward the Indians, and even worked for the removal of the disabilities of Southern men. His colleagues watched with unusual interest to see what attitude he would take on the bill excluding the Chinese. As to this he said: "Mr. President, I desire to submit a single remark. Representing as I do a people who but a few years ago were considered essentially disqualified from enjoying the privileges and immunities of American citizenship, and who have since been so successfully introduced into the body politic, and having a large confidence in the strength and assimilative power of our institutions, I shall vote against this bill."

Naturally much of Bruce's time had to be given to the disputed elections and the political disorders in the South. His very first speeches were prompted by this general subject; and when there was question as to the admission of Governor Pinchback, of Louisiana, in a strong speech he showed his intimate acquaintance with the conditions that prevailed. When, on March 31, 1876, a resolution was introduced for the investigation of a recent election in Mississippi, he took occasion to give an exposition of the whole situation. "The conduct of the late election in Mississippi," he said, "affected not merely the fortunes of the partisans— as the same were necessarily involved in the defeat or success of the respective parties to the contest—but put in question and jeopardy the sacred rights of the citizens; and the investigation contemplated in the pending resolution has for its object not the determination of the question whether the offices shall be held and the public affairs of the State be administered by Democrats or Republicans, but the higher and more important end, the protection in all their purity and significance of the political rights of the people and the free institutions of the country." To the charge that had been made that in some instances in recent disorders the Negro was cowardly, he replied with a defense of the courage of the black man as shown on many a battle-field, and with emphasis on the kindly feeling of the Negro people toward their white fellow-citizens, and their abhorrence of a war of races. He then said: "The sober American judgment must obtain in the South as elsewhere in the Republic, that the only distinctions upon which parties can be safely organized and in harmony with our institutions are differences of opinion relative to principles and policies of government, and that differences of religion, nationality, or race can neither with safety nor propriety be permitted for a moment to enter into the party contests of the day. The unanimity with which the colored voters act with a party is not referable to any race prejudice on their part. On the contrary, they invite the political coöperation of their white brethren, and vote as a unit because proscribed as such. They deprecate the establishment of the color line by the opposition, not only because the act is unwise, but because it isolates them from the white men of the South and forces them, in sheer self-protection, and against their inclination, to act seemingly upon the basis of a race prejudice that they neither respect nor entertain."

On May 19, 1881, just a few weeks after the close of his term as senator, Bruce was appointed by President Garfield register of the Treasury, in which office he served at this time four years, being the first man of Negro descent to hold the position. Already, on June 24, 1878, in the middle of his term in the Senate, he had married Josephine B. Wilson, of Cleveland, Ohio. The wedding was a brilliant social event, followed by a tour of the chief cities of Europe. The son born of the marriage was named after his father's first friend in the Senate, Roscoe Conkling.

Under President Cleveland, in both the first and the second term, Bruce was out of office. His personal property, however, engaged his thought. In addition he was in charge of the Negro exhibit at the World's Cotton Exposition in New Orleans in 1884, he appeared on the lecture platform, and was a trustee of Howard University. Under President Harrison he served for two years as recorder of deeds for the District of Columbia. On December 2, 1897, he was appointed by President McKinley as register of the Treasury for a second term, but he died at his home in Washington not long thereafter, on March 17, 1898. Throughout his career he had placed himself upon the broad plane of statesmanship; at the same time he kept ever in mind the people he represented.

21

Robert B. Elliott and His Civil Rights Speech

One of the large questions engaging the attention of the Negro men in Congress was that of Civil Rights. In general the idea was so to extend the provisions of the Fourteenth Amendment as to cover the exclusion of Negroes from juries and to guarantee to them equal privileges in schools, public conveyances, hotels, and theatres. Legislation to this end was urged by Charles Sumner even until his death, and a provision was offered as an amendment to the Amnesty Bill of 1872 and defeated by only one vote. It was again presented in the House in December and referred to a committee. On April 30, 1874, it passed the Senate, but the House rejected it. In February, 1875, it finally passed both houses, and was duly signed on March 1. Test cases were not long in coming up; these served more and more to invalidate the enactment; and the whole provision was finally declared unconstitutional by the Supreme Court in 1883.

It was early in January, 1874, that there took place on the bill one of the most notable debates in Congress in the decade after the Civil War. The setting was dramatic, for men from the states formerly in rebellion had now been returned to Congress, and among those to greet them there were representatives of the people recently enslaved. Prominent in the presentation of the Southern point of view were Alexander H. Stephens, of Georgia, James B. Beck, of Kentucky, and John T. Harris, of Virginia. At the moment there were seven Negroes in the House of Representatives—James T. Rapier, of Alabama, Josiah T. Walls, of Florida, John R. Lynch, of Mississippi, and Robert B. Elliott, Richard H. Cain, Joseph H. Rainey, and Alonzo J. Ransier, of South Carolina. It fell to Elliott to make the most notable speech on the bill on January 6.

Robert Brown Elliott was born in Jamaica August 11, 1842, but was taken by his parents while still young to Boston, Massachusetts. As a boy he attended High Holborn Academy in London, and in 1859 was graduated at Eton. Having studied law, he was admitted to the bar in South Carolina, and began practice in Columbia. He was a member of the state constitutional convention in 1868; was in the state House of Representatives from July 6, 1868, until October 23, 1870; and was assistant adjutant general of South Carolina from 1869 to 1871. Elliott was elected as a Republican to the Forty-second and Forty-third Congresses, and served from March 4, 1871, until his resignation, which was effective November 1, 1874, when he again went to the state House of Representatives, where he served as speaker until 1876. He then became a special agent of the Treasury, with headquarters at Charleston; later he was transferred to New Orleans; and when the death of President Garfield in 1881 threw him out of office, he remained in New Orleans engaged in the practice of law. He was a member of the National Republican Conventions of 1872, 1876, and 1880, and in the last seconded the nomination of John Sherman for the presidency. He died August 9, 1884.

Elliott was a man of fine personal presence, dark brown in color, and with a manner that suggested precision and

culture. He was temperate in his personal habits, though
generous to a fault in dealing with his friends. As a speaker
he had firm mastery of the principles of organization; he
had also a fine conception of style, and the special gift of a
vein of irony to which the debate on the Civil Rights Bill
gave full opportunity. His chief opponent was Alexander
H. Stephens, former vice-president of the Confederacy.

Elliott rose to speak before a House quivering with interest. "No language," he said, "could convey a more complete assertion of the power of Congress over the subject
embraced in the present bill than is here expressed. If the
States do not conform to the requirements of this clause,
if they continue to deny to any person within their jurisdiction the equal protection of the laws, or, as the Supreme
Court has said, 'deny equal justice in its courts,' then Congress is here said to have power to enforce the constitutional
guarantee by appropriate legislation. That is the power
which this bill now seeks to put in exercise. It proposes to
enforce the constitutional guarantee against inequality and
discrimination by appropriate legislation. It does not seek
to confer new rights, or to place rights conferred by State
citizenship under the protection of the United States, but
simply to prevent and forbid inequality and discrimination
on account of race, color, or previous condition of servitude. Never was there a bill which appealed for support
more strongly to that sense of justice and fair play which
has been said, and in the main with justice, to be a characteristic of the Anglo-Saxon race. The Constitution warrants it; the Supreme Court sanctions it; justice demands it."

In the course of his speech Elliott had to deal with somewhat discourteous remarks by Representatives Beck and
Harris. As to the former he recalled that, fifty years before, General Andrew Jackson, in speaking of the action
of the soldiers of Kentucky on one occasion, had said that

they "ingloriously fled." "In quoting this indisputable piece of history," he continued, "I do so only by way of admonition, and not to question the well attested gallantry of the *true* Kentuckian, and to suggest to the gentleman that *he* should not flaunt his heraldry so proudly while he bears this bar sinister on the military escutcheon of his State—a State which answered the call of the Republic in 1861 by coldly declaring its neutrality in the impending struggle."

Much had been made by Stephens and others who entered the discussion of the technical difference between citizenship of the United States and citizenship of the states. As to this Elliott said further: "The distinction between the two kinds of citizenship is clear, and the Supreme Court has clearly pointed out this distinction, but it has nowhere written a word or line which denies to Congress the power to prevent a denial of equality of rights whether those rights exist by virtue of citizenship of the United States or of a State. Let honorable members mark well this distinction. There are rights which are conferred on us by the United States. There are other rights conferred on us by the states of which we are individually the citizens. The Fourteenth Amendment does not forbid a State to deny to all its citizens any of those rights which the State itself has conferred with certain exceptions which are pointed out in the decision which we are examining. What it does forbid is inequality, is discrimination, or, to use the words of the amendment itself, is the denial 'to any person within its jurisdiction, the equal protection of the laws.'"

Turning to his chief opponent, Stephens himself, Elliott turned loose all his guns: "Now, sir, recurring to the venerable and distinguished gentleman from Georgia who has added his remonstrance against the passage of this bill, permit me to say that I share in the feeling of high personal regard for that gentleman which pervades this House. His years, his ability, and his long experience in public affairs entitle him to the measure of consideration which has been accorded to him on this floor. But in this discussion I can not and will not forget that the welfare and rights of my whole race in this country are involved. When, therefore, the honorable gentleman from Georgia lends his voice and influence to defeat this measure, I do not shrink from saying that it is not from him that the American House of Representatives should take lessons in matters touching human rights or the joint relations of the State and National governments. While the honorable gentleman contented himself with harmless speculations in his study, or in the columns of a newspaper, we might well smile at the impotence of his efforts to turn back the advancing tide of opinion and progress; but when he comes again upon this national arena, and throws himself with all his power and influence across the path which leads to the full enfranchisement of my race, I meet him only as an adversary; nor shall age or any other consideration restrain me from saying that he now offers this Government which he has done his utmost to destroy, a very poor return for its magnanimous treatment, to come here and seek to continue, by the assertion of doctrines obnoxious to the true principles of our Government, the burdens and oppressions which rest upon five millions of his countrymen who never failed to lift their earnest prayers for the success of this Government when the gentleman was seeking to break up the Union of these States and to blot the American republic from the galaxy of nations.

"Sir, it is scarcely twelve years since that gentleman shocked the civilized world by announcing the birth of a government which rested on human slavery as its cornerstone. The progress of events has swept away that pseudo-government which rested on greed, pride, and tyranny; and the race whom he then ruthlessly spurned and trampled on is here to meet him in debate, and to demand that the rights which are enjoyed by its former oppressors—who vainly sought to overthrow a government which they could not prostitute to the base uses of slavery—shall be accorded to those who even in the darkness of slavery kept their allegiance true to freedom and the Union. Sir, the gentleman from Georgia has learned much since 1861; but he is still a laggard. Let him put away entirely the false and fatal theories which have so greatly marred an otherwise enviable record. Let him accept, in its fullness and beneficence, the great doctrine that American citizenship carries with it every civil and political right which manhood can confer. Let him lend his influence with all his masterly ability, to complete the proud structure of legislation which makes this nation worthy of the great declaration which heralded its birth, and he will have done that which will most nearly redeem his reputation in the eyes of the world, and best vindicate the wisdom of that policy which has permitted him to regain his seat upon this floor."

Of such nature was the speech that helped toward the actual passing of the bill in 1875, though then Elliott was no longer in Congress. It would be hard to overemphasize the significance of the occasion, or the interest awakened in political circles. Wendell Phillips rode all the way from Boston to hear and to cheer the Negro orator. Frederick Douglass said: "Robert Brown Elliott was to me a most grateful surprise, and in fact a marvel. Upon sight and hearing of this man I was chained to the spot with admiration and a feeling akin to wonder." It was as if all the years that went before had been but to prepare a man for one great moment. When the time came to say a needed word for his people he was ready. Thus it was that he won their praise; thus it is that he deserves their gratitude.

22

JOHN MERCER LANGSTON AND
THE NEGRO EXODUS

PROMINENT IN THE generation after the Civil War in both education and public affairs was John Mercer Langston. This man, an Oberlin graduate, became the first president of what is now the Virginia State College, and he was the first and only man of color ever to represent Virginia in the Congress of the United States.

Langston was born in Louisa County, Virginia, December 14, 1829. He was the son of Ralph Quarles, the owner of a large estate, and Lucy Langston, who was of African and Indian descent. Quarles was a man of enlightened social outlook, and believed that slaves should be emancipated as rapidly as possible by the voluntary act of owners. Accordingly he manumitted his three children by another mother and sent them to Ohio. The two daughters died early, but the son, William, became a carpenter and joiner and settled in Chillicothe, in Ross County. Quarles and Lucy Langston became the parents of four children, a daughter, Maria, and three sons, Gideon, Charles, and John. The father was legally estopped from giving these children his name, but he showed solicitude for their welfare, made provision for each of the sons, and was especially interested in John.

Both Ralph Quarles and Lucy Langston died in 1834, when John was still in his fifth year. In line with the father's wishes, the boy passed to the guardianship of a special friend, Colonel William D. Gooch, of Chillicothe, Ohio, who cared for him just as he would have done for a son. Mrs. Gooch and her three daughters also became attached to John, and the youngest of the daughters, Virginia, laid the foundations of his education.

When the boy was about ten years of age, Colonel Gooch decided to remove to Missouri, a slave state, and naturally he thought to take John along with the members of the family. He had already gone some miles on his way when he was overtaken by John's half-brother, William, and an officer, the point being made that he had no right to take the boy beyond the jurisdiction of the court that made him guardian. It was not felt that Gooch himself contemplated any wrong, but that neither he nor anyone else could tell what might not happen in a slave state. The court decided that John could not leave Ohio. The family of Gooch parted sorrowfully with him, and he passed into the care of Richard Long, an abolitionist from New England and an elder in the Presbyterian Church of Chillicothe. The difference between the household of Gooch and that of Long was the difference between one with a leisurely and indulgent air and one in which strict and even severe discipline was the rule. John was as well treated as before, but he now had to attend to his chores with promptness and be regular in attendance at Sunday School. For the ultimate development of his character the change would seem to have been providential.

After about three years in the home of Richard Long,

young Langston was sent to a private school in Cincinnati, where he remained two years. In 1844 he entered the preparatory department of Oberlin College. Oberlin was still a young institution, having been founded in 1833. In 1835 Professor Asa Mahan, of Lane Seminary in Cincinnati, was offered the presidency. He said he would accept only if Negroes were admitted on the same terms as other students. After a warm debate the trustees decided in his favor. Though before this, individual Negroes had occasionally found their way into colleges in the North, it was here at Oberlin that they first received a genuine welcome. The institution became known as one founded on abolitionist principles, and at the outbreak of the Civil War nearly a third of the students were of the Negro race.

Here young Langston again found favorable situation, as he was taken into the home of one of the professors, George Whipple, later the secretary of the American Missionary Association. He made rapid progress, and in due time, in 1849, was graduated from the college. Remaining at Oberlin, he took the theological course also, as that seemed at the moment the best thing to do; for it must be remembered that, a hundred years ago, institutions founded under religious auspices frequently offered theology when they had no other professional department. Langston's real inclination, however, was toward the law. He had applied at the Albany Law School, and had been informed that he could enter if he claimed anything other than African descent. Declining to enter on such terms, he read law privately with Philemon Bliss, of Elyria; and in September, 1854, after an examination in open court, was admitted to the bar in Ohio. The next month he married Caroline M. Wall, a senior in the literary department of Oberlin College.

Langston began the practice of law in Brownhelm, but

two years later removed to Oberlin. In 1855 he was nominated by the Liberty Party for the position of clerk of Brownhelm township, and elected. This is generally thought to have been the first time that a man of Negro descent was ever chosen for an elective office in the United States. During the Civil War he served as an agent for Negro troops, and helped to recruit men for the Fifty-fourth and Fifty-fifth Massachusetts regiments, and the Fifth Ohio. From 1865 to 1867 he was a member of the Council of the City of Oberlin, and then for a year a member of the Board of Education. As to his life at this time another graduate of Oberlin, Fanny Jackson Coppin, has said that his comfortable home was always open with a warm welcome to the colored students, or to any who cared to share its hospitality.

In 1868 Langston was called to Washington and appointed inspector general of the Freedmen's Bureau. Within the next year he greatly broadened his horizon, visiting the South, studying conditions at first hand, and making many tactful addresses. His work brought him in close touch with General O. O. Howard, and within a few months he was summoned to the recently established Howard University to organize the Law Department. This was formally opened January 6, 1869. With Langston, who was dean, was associated one other teacher, Professor A. B. Riddle, and in the first law class were six students, classes being held three evenings a week. At the first commencement at Howard, that of 1871, Charles Sumner served as orator in compliment to the dean of the Law Department, and at least once Ralph Waldo Emerson was secured for a Sunday morning lecture on Ethics. On the resignation of General Howard in 1873, Langston was appointed vice-president, and his duties were really those of the acting president until 1875, when he retired from the institution.

Meanwhile he steadily broadened the range of his activities. In 1871 he was appointed by President Grant to the Board of Health of the District of Columbia, and he became the attorney of the Board. In 1877, by appointment of President Hayes, he became resident minister to Hayti and chargé d'affaires to Santo Domingo. For such service he was admirably fitted, his tact, his ease of manner, and his courtly address all serving in good stead. He remained in the diplomatic service until 1885, when the Democrats came into power. President Cleveland invited him to continue, but he said that as he had opposed that high official's election, he could not conscientiously serve in his administration.

On his return to the United States Langston became president of the recently organized Virginia Normal and Collegiate Institute at Petersburg, Virginia, now the Virginia State College. His wisdom, his culture, and his public spirit made a deep impression; and when after a few years his political interests made it necessary for him to leave the work, he was given a resolution of thanks "for his matchless administration of the affairs of the institute, and his invaluable services in behalf of its students." In 1888 he was the Republican nominee for Congress from his district, though he was vigorously and even bitterly opposed by General William Mahone, chairman of the State Republican Committee. He successfully contested the election of Edward C. Venable, and actually served in Washington from September 23, 1890, until March 3, 1891. An unsuccessful candidate for reëlection, he retired to his home in Washington and worked on his book, *From the Virginia Plantation to the National Capitol*, which appeared in 1894.

Already, in 1883, while still in the diplomatic service, Langston had brought together the more notable of his public addresses in a volume with the title, *Freedom and*

Citizenship. The introductory sketch for this was written by Dr. Jeremiah E. Rankin, later president of Howard University, who said of the author, "With less massive movement of mind and dignity of address than the great orator Douglass, for platform speech he is keener and more magnetic." Langston's concern with public affairs and the range of his interests may be seen from the subjects of the successive addresses: The World's Anti-Slavery Movement, Daniel O'Connell, Citizenship and the Ballot, Bishop Richard Allen, Equality before the Law, Eulogy on Charles Sumner, Our Patriot Dead, Our Political Parties, Pacific Reconstruction, The Exodus, The Future of the Colored American. If some of these subjects remind one of the old nineteenth-century lyceum, there is not one of the addresses that is not a capable presentation, while several show the speaker as thoroughly alert to the problems and issues of the day.

In the perspective the most important is that dealing with the Exodus of 1879. By this year, three years after the withdrawal of Federal troops, conditions in the South were so changed that, especially in South Carolina, Mississippi, Louisiana, and Texas, the state of affairs was no longer tolerable for the Negro people. Within fourteen years more than three thousand of them had been summarily killed, largely through the activities of the KuKlux Klan. The race began to feel that a new slavery in the form of peonage was approaching, and that the disposition of the men in power was to reduce to the minimum the advantages of the laborer as free man and citizen. The fear developed into a panic, and naturally it called forth organization to the end that there might be migration to some more favorable section. About this, one notable fact was that the political leaders of the last few years were regularly distrusted and ignored, the movement being secret in its origin and committed either to the plantation laborers themselves or to their direct representatives. A convention to consider the whole matter was held in Nashville in 1879. At this the politician managed to put in an appearance and there was much wordy discussion. At the same time much of the difference of opinion was honest; the meeting was on the whole constructive; and the resolution adopted favored "reasonable migration." Already, however, thousands of Negroes had left their homes in the South, going in greatest numbers to Kansas, Missouri, and Indiana. Within twenty months Kansas alone thus received an addition to her population of forty thousand persons. Many of these people arrived at their destination without funds and without prospect of immediate employment; but help was given by relief agencies in the North, and they themselves showed initiative and sturdiness in adapting themselves to the new conditions.

Some leaders, Frederick Douglass among them, opposed the so-called Exodus. They felt that it was for the best interest of the Negro to fight out his problem in the South; also that the new movement tended to aggravate conditions throughout the country. These men unfortunately did not fully sense the deeper striving of the people, or the disposition they have sometimes exhibited to face death in the unknown rather than be bound forever in servitude. Langston took a very different view of the situation. "Let the freedman come to the North," he said; "let him go to the West, and his contact with new men, new things, a new order of life, new moral and educational influences will advance him in the scale of being in an incomparably short time, even beyond the expectations of the most sanguine." Further: "In view then of the considerations presented; to secure the highest good of all the parties concerned by the overthrow of the plutocracy of the South and the reconstruction of the industrial system of that section, on the basis of free labor, justice, and fair dealing; to relieve the ex-slave from his dependent and practical slavery, and while giving him the fact and consciousness of his freedom and independence, furnish him the opportunity to cultivate not only ordinary labor, but to build up his present interests, industrial, material, educational, and moral, with reference to that future of which his past conduct, his capabilities and powers, his loyal and Christian devotion, give such reasonable promise, I do most reverently and heartily accept the lesson contained in the words, 'And the Lord said, I have surely seen the affliction of my people which are in Egypt, and have heard their cry by reason of their taskmasters; for I know their sorrows; and I am come down to deliver them out of the hand of the Egyptians, and to bring them up out of that land unto a good land and a large, unto a land flowing with milk and honey.' "

This was but one of many instances in which Langston showed his keen perception of the problems of his people, even of those who lived in a section far from that in which he was reared. He died at his home in Washington November 15, 1897. One who knew him described him as "little above the medium stature, slender and straight as an arrow." He was a man who had unusual advantages. One can but hope that all who have such advantages will also have the wisdom to use them so well.

23

Booker T. Washington and Industrial Education

THE OUTSTANDING LEADER of the Negro people in the United States about the turn of the century was Booker T. Washington. This famous educator was born near a cross-roads post-office named Hale's Ford, in Franklin County, Virginia, April 5, 1856; he attracted national attention by a speech at the Cotton States Exposition in Atlanta in 1895, and died November 14, 1915. The story of his early years and his rise to prominence he himself has told in his autobiography, *Up from Slavery*.

In his youth he experienced the utmost hardship. The first home that he knew was a cabin that did not even have a wooden floor. His mother was the cook of the plantation on which she was a slave; and he, an older brother, and a sister got what they could to eat but never sat at table together as in a well ordered home. In the course of the Civil War their stepfather made his way to West Virginia and, when freedom was declared, sent word to his wife to come with the children to Malden, a town five miles from Charleston. There, when he was a mere child, Booker was sent with his brother to work in a salt-furnace, and often he had to begin the day's labor at four o'clock in the morning. After two ~~or three~~ years he was placed in a coal-mine that supplied fuel for the salt-furnace. In it he had to walk a mile from the opening of the mine to the face of the coal, and often he would lose his way in the blackness. The work was dangerous as well as hard, for one might at any time be blown to pieces by an explosion or be crushed by falling slate.

One day while he was at work in the mine, Booker heard two men talking about a school, Hampton Institute, that had been founded in Virginia. He gleaned that this was not only for Negro youth but that poor and worthy students could work out all or at least a part of the cost of board and at the same time learn a trade. Inspired by a new hope, he worked a few months longer in the mine; then he was employed in the home of General Lewis Ruffner, owner of the related industries. The wage was only five dollars a month, and Mrs. Ruffner had the reputation of being hard to please, but Booker soon realized that she simply wanted promptness and cleanliness. By reason of the training then received, never in later years could he bear to see scraps of paper lying about a yard or street.

When he first had opportunity to go to school, the lad observed that the other children had two names and even three, while he had never thought of having more than one; still, when the teacher asked what his full name was, something prompted him to say "Booker Washington." Later he learned that his mother had given him the name *Talia-ferro* soon after he was born. It was then as "Booker T. Washington" that, in the autumn of 1872, at the age of sixteen, he set out for Hampton Institute. On his way thither, in Richmond, he slept for some nights under a board sidewalk with his satchel for a pillow. On his arrival he did not make a prepossessing appearance, and he waited for some hours while the head teacher, Miss Mary F. Mackie, seemed to wonder whether to admit him or not. At length she said, "The adjoining recitation-room needs sweeping. Take the broom and sweep it." Here was his chance and he was determined to make the most of it. All the training he had received from Mrs. Ruffner came to his aid. He swept the room three times, then dusted it four times, being careful to move every piece of furniture and to see that every corner was thoroughly cleaned. When at length the teacher returned and was not able to find any dirt on the floor or a particle of dust on the furniture, she said quietly, "I guess you will do to enter this institution."

Miss Mackie now offered young Washington a position as janitor and in course of time became his steadfast friend. Another teacher, Miss Nathalie Lord, helped him to improve in speaking. He also came in touch with the principal of the institution, General Samuel C. Armstrong. The work was heavy, for there was a large number of rooms to be cared for, and he had to rise at four in the morning in order to make the fires and have a little time for his lessons. The charge for board was then ten dollars a month and a student was expected to pay at least a part of this in cash; but, aside from a few dollars that his brother sent him occasionally, Washington had no means for any such payment. He determined accordingly to make his work as a janitor so good that his services would be indispensable, and he labored to such advantage that he was soon informed that he would be allowed the full cost of his board. The cost of tuition still remained, being seventy dollars a year. General Armstrong got a friend of the institution, S. Griffitts Morgan, of New Bedford, to be responsible for this throughout the student's course. Years afterward, at the height of his fame, Dr. Washington visited Mr. Morgan at his home in Massachusetts and thanked him for the assistance he had given.

At the close of his second year at Hampton, aided by a little money from his brother and his mother and a small gift from one of the teachers, Washington returned to his home in Malden. The people were happy to see him and commented on his improved appearance, but in general the outlook did not appear promising to him, as the salt-furnaces were not running and the coal-mines were closed by a strike. Early one morning moreover, after he had been away seeking work, his brother came to inform him that his mother had died. This was a hard blow, for his hope had been to make her more comfortable and happy. The little home was naturally in confusion, and for a while it seemed that all thought of returning to school would have to be given up; but before the vacation was over, Mrs. Ruffner assisted in various ways, and work was secured at a mine some distance away.

A third year passed, and in 1875 Booker T. Washington completed his course at Hampton Institute. Returning to Malden, he taught school for three years. He then attended for a year Wayland Seminary in Washington, now incorporated in Virginia Union University in Richmond, and in 1879 he was appointed as instructor at Hampton. In 1881 there came to General Armstrong a call from the town of Tuskegee, Alabama, for someone to organize and become the principal of a school that the people wanted to start. He recommended Mr. Washington, and school was opened in an old church on the Fourth of July. The teacher was then twenty-five years of age, and he worked for fourteen years before he was known to the larger American public. From the first he resolved to represent in the far South the Hampton ideal of practical training, and to attempt nothing that would not be adapted to the

BOOKER T. WASHINGTON

lives of those to whom he ministered. Said he: "We found that most of our students came from the country districts, where agriculture in some form or other was the main dependence of the people. We learned that about eighty-five per cent of the colored people in the Gulf states depended upon agriculture for their living. Since this was true, we wanted to be careful not to educate our students out of sympathy with agricultural life, so that they would be attracted from the country to the cities, and yield to the temptation of trying to live by their wits. We wanted to give them such an education as would fit a large proportion of them to be teachers, and at the same time cause them to return to the plantation districts and show the people there how to put new energy and new ideas into farming, as well as into the intellectual and moral and religious life of the people."

Meanwhile the Negro people were passing through one of the most critical periods of their history in America. One of the gravest evils affecting their lives was peonage, often an outgrowth of the convict lease system. Legislation in the South after the Civil War imposed severe penalties on vagrancy. The freedmen were arrested on the slightest pretexts, and their labor as that of convicts was leased to men in business. When some, dissatisfied with their returns under the developing "share" system, began a movement to the cities, there arose a tendency to make the legislation even more harsh, so that a laborer could not stop work without technically committing a crime. There was also notable increase in lynching. About 1870 the number of Negroes lynched in the South was eleven or twelve a year; but between 1885 and 1915 the number of persons lynched in the country was 3,500, the great majority being black men in the South. For the year 1892 alone the figure was 255. In addition, separate and inferior traveling accom-

modations, meagre provision for education, inadequate
street, light, and water facilities, and the general lack of
protection of life and property, especially in the rural districts, made life even more hard for a struggling people.

✗ As if it was not enough for the Negro to have to labor
under such disadvantages, he was now formally to be de-
prived of his voice as a citizen. Though previously his vote
may have been suppressed in actual practice, it was not
until 1890 that he was disfranchised in any state by direct
legislation. In that year the Constitution of Mississippi was
so amended as to exclude from the suffrage any person who
had not paid his poll-tax or who was unable to read any
portion of the Constitution or to give a reasonable inter-
pretation of it. The effect of the administration of this provision was to exclude the great majority of Negroes, as they
could not control the discretion of registrars. In 1895
South Carolina amended her Constitution to similar purpose.
In 1898 Louisiana passed an amendment inventing the so-
called "grandfather clause." This excused from the operation of her disfranchising act all descendants of men who
had voted before the Civil War, thus admitting to the suffrage white men who were illiterate and without property
at the same time that it excluded others. Within the next
few years other Southern states passed similar enactments.

✗ Thus by 1895 the tide had fully set in against the Negro.
The race was bewildered as indignity after indignity was
heaped upon it, and the older leaders seemed powerless before the demands of the new day. Meanwhile the South
had entered upon a new era of industrial development, and
there were those who urged that in this the black man be
ignored completely, and that a labor supply be imported
from Italy or Greece or Poland. Such was the situation
when the principal of Tuskegee Institute was invited to

speak at the Cotton States Exposition in Atlanta on September 18, 1895.

It had been suggested that, as the Negro people had been asked to take a part in the Exposition, it would be a fine thing to have a member of the race deliver one of the opening day addresses. Some were opposed to such recognition, but the Board of Directors decided to act upon the suggestion. "What were my feelings," said Booker T. Washington, "when this invitation came to me? I remembered that I had been a slave, that my early years had been spent in the lowest depths of poverty and ignorance, and that I had little opportunity to prepare for such a responsibility as this. I knew, too, that this was the first time in the entire history of the Negro that a member of my race had been asked to speak from the same platform with white Southern men and women on any important national occasion. I knew, too, that while the greater part of my audience would be composed of Southern people, yet there would be present a large number of Northern whites, as well as a great many men and women of my own race."

Upon one thing at least he was resolved, and that was to say nothing he did not feel from the bottom of his heart to be true. The newspapers took up the discussion of the coming speech, and as the appointed day drew nearer, Mr. Washington's heart became heavier. He only hoped that his effort would not end in disappointment. His anxiety extended to his friends. On the opening day one of the trustees of Tuskegee Institute, a prominent business man of the North, William H. Baldwin, Jr., was in Atlanta, and he could not persuade himself to go into the building, but walked back and forth about the grounds until the formal exercises were over.

Mr. Washington began crisply: "One-third of the population of the South is of the Negro race." It was obvious that nothing affecting the material or moral welfare of the section could overlook this element of the population, and the Directors of the Exposition were to be thanked for their recognition of the value and manhood of the race. The speaker then passed to an illustration that became famous. "A ship lost at sea for many days suddenly sighted a friendly vessel. From the mast of the unfortunate vessel was seen a signal, 'Water, water; we die of thirst!' The answer from the friendly vessel at once came back, 'Cast down your bucket where you are.' A second time the signal, 'Water, water; send us water!' ran up from the distressed vessel, and was answered, 'Cast down your bucket where you are.' And a third and fourth signal for water was answered, 'Cast down your bucket where you are.' The captain of the distressed vessel, at last heeding the injunction, cast down his bucket, and it came up full of fresh sparkling water from the mouth of the Amazon River."

This illustration Mr. Washington applied first to his own people, to those who thought of bettering their condition in a foreign land or who underestimated the importance of cultivating friendly relations with their Southern white neighbor. They were to cast down their bucket by making friends in every manly way with the people by whom they were surrounded. "No race," he said, "can prosper till it learns that there is as much dignity in tilling a field as in writing a poem. It is at the bottom of life we must begin, and not at the top. Nor should we permit our grievances to overshadow our opportunities." Then he turned to the white people, to those who might look to the incoming of persons of foreign birth and strange tongue and habit for the prosperity of the South. For them he had the same message: "Cast down your bucket where you are. Cast it down among the eight millions of Negroes whose habits you know, whose fidelity and love you have tested in days when to have proved treacherous meant the ruin of your firesides. ... In all things that are purely social we can be as separate as the fingers, yet one as the hand in all things essential to mutual progress."

There were other sentences that were provocative or full of pith and wisdom. "No race," said the speaker, "that has anything to contribute to the markets of the world is long in any degree ostracized." Further: "The opportunity to earn a dollar in a factory just now is worth infinitely more than the opportunity to spend a dollar in an opera-house." Still further: "There is no defense or security for any of us except in the highest intelligence and development of all."

The first thing that Mr. Washington knew when he had finished was that the presiding officer, Ex-Governor Rufus B. Bullock, had rushed across the platform to shake his hand. So many pressed forward to congratulate him that he found it difficult to get out of the building. The next morning he appeared in the business section of the city, but attracted so much attention that he returned to his boarding-place. At every station on the way back to Tuskegee there was a crowd of people eager to shake his hand. Mr. Clark Howell, editor of the *Atlanta Constitution*, telegraphed to a New York paper: "I do not exaggerate when I say that Professor Booker T. Washington's address yesterday was one of the most notable speeches, both as to character and as to the warmth of its reception, ever delivered to a Southern audience. The address was a revelation." The *Boston Evening Transcript* said in an editorial: "The speech of Booker T. Washintgon at the Atlanta Exposition this week seems to have dwarfed all the other proceedings and the Exposition itself. The sensation that it has caused in the press has never been equalled."

Many intelligent Negro men, however, were taken aback. They felt that in the so-called Atlanta Compromise Mr. Washington had conceded altogether too much. Dr. W. E. Burghardt DuBois became prominent in the opposition, and Monroe Trotter, of the Boston *Guardian*, was especially outspoken. Some other critics were also not enthusiastic. Mr. H. I. Brock, of the staff of the *New York Times*, writing in *The South in the Building of the Nation*, said: "The capable Booker T. Washington is in type and in fact exactly like Peter the successful barber and Walker who runs a profitable carrier's business in a certain Southern town, though neither Peter nor Walker can read or write. It is Washington's native shrewdness which has made him what he is, which has enabled him (as did Walker also) to stand well with the white community while he leads the blacks." But no matter what may have been the opposition or the discount, Mr. Washington became more than ever the leader of his people. For years presidents of the United States sought his advice in large matters affecting the Negro. In 1896 Harvard conferred on him the degree of Master of Arts, and five years later Dartmouth conferred that of Doctor of Laws. He was overwhelmed with requests for addresses and appeared on many distinguished occasions—at the unveiling of the Robert Gould Shaw Monument in Boston in May, 1897, at the Chicago Peace Jubilee in October, 1898, at the National Education Association in St. Louis in 1904. Institutions modeled after Tuskegee appeared in different parts of the South. The National Negro Business League was organized, Mr. Washington becoming president. Banks were founded and stores and business enterprises to the number of twenty thousand. Of course much of this progress would have been realized if the Negro Business League had never been organized; but everyone knew to whom the inspiration was due, and knew too that in the development so rapidly taking place the genius of the leader at Tuskegee was the chief directing force.

Mr. Washington was married three times. His first wife was Fannie N. Smith, of Malden, West Virginia, a graduate of Hampton, to whom he was joined in the summer of 1882, one year after he began work at Tuskegee. She helped to make a home for the teachers in the early days of the institution, became the mother of a daughter, Portia, and died in 1884. A year later took place the marriage to Olivia A. Davidson, of Ohio, a graduate of Hampton, also of the State Normal School in Framingham, Massachusetts, who had been teaching at Tuskegee for four years. This wife exhausted herself by her labors for the institution and died in 1889, leaving two sons, Booker Taliaferro and Ernest Davidson. In 1893 Mr. Washington married Margaret J. Murray, a native of Mississippi and a graduate of Fisk University, who was then serving at Tuskegee as lady principal and now became his companion in his larger labors. She survived him ten years. 1915

24

Paul Laurence Dunbar

In the closing decade of the last century appeared a young Negro writer who, more than anyone of his race who had preceded him, had the heart and the mind of a poet. He became famous when only twenty-four years of age. Two years later his success was so great that it created a vogue.

Paul Laurence Dunbar was born in Dayton, Ohio, June 27, 1872, the son of Joshua and Matilda Dunbar. Joshua Dunbar, a plasterer, had been held in slavery in Kentucky before the Civil War, but escaped to Canada by "underground railroad." Returning to the United States in the course of the war, he enlisted in the Fifty-fifth Massachusetts, the second regiment of Negro men recruited in the North. In 1871, already advanced in years, he married a young widow, Mrs. Matilda Murphy, who by her first marriage had become the mother of two sons. Mrs. Dunbar proved to be a woman of initiative. She was bright and witty and, though without formal education, had a keen sense of literary values.

When Paul was not more than four years of age, his

mother began to teach him his letters. When he was six or seven, he began to make attempts at rhyming. What he afterward spoke of as his "first poetical achievement" was the reciting of some original verse at a Sunday school Easter celebration when he was thirteen. In school he showed an inclination toward literary studies, excelling in reading, spelling, and grammar. Often in the long winter evenings he would listen to the stories his mother told of old days in Kentucky.

Joshua Dunbar died when his son was twelve years old; a little sister of Paul's died in infancy; and the two Murphy brothers went away to Chicago to work. As a lad Paul was thus left alone with his mother, and between the two there was always deep sympathy. The boy was not robust in health, rather delicate in fact, and engaged little in outdoor sports. Even if he had been so inclined, there would have been little time, for he had to help in the home. His mother supported herself by washing clothes or doing any other work she could find, and he would carry out the bundles or help about the hotels in the city when opportunity offered. Paul made steady progress in his studies and in due course passed on to the Central High School, now superseded by the Steele High School, where he was the only Negro in his class. His schoolmates perceived his merit and liked him, and he also won the good will of the teachers. In his second year he was admitted to the Philomathean Society, a literary organization, and soon began to contribute to the *High School Times*. In his last year he was chosen both president of the society and editor of the paper. For the graduation exercises in 1891 he wrote the class song.

The next few years were the most critical in the life of Paul Laurence Dunbar. As long as there were lessons to get, and the completion of a course to be kept in mind, the way was clear; but now that all was over, what was next?

He was ceasing to be a boy and drawing toward manhood: how best could he give of himself to the world? Primarily, he hoped, by something of a literary nature. College by all means was to be considered—perhaps a profession, the law, or, as he later thought, the ministry. For the moment, however, there was the pressing need of earning a living and helping his mother. Everything else must wait.

Then it was that there came to Paul Dunbar the problem faced by thousands of young Americans since, and in his case rendered doubly difficult. Was there anything he could do, in an office, on a newspaper—anything of a clerical nature? No; it seemed that there was no one who wanted a Negro youth in such capacity. At last, however, he found a place as elevator boy in the Callahan Building on Main Street. The wage was only four dollars a week, but—that was four dollars. It did not seem quite right: there were young men who had never been to high school who could run an elevator; but the days were passing, and hunger was insistent.

One thing at least he could do, and that was to hold to his vision. Thus it was that he gave readings from time to time, and he sent to newspapers and magazines some of the poems he composed. Very often the little manuscripts came back immediately, but sometimes also the young author did not see his poems again until they were in print. In June, 1892, he made a favorable impression at the meeting in Dayton of the Western Association of Writers. One of his former teachers had arranged that he would be invited to deliver the address of welcome, and he decided to use verse as the medium for what he had to say. On the appointed day, as the hour for his part drew near, he got leave from the elevator, hastened to the assembly hall, and duly said his piece. The next day the presiding officer and two of his associates sought out the young writer at his work. Another man who became interested was the well known poet, James Whitcomb Riley, who sent a letter of good cheer and encouragement.

Thus it was that in the late autumn of 1892, when he was but twenty years of age and only a year and a half out of high school, Paul Dunbar conceived the idea that he too would like to publish a book of poems. One evening, after a hard day on the elevator, he came home and asked his mother for the newspapers containing different pieces that she had been keeping for him; and that night he spent in selecting and arranging such pieces as he wanted to use. Going, however, the next morning to the United Brethren Publishing House, which he often passed on his way to the heart of the city, he was doomed to be disappointed. The representative of the firm informed him that his poems could not be published on a regular royalty basis, that the house could not assume any responsibility, and that the collection could be printed only at the author's risk, the cost to be one hundred and twenty-five dollars. Would the firm then print the book and permit him to pay after a few weeks? No, not unless there was ample security.

The young author had turned away and was leaving in dejection when the business manager of the firm, William Lawrence Blacher, who knew his worth, called him to his desk. "What's the matter, Paul?" he asked. "Oh," said Dunbar, "I wanted to have a volume of poems printed, but the house can't trust me and I can never get one hundred and twenty-five dollars to pay for it in advance." Mr. Blacher talked with him a little further and then thrilled him by saying that he would give his personal guarantee for the book and that it would be out in time for the Christmas holidays.

Day after day, in the busy season now at hand, Paul Dunbar, with a new hope in his eyes, asked those who came into the elevator if they would buy his book. More than one had reason to know him pleasantly and showed kindly interest. When some others paused and remarked that the book was a very small one to cost a dollar, the author replied with a touch of humor but also with confidence that it was not selling on its size but its merits. Within just two weeks after the appearance of the work, he was able to call again at the Publishing House and place in the hands of Mr. Blacher the full amount of his obligation. To-day his little volume, entitled *Oak and Ivy*, is one of the rarest and most valuable items in the whole range of Negro literature.

As one might suppose, there is in the book some imitation of Riley and other popular poets of the day, especially those who wrote in sentimental vein. What is really notable, however, is that by the time he was twenty Dunbar had not only written some of the best of his poems in classic English, such as "A Drowsy Day," "October," and "Life," but had also struck the note in dialect that was to make him famous. This is perhaps best seen in "The Ol' Tunes."

> You kin talk about yer anthems
> An' yer arias an' sich,
> An' yer modern choir-singin'
> That you think so awful rich;
> But you orter heerd us youngsters
> In the times now far away,
> A-singin' o' the ol' tunes
> In the ol'-fashioned way.

The next three years in the life of Paul Laurence Dunbar were years of feverish activity in composition but also of increasing doubt and discouragement. Only occasionally was there a ray of sunlight. For a time a group of interested men thought of helping him to go to college, but somehow the plan failed to materialize. In the summer of 1893 he went to Chicago with the hope of finding work, as the World's Columbian Exposition had opened; but day after day he was baffled. Finally, Frederick Douglass, who was commissioner in charge of the exhibit from Hayti, employed him as a clerical assistant, paying him five dollars a week. After a few months the exposition was over, and he was again in Dayton, facing another hard winter of struggle and defeated hopes. From time to time he would give readings, but in general he was uncertain for still another year. One special friend whom he found in this trying period, however, and one who did much to lift him from the gloom was Dr. H. A. Tobey, superintendent of the State Hospital for the insane. This acquaintance led to other engagements, and, after a notable recital in Toledo, a group of friends generously undertook to assist him with the publishing of another book of verse.

The collection thus arranged for was *Majors and Minors*, privately printed in Toledo. The date was 1895, and the poet hoped that the book might be out in time for the Christmas holidays; but it did not appear until early in the new year. As a piece of book-making *Majors and Minors* was not as good as *Oak and Ivy*. The paper was thinner and duller, and the binding not especially attractive. Even a sympathetic critic spoke of it as a "countrified" little volume. All that is true. At the same time, if we consider only original work, that is, the number of pieces that had not previously appeared in a book, *Majors and Minors* is the most notable collection of poems ever issued by a Negro in the United States. Among the new pieces were "The Poet and his Song," "Ships that Pass in the Night," "Ere Sleep Comes Down to Soothe the Weary Eyes," "The Party," "The Deserted Plantation," "The Rivals," and "When Malindy Sings."

A song is but a little thing,
And yet what joy it is to sing!
In hours of toil it gives me zest,
And when at eve I long for rest;
When cows come home along the bars,
    And in the fold I hear the bell,
As Night, the shepherd, herds his stars
    I sing my song, and all is well.

Dr. Tobey, who had the zeal of a missionary in advancing his young friend's work, saw that a copy was received by James A. Herne, a prominent actor who was appearing in the state in *Shore Acres*. Mr. Herne wrote to Dunbar from Detroit, speaking enthusiastically of the poems and saying that he would bring the book to the attention of William Dean Howells. So he did, and that distinguished author and critic wrote a review of nearly a page in his regular discussion of "Life and Letters" in *Harper's Weekly*. The issue was that reporting the nomination of William McKinley for the presidency. The date was June 27, 1896, Dunbar's twenty-fourth birthday. Like Byron at the same age, he awoke one morning and found himself famous.

A prominent firm in New York, Dodd, Mead and Company, now undertook formally to publish a collection of the new author's poems, and thus appeared in 1896 *Lyrics of Lowly Life*, the book by which Dunbar is best known, though the contents were mainly drawn from the two previous collections, privately issued. Howells wrote the Introduction and said among other things: "So far as I could remember, Paul Dunbar was the only man of pure African blood and of American civilization to feel the Negro life aesthetically and express it lyrically."

Early the next year, supposedly in charge of a manager, Dunbar went to England as a reader; but financially the trip proved to be disastrous. On his return he worked for

a little more than a year in the library of Congress in Washington; then he realized that the confining nature of his employment was undermining his health. In New York in
1899 he was critically ill. As soon as he was able to travel
he went to Colorado for several months.

Meanwhile he had married Alice Ruth Moore, a gifted
young woman from New Orleans, and books were appearing in rapid succession. Within the next few years *Lyrics
of the Hearthside, Lyrics of Love and Laughter,* and *Lyrics
of Sunshine and Shadow* were published. Many of the
poems in these books, especially those in dialect, were re-
issued in specially illustrated volumes. Of these there were
six: *Poems of Cabin and Field; Candle-Lightin' Time;
When Malindy Sings; Li'l' Gal; Howdy, Honey, Howdy;*
and *Joggin' Erlong.* There were also four novels, *The Un-
called, The Love of Landry, The Fanatics,* and *The Sport
of the Gods,* and four collections of stories and sketches,
*Folks from Dixie, The Strength of Gideon, In Old Planta-
tion Days,* and *The Heart of Happy Hollow.* In 1913
Dodd, Mead and Company issued the *Complete Poems,* and
the next year a little gift book, *Speakin' o' Christmas.*

Dunbar's later years witnessed increasing fame but also
an unavailing quest for health. Everything that the devotion of friends could contribute was his, but he died on
February 9, 1906. He was finally laid to rest in Woodland
Cemetery in Dayton. The grave is on a slight elevation,
near the roadway, and by it grows a small willow. Just a
few feet beyond is a small lake, while not far away, still
closer to the road, stands a giant oak.

Three years later, on the occasion of his birthday, leading
citizens of Dayton paid tribute to the poet by unveiling a
monument erected by popular subscription. More than a
thousand persons were present on that beautiful morning in
June. Several came from other cities. James Whitcomb

Riley was there, and the Philharmonic Society sang words of the poet set to music. It was all a noble tribute to one who was worthy of it.

Paul Laurence Dunbar was unique in the literature and the life of his time. His genius commanded the attention of the great, the wise, and the good; and his modesty increased their admiration. Of his deeper striving the world knew little, but to his own people he was such an inspiration as they have seldom had. About the turn of the century there was hardly a Negro college in the country in which there were not three or four young men who were trying to write verses like his; and many students earned money for their schooling by reciting his poems.

As a poet of his people he has sometimes been compared with Burns. The comparison is apt, and yet it must not be pressed unduly. As Brand Whitlock said, there was in Dunbar something that soared above race and that touched the heart universal. He came on the scene just at the time when America was being launched on the machine age, and when the country was beset by problems. Against the bullying forces of industrialism he resolutely set his face. In a world of discord he dared to sing his song, about nights bright with stars, about the secret of the wind and the sea, and the answer one finds beyond the years. In doing this he vindicated the spirit of youth—youth that is the same in all climes and all ages, youth that believes in itself and is not overcome. Thus it was that he could truthfully write:

> When all is done, say not my day is o'er,
> And that thro' night I seek a dimmer shore:
> Say rather that my morn has just begun,—
> I greet the dawn and not a setting sun,
>   When all is done.

25

Charles Young and the Tenth Cavalry

When the Spanish-American War broke out in 1898, there were four regiments of Negro regulars in the Army of the United States, the Twenty-fourth Infantry, the Twenty-fifth Infantry, the Ninth Cavalry, and the Tenth Cavalry. Negroes enlisted in the volunteer service in several states. The Eighth Illinois regiment was officered throughout by Negroes, with J. R. Marshall in chief command; and Major Charles Young, later Colonel Young, a West Point graduate, was in charge of the Ohio battalion.

Negro troops were conspicuous in the fighting around Santiago, and they also faced danger in other ways. Having learned that General Nelson A. Miles desired a regiment for the cleaning of a yellow fever hospital and the nursing of some victims of the disease, the Twenty-fourth Infantry volunteered its services and reported at dawn the following morning. An hour later the men were put to work, and before sunset the lines of the tents were straightened out, the waterworks put in operation, and the debris of the burned buildings cleared away. Thus it was that within a few days the number of those ill was greatly reduced.

On July 1 it seemed necessary to attack a garrison at El Caney, a position important for securing possession of a line of hills along the San Juan River, a mile and a half from Santiago. This was but one of several places where the Spaniards had taken advantage of the Cuban terrain. The natural features of the country were plains and highlands that sloped sharply into marshes covered with vines, and in the jungle passage might be greatly impeded by the skillful placing of barbed wire. Blockhouses were so stationed as to command the points awaiting the unsuspecting, and those who had just disembarked and were making their way inland were especially exposed to attack.

The charge at El Caney was made by the First Volunteer Cavalry, commonly known as the "Rough Riders," led by Colonel Theodore Roosevelt. These men were making their way through the jungle and up the hillside when there was suddenly turned loose upon them the merciless fire of Spanish sharpshooters. For some moments there was confusion, and meanwhile the officers sought to get their bearing and to discover the source of the concealed fire. Then the men of the Tenth Cavalry, having heard of the plight of their comrades, hurriedly mounted and galloped to the front, just in time to rescue the famous regiment; and they did not return from their work until the Spaniards were routed and the event recorded as another victory for the American arms.

The exploit made a profound impression on the country. Kenneth Robinson, one of those wounded in the charge, said of the men of the Tenth: "They have been the best friends that the 'Rough Riders' have had, and every one of us, from Colonel Roosevelt down, appreciates it." A corporal who was in the fight said: "If it had not been for the Negro cavalry, the 'Rough Riders' would have been exterminated. I am not a Negro lover. My father fought with Mosby's rangers, and I was born in the South, but the Negroes saved that fight, and the day will come when General Shafter will give them credit for their bravery."

A correspondent of the Atlanta *Evening Journal* said under date July 30, 1898: "I have been asked repeatedly since my return about what kind of soldiers the Negroes make. The Negroes make fine soldiers. Physically the colored troops are the best men in the army, especially the men in the Ninth and Tenth Cavalry. Every man of them is a giant. The Negroes in the Twenty-fourth and Twenty-fifth Infantry, too, are all big fellows. These colored regiments fought as well, according to General Sumner, in whose command they were, as the white regiments. What I saw of them in battle confirmed what General Sumner said. The Negroes seemed to be absolutely without fear, and certainly no troops advanced more promptly when the order was given than they."

To this word of commendation we may add the editorial comment of the *Review of Reviews* (October, 1898): "One of the most gratifying incidents of the Spanish War has been the enthusiasm that the colored regiments of the regular army have aroused throughout the whole country. Their fighting at Santiago was magnificent. The Negro soldiers showed excellent discipline, the highest qualities of personal bravery, very superior physical endurance, unfailing good temper, and the most generous disposition toward all comrades in arms, whether white or black. There is not a dissenting voice in the chorus of praise. Men who can fight for their country as did these colored troops ought to have their full share of gratitude and honor."

Such being the record of Negro regiments in the Spanish-American War, it may now be worth while to pause and study at closer range the career of the man who became famous at the time and who for years was the Negro of highest rank in the Army of the United States.

Charles Young was born in Mayslick, Kentucky, March 12, 1864. When nine years of age he was taken by his parents to Ripley, Ohio, where he attended high school. After some service as a public school teacher, he was recommended to the United States Military Academy and duly admitted June 15, 1884. His life at West Point, with the ostracism to which he was subjected and the petty indignities visited upon him, was such as might have daunted the stoutest heart. He was determined, however, not to be overcome; he performed every duty punctiliously; and thus it was that he was graduated August 31, 1889, and commissioned as second lieutenant in the Tenth Cavalry. After a year with this organization he was transferred to the Thirty-fifth Infantry, then to the Ninth Cavalry, and from 1894 to 1898 was professor of Military Science and Tactics at Wilberforce.

When the Spanish-American War began, Young took charge of the Ninth Ohio Regiment, this being composed of Negro volunteers, and he served with the organization from May 14, 1898, until January 28, 1899, when it was mustered out, his rank for the period of the war being that of major. In the regular service he became captain February 2, 1901, major August 28, 1912, and lieutenant colonel June 1, 1916. In the meantime he was on duty not only at different places in the United States but also in the Philippines, Mexico, and Hayti. Meanwhile also he was steadily rising in the affection of his people throughout the country. After the death of Dunbar there was no man whose career they followed with more intense interest. The high courage he exhibited, the slights he suffered, and his hopes that were baffled or unfulfilled, were all a part of their own daily striving.

CHARLES YOUNG

When the United States entered the World War in April, 1917, the Negro people expected that Colonel Young would be given some post commensurate with his experience and rank. Instead of that he was suddenly retired June 22, 1917, for what was said to be physical disability. This action amazed the Negroes throughout the country. After all that they had seen their heroes suffer in the organized forces of the nation, the move seemed to them one deliberately intended to keep a worthy man from rendering the service and having the honor that was his due. The outcry was so great that Colonel Young was at length recalled from his retirement—not, however, until the war was nearly over. He served at Camp Grant from November 6, 1918, until March 5, 1919, and then eight months later was appointed military attaché to the American embassy in Liberia, in which capacity he assisted with the training of the forces of the republic. The opening of the year 1922 found him on an expedition to Nigeria. He died at Lagos, far from home, on January 8. His wife, the companion of many of his travels, and two children, a son and a daughter, survive him.

He was interred with military honors by British troops. As by English law a body was not allowed to be exhumed within a year, it was not until February, 1923, that he was disinterred and the journey homeward begun. Even then there was lack of due honor, for he was brought from Liberia to the United States not on a war vessel but on a tramp steamer. Thus another sword pierced the soul of the Negro.

On May 27, shortly after the arrival of the body in New York, there was a service sponsored by the American Legion at the College of the City of New York. The chief speaker was Theodore Roosevelt, son of the former president and Assistant Secretary of the Navy, who lauded

Colonel Young as one who "by sheer force of character overcame prejudices which would have discouraged many a lesser man." The final service and interment were at Arlington Cemetery, and in the host assembled were representatives of the United States Army, the Grand Army of the Republic, United Spanish War Veterans, the Army and Navy Union, and the American Legion.

Charles Young's public life was that of a soldier and a hero, but those who knew him best think first of his laughter, his ready sympathy, his joy in living. He spoke several languages and had interest in music and poetry; yet beyond all such things as these was his patience, his ability to forgive. As few others he knew the meaning of suffering, but he also had infinite faith. To a friend who was joining the Tenth Cavalry and asked what one should bring, he said: "Send your family home; get your life insured in their favor; bring your Bible and yourself."

One who knew him well remembers him as he sat in the living-room of his home in Liberia. All around were tokens of sojourns in many lands. In front was the long veranda looking over the Bay of Monrovia, and the heat of the afternoon was tempered by the breezes that came from over the water. That day he was more gay and carefree than ever. He had been to Liberia before, and knew that in being sent there again he was receiving sentence of death. Yet he did not quail. This was the service that his country demanded; it was for him to do his duty.

26

Matthew A. Henson: Negro Explorer

When in 1909, after a series of unsuccessful attempts, Commander Robert E. Peary crowned his lifework by reaching the North Pole, the only one of his countrymen who was with him in the exploit was a man of Negro descent, Matthew A. Henson. The trials and hazards of the expedition can hardly be appreciated in this day of the radio and aeroplane. Other men turned back or fell by the way, but Henson persevered until the end. By his courage and hardihood, his moral fibre as well as his physical stamina, he had proved himself worthy of the highest confidence, a fit companion for the noble but dangerous enterprise.

Peary's diary contains the entry from the North Pole, 90 degrees North Latitude, under date April 6, 1909: "Arrived here to-day, 27 marches from C. Columbia. I have with me 5 men, Matthew Henson, colored, Ootah, Egingwah, Seegloo, and Ookeah, Eskimos; 5 sledges and 38 dogs. My ship, the S. S. *Roosevelt*, is in winter quarters at C. Sheridan, 90 miles east of Columbia." As to Henson himself he said in 1910: "Matthew A. Henson, my Negro assistant, has been with me in one capacity or another since my second trip to Nicaragua, in 1887. I have taken him with me on each and all of my northern expeditions, except the first, in 1886, and almost without exception on each of my 'farthest' sledge trips. This position I have given him primarily because of his adaptability and fitness for the work; secondly, on account of his loyalty. He has shared all the physical hardships of my arctic work. He is now about forty years old, and can handle a sledge better, and is probably a better dog-driver, than any other man living, except some of the best of the Eskimo hunters themselves." [1]

Matthew Alexander Henson was born August 8, 1866, in Charles County, Maryland, on the Potomac River about forty miles below Washington. His parents were Lemuel and Caroline Henson. Left an orphan at the age of eight, he passed into the care of an uncle in Washington, and for six years attended the N Street School. Then, while still not more than a lad, he went to Baltimore and shipped as cabin boy on a vessel bound for China. There followed other trips, to Japan, France and Spain, North Africa, Russia, and the Philippines, from which he returned at length an experienced and able-bodied seaman.

In 1888, in Washington, Henson met Robert E. Peary, then a civil engineer in the United States Navy, to whom he felt drawn by the air of confidence that he radiated. He accompanied Peary to Nicaragua as personal attendant, then became his messenger at the League Island Navy Yard, and on the second of the expeditions to the Arctic regions (1891) and thereafter was constantly with the explorer. Instead of being a mere servant he became more and more a trusted helper and friend. He did any work that was

---

[1] As is said in the Preface, the quotations in this chapter are used with the permission of the Frederick A. Stokes Company, owners of copyright on books of Peary and Henson.

necessary, whether as blacksmith, carpenter, or cook; came to know the customs and language of the Eskimos; and could skin a musk-ox with the utmost celerity. He not only learned the art of navigation but also knew at first hand the frozen wilderness in the North. Thus it was that when the most notable of all the expeditions set forth on July 8, 1908, on one of the most difficult tasks ever attempted by man, he was not only a useful and trusted member but even an indispensable assistant. With his own hands he built the sledges with which the journey to the Pole was completed.

So great were the hazards and hardships that on April 3, just three days before the conquest of the Pole, it seemed that the whole purpose of the expedition might be defeated. Henson himself came near to losing his life. Says he: "The ice was so rough and jagged that we had to use our pickaxes constantly to cut a trail. Once the runner of Egingwah's sledge cut through the 'young ice,' but the two Eskimos acted quickly and saved the sledge and dogs from being submerged. This averted a very serious accident, for that particular sledge contained the Commander's sextant and other instruments very necessary to the success of the expedition."

However, three days later the goal was won. Says Henson: "When we halted on April 6, 1909, and started to build the *igloos* (huts), the dogs and sledges having been secured, I noticed Commander Peary at work unloading his sledge and unpacking several bundles of equipment. He pulled out from under his *kooletah* (thick fur outer garment) a small folded package and unfolded it. I recognized his old silk flag, and realized that this was to be a camp of importance. ... He fastened the flag to a staff and planted it firmly on the top of his *igloo*. For a few minutes it hung limp and lifeless in the dead calm of the haze, and then a slight breeze, increasing in strength, caused the folds to straighten out, and soon it was rippling out in sparkling color. The Stars and Stripes was 'nailed to the Pole'."

Naturally Henson as well as Peary was acclaimed on his return to the country. In New York, in October, 1909, there was a formal testimonial, with the presentation of a gold watch and chain by his admirers. Two years previously, on September 5, 1907, he had been married to Lucy Jane Ross. He now wrote his book, *A Negro Explorer at the North Pole*. In 1913 he entered the service of the United States Government, as an employee in the Correspondence Division of the Collector of Customs, New York, from which work he retired in 1936.

After a quarter of a century of adventure on the seas, from the blazing tropics to the distant regions of the North, the joy and peace of civil life were well earned; yet even they could not wholly dispel the yearning for the toils and the triumphs of other years. Suddenly, at any moment, would come the call to high adventure; and memories were made more poignant by the death in 1920 of Commander Peary. Thus it is that we have the word of Henson himself:

"I long to see them all again! the brave cheery companions of the trail of the North. I long to see again the lithe figure of my commander, and to hear again his clear ringing voice urging and encouraging me onward, with his 'Well done, my boy.' I want to be with the party when they reach the untrod shores of Crocker Land; I yearn to be with those who reach the South Pole. The lure of the Arctic is tugging at my heart; to me the trail is calling!

'The Old Trail!
The trail that is always New.'"

27

John Merrick: Pioneer in Business

One of the large fields of activity deserving the attention of Negro Americans is that of business. This is the more important because the United States is comparatively a young country, one in which enterprises are still in the making. Because at the close of the Civil War nine-tenths of the Negro people in the country were illiterate, and because they were uncertain as to the future, emphasis was at first on mental and moral training. The leadership of the race thus tended to rest with the ministers, many of whom were also teachers. Because there was opportunity for representation in state legislatures and the National Congress, at least a few Negroes went into the public service. Meanwhile the great majority of the people were tillers of the soil. As such they were often exploited by those who took advantage of their poverty or ignorance. Few men as yet had either the training or the minimum capital to warrant their entering the field of business. All the more then is credit due those spirits who, in spite of all the handicaps, had the initiative to succeed in this line of endeavor. One such man was John Merrick, of Durham, North Carolina.

Merrick was born in Clinton, Sampson County, North Carolina, September 7, 1859. When not more than twelve years of age, he helped to support his mother by work in a brickyard at Chapel Hill. From the first his alertness, his willing spirit, and pleasant manner impressed anyone who employed him. After he had been six years at the brickyard, the family goods were one day placed on a cart and taken to Raleigh; and there, working as hod-carrier or brickmason, the youth helped with the erecting of the first of the large buildings at Shaw University. When such employment became uncertain, he worked as a boot-black in a barber shop, and thus he learned the trade on which he was to build his future. Meanwhile he formed a friendship with John Wright, the foreman of the shop in which he was employed.

It was suggested to Wright by some prominent white citizens of Durham, General Julian S. Carr, Colonel W. T. Blackwell, and Washington Duke, organizer of the American Tobacco Company, that he might do well if he would come to that town and open a shop. Merrick decided to go with him. Durham was, about 1880, by no means the busy industrial city it has since become. None of the large buildings that one now sees there had as yet been erected. Along the railroad track were a few shops and stores, but houses were sometimes far apart. The town was just at the beginning of its period of rapid expansion, though its possibilities had been recognized by at least a few discerning men. This was the place to which the two young barbers had come. Merrick was now married, and he and his partner decided to buy a lot and build their homes next to each other. His first house was a little three-room cottage on Pettigrew Street facing the railroad. After a few years his growing family made larger quarters necessary, and he removed to a comfortable six-room house on Fayetteville Street, and later to an even more commodious home on the same street. The example thus set was an incentive and encouragement to others, and to-day Fayetteville Street in Durham is one of the best known for Negro home owners in the United States.

After twelve years in Durham, Wright decided to move to Washington, and he sold to his friend his interest in the shop. At the age of thirty-three John Merrick thus found himself the sole proprietor of his enterprise. His business expanded rapidly, and soon he was the owner of five barber shops, three for white patrons and two for colored. He now began to invest in real estate and to build houses to rent, especially as many people were coming to Durham to work in the factories. To this end his early experience in the brickyard stood him in good stead. He was his own contractor, and would carefully figure the cost of the lumber he needed, do any hauling with his own horse and wagon, and serve as his own chief carpenter. Meanwhile he experimented with a preparation that he named Merrick's Dandruff Cure, and of this some advertisements with rather weird spelling have been preserved. Thus in one way or another there was token of the initiative of the young business man and his promptness in taking advantage of any opportunity to broaden his horizon. One day in the year 1896, in the course of his first campaign for the presidency, William Jennings Bryan came to the shop and, after being served, gave to the barber a dollar with the word that it was not to be spent until he, Bryan, had become president of the United States. That dollar is still in the possession of the Merrick family.

To the shop in the heart of the city came several men who were just rising to wealth, and the proprietor heard much about politics and business. The very first trip he ever made to New York was with his patron and friend, Washington Duke, whose personal barber he was. Years afterward he went as usual one Sunday morning to serve the family. In the course of his work he spoke to Mr. Duke about a rally his church was having that day, and asked if a contribution was possible. He was told to come back and report after the congregation had raised all the money it could. The obligation was for $3,500, and the membership raised about $1,000. Mr. Duke wrote a check for the balance.

Meanwhile John Merrick was more and more becoming a leader and an organizer for community uplift. In course of time two other men became associated with him, Dr. Aaron McDuffie Moore, a physician, who after completing his course at Shaw had decided to come to Durham, and a man still younger, a nephew of Dr. Moore, Charles Clinton Spaulding. As the years passed, these three men worked together so much that sometimes it was difficult to say just which one was responsible for a new effort. When Dr. Moore in 1901 led in founding the Lincoln Hospital, Merrick helped and became president of the Board of Trustees. When the Mechanics and Farmers Bank was established in 1908, he became a stockholder and vice-president, and two years later assumed the presidency of the organization. In the same year he assisted in founding the Bull City Drug Company, and two years later incorporated the Merrick-Moore-Spaulding Real Estate Company.

Among the buildings belonging to Mr. Merrick was one on a triangular plot facing the railroad, diagonally across from his home. Dr. Moore suggested that this be rented for a library, and he gladly consented. When later the citizens decided to purchase the building and make the library a permanent institution, he gave back one thousand dollars of

JOHN MERRICK

the four thousand agreed on as the purchase price. He gave of his means in other ways, to his church, to educational institutions, to the aged and destitute; and many of his good deeds will never be known. When he became the owner of scores of houses, each year at Christmas he would remit for each of his tenants a week's rent, and also distribute loads of toys and provisions.

Foremost of the organizations that he helped to build was the North Carolina Mutual and Provident Association, now the North Carolina Mutual Life Insurance Company. When the Association was started by seven men in October, 1898, Merrick became president and Moore the treasurer and medical director. Each of the organizers invested fifty dollars as a guarantee fund for the mutual assessment corporation, and business began as of April 1, 1899. Progress was slow at first; few people had faith in a Negro insurance company. After a while some of the men were disposed to close up the business. Merrick and Moore then bought out the others, attached to themselves the young and active C. C. Spaulding, and rented space in Dr. Moore's office for two dollars a month. A carpenter made a desk for four dollars, and this with one or two chairs was at first the only equipment of the organization.

R. McCants Andrews, who wrote a brief biography of John Merrick, says: "The directors got together and allotted the work of the Association among them. Mr. Merrick was to handle the finances, Dr. Moore was to examine and pass upon the policy-holders, and Mr. Spaulding was to hustle and develop the field." The third of these men, the president of the Company in more recent years, says: "When I became general manager of the Association it was doing an industrial business on the assessment plan and paid sick and death benefits. Its debit or weekly collection was $29.40. I was manager, agent, clerk and janitor, and had to do local collecting as well as organize new fields in the adjacent counties. Dr. Moore and Mr. Merrick served without salaries, each continuing to follow his chosen business while I took the field on a commission basis."

The story of the development of the North Carolina Mutual Life Insurance Company from the day of small things to its present far-flung activities is one of the romances of Negro business. In 1921 a new office building, with six stories and basement, was erected at a cost of $250,000. In the year 1935 the total number of persons employed in the organization, including medical examiners, was 1,153; in the home office in Durham alone there were 93; payments to policy-holders and beneficiaries amounted to $785,347, and admitted assets were $4,345,145. This growth would never have been possible if the men chiefly responsible for the organization had not had faith in themselves and their effort, and if they had not been scrupulously honest. Not one had had previous experience in insurance, and each had not only to learn the technique of the business but also to carry on his part of the work while he did so. Especially did the others owe much to the encouragement of the first president of the organization.

Something of what John Merrick meant to those associated with him may be seen from his word to T. J. Russell, the first full-time local agent of the Company. Russell had been employed in the Duke Tobacco Factory at a wage of six dollars a week. He went into the insurance work but found for two weeks that things did not move very fast. One day his old superintendent met him on the street and said that if he cared to return, he would be paid twelve dollars a week. This was not only twice the old wage, but much more than he was earning with the insurance company. He decided to talk the matter over with the president. Merrick, having heard of the new offer, said that it was pretty good and that there was no doubt that he was worth it. Then with a smile he added, "Why don't you brighten up and take fresh courage and make fifteen dollars a week out of your job with us?" So Russell did, in time earning much more than fifteen dollars, and never regretting the decision.

In June, 1919, the North Carolina Mutual Life Insurance Company celebrated its twentieth anniversary, the meetings being held at the White Rock Baptist Church in Durham. Two hundred and fifty agents and other employees came from ten states and the District of Columbia to review together the past and to plan for the future. The president, however, was a very sick man, and for months had been forced to use a crutch. No one who was present that day will ever forget the scene as he came into the church assisted by his daughter. The hopes and fears and the aspiration of years were all crowded into one intense moment. It was clear that he had not many weeks to live. "I am glad to see you," he said, amid the deepest emotion. "Yes, I came anyway. I am not going to talk loud or long, but I have come in here to look on some of the friends that I haven't seen in two or three years, and some that I have never seen." Then, glancing at the symbol of his affliction, he continued: "I don't want anybody in the house to think that I am shedding a tear because of *this*. I am not shedding tears for that, but I am thanking God that there is this much of me left and that I can come in here and see you. I have more to thank God for than everybody put together in this house. . . . As long as it is God's will I want this institution to move, for men to support their families; and God will let it live. That is what I am interested in, and God knows it. I want this institution to live, and she will. God bless you all."

He passed August 6, 1919.

Tributes came from all parts of the country. C. C. Spaulding said: "He was not only a loyal business partner and a firm and loving friend, but he was also a big-hearted sympathetic brother. I never made an important decision without consulting him, and always placed the utmost confidence in his judgment, because I knew he considered my interests his." The *Greensboro Daily News* said in an editorial: "John Merrick was not schooled in the institutions, but he was a race philosopher who found in his few choice books the ways of all men. He had utterly no patience with those race leaders who sought near-cuts to place and power through gifts of philanthropy rather than through elemental excellences. . . . Along with his patience was a clever trade principle which held it the quintessence of folly to hope for the admiration of the world while asking only its pity. The race had something to sell, artisan's work, agricultural products, manufactured articles: it had supply and demand, he said; and no market is afforded for the race, he taught, which declares itself bankrupt."

John Merrick was essentially a man of action, a *doer;* but, though his conception of life was realistic, he was also a man of faith. He believed the best of people, found no place for the merely showy or superficial, and felt that in sobriety, industry, and truth lies the true welfare of men as well as nations. Unlike many leaders, he was neither a speaker nor a writer; and, even if he had had more academic training, it is doubtful if he would have been either. Having faith in himself, his people, and his country, he not only rounded out a successful career but also laid down the lines that must be followed by any who in the world of business might hope for distinguished achievement.

28

W. E. Burghardt DuBois

THE YEARS ABOUT the turn of the century were critical for the Negro. More than ever he was the subject of dispraise. Propaganda was rife; scurrilous articles were appearing; and sometimes there were furious outbreaks. Some even contended that education was ineffective. If ministers and college professors wrote in this fashion, one would hardly expect less of the politician. The reaction from reconstruction was complete. What was needed was for some man of vision to bring the discussion to the bar of truth, separate fact from falsehood, and give to the American people a solid foundation for their thinking. The man was ready in the person of a scholar from Harvard and Berlin, W. E. Burghardt DuBois.

This emphasis on accuracy in studies relating to the Negro was only one of several contributions. A number of thoughtful men raised question about the larger influence of Booker T. Washington, feeling that in his Atlanta speech he had conceded too much. One of the most militant opponents was William Monroe Trotter, editor of the *Guardian*, a weekly paper published in Boston. The

Guardian, however, reached only a limited number of people. Someone, by articles in prominent magazines, had to touch the larger thought of the nation and quicken its conscience into action. Here again Dr. DuBois served, and the prose style he exhibited gave him place as a man of letters. All this was aside from his work in the classroom, where for years he did yeoman service.

William Edward Burghardt DuBois was born in Great Barrington, Massachusetts, February 23, 1868, the son of Alfred and Mary DuBois. In 1888 he received the degree of Bachelor of Arts at Fisk University, the same degree at Harvard in 1890, that of Master of Arts at Harvard in 1891, and, after a period of study at the University of Berlin, that of Doctor of Philosophy at Harvard in 1895, his thesis being *The Suppression of the African Slave-Trade to the United States of America.* He taught for a short while at Wilberforce University and was also for some time an assistant at the University of Pennsylvania, producing in 1899 his study, *The Philadelphia Negro.* Already, in 1896, he had accepted the professorship of History and Economics at the old Atlanta University, and there he remained until 1910. He was the moving spirit of the Atlanta Conference, which assembled each year in commencement week; and by the "Studies of Negro Problems" which he edited annually in this connection he became known as one of the leading sociologists of the day. He contributed to the *Atlantic Monthly,* the *World's Work,* and other magazines, and in 1903 brought together a number of his papers in the book, *The Souls of Black Folk.*

In 1896 Dr. DuBois married Nina Gomer, of Cedar Rapids, Iowa. A son, Burghardt Gomer, came into the home, and his early death has been recorded in "Of the Passing of the First-Born," included in *The Souls of Black Folk.* There was also born a daughter, Nina Yolande,

In 1905 twenty-nine men of the race launched what was known as the Niagara Movement. The aims of the organization included the abolition of all distinctions based on race or color, the recognition of the principle of human brotherhood as a practical present creed, and the recognition of the highest and best training as the monopoly of no class or race. The first meeting, at Niagara Falls, had "all the earnestness of self-devotion"; the second, at Harper's Ferry, "the solemnity of a holy crusade." Dr. DuBois had most to do with the writing of the manifestoes, which impressed some as a little dictatorial in tone. The movement, with all of its high principle, lacked coherence, and it died after three or four years, but not until it had paved the way for a larger and stronger organization.

In 1909, on Lincoln's birthday, some persons of both races, in and about New York, determined upon a new effort for the full freedom of the Negro. The result was the National Association for the Advancement of Colored People. Dr. DuBois was called from Atlanta the next year to be Director of Publicity and Research, and he began to edit the *Crisis,* the organ of the Association. He remained in the work for twenty-four years. In 1919 he organized the Pan-African Congress, which had its first meeting in Paris, and in 1920 was awarded the Spingarn Medal.[1] In 1934 he went to the new Atlanta University, to devote his time mainly to historical research. In 1935 he published *Black Reconstruction,* which was immediately recognized as revising the conventional attitude toward the period with which it dealt. The next year he was formally approved

[1] In 1914 Dr. Joel E. Spingarn, formerly a professor in Columbia and later president of the National Association for the Advancement of Colored People, established the annual award of a gold medal of the value of one hundred dollars, to be given to that man or woman of Negro descent who should have reflected most credit upon the race in any field of honorable endeavor.

as chairman of the Board of Editors of a new work that had
been projected, the *Encyclopedia of the Negro*. Among the
books that have so far not been mentioned are *John Brown*
(1909), a contribution to the series of "American Crisis
Biographies"; two novels, *The Quest of the Silver Fleece*
(1911) and *Dark Princess* (1928); and *Darkwater* (1920),
another collection of essays.

No one can consider such a career without seeing that
there have been many soul crises. For W. E. Burghardt
DuBois disillusion began even in his school days. It continued later at Wilberforce, his introduction to the world
of the Negro. In Atlanta, however, he was reborn. He
learned to play as well as work, and formed some of his
strongest friendships. In *The Souls of Black Folk*, the fruitage of these years, there was cynicim, even bitterness, but
a great sympathy. Formerly he had been the sharp critic
of his people, but now he became their defender. Said he:
"I saw the race-hatred of the whites as I had never dreamed
of it before,—naked and unashamed! The faint discrimination of my hopes and desires paled into nothing before this
great, red monster of cruel oppression. . . . I emerged into
full manhood, with the ruins of some ideals about me, but
with others planted above the stars; scarred and a bit grim,
but hugging to my soul the divine gift of laughter and
withal determined, even unto stubbornness, to fight the
good fight."

In his criticism of Booker T. Washington in 1903 Dr.
DuBois maintained that that leader acquiesced in the dis-
franchisement of the Negro, in proscription in civil life, and
in the withdrawal of aid from institutions of higher learning. The impression given, he said, was that in general the
South was justified in its attitude. Such being his well
known position, many were startled thirty years later when
Dr. DuBois himself swerved toward segregation, the very

core of Dr. Washington's program. The surprise was natural, for there had certainly been a change of viewpoint. One might have remembered of course that the times had also changed. In 1903 the issue was still largely political; if a man wanted to work, there seemed to be plenty of work to be done. Thirty years later, when millions were unemployed, the Negro needed all his resources. As to the basic rights of citizens there was no change of attitude.

The divergence between these two men was the same as that between Douglass and Richard Allen. Just as Douglass was not always consistent, so neither was his successor. Dr. Washington sometimes quoted Dr. DuBois, and Dr. DuBois could see the good in his opponent's program.

In *The Souls of Black Folk* the sentences move with a tremulous flow; over all is the glow of allusion and poetry. "The Problem of the Twentieth Century is the problem of the color-line." "So, wed with Truth, I dwell above the Veil." "How many heartfuls of sorrow shall balance a bushel of wheat?" That was the DuBois who became famous. Different was the tone of *Darkwater*; the writing is high-keyed, the work of a battle-scarred veteran, and sometimes the notes are harsh. Much better is *Black Reconstruction*.

No one interested in information tersely put, or in pitiless satire, can overlook the last chapter of this late work. "Not a single great leader of the nation during the Civil War and Reconstruction has escaped attack and libel. The magnificent figures of Charles Sumner and Thaddeus Stevens have been besmirched almost beyond recognition. We have been cajoling and flattering the South and slurring the North, because the South is determined to rewrite the history of slavery and the North is not interested in history but in wealth." "The chief witness in Reconstruction, the emancipated slave himself, has been almost barred from court. His written Reconstruction record has been largely destroyed and nearly always neglected. Only three or four states have preserved the debates in the Reconstruction conventions; there are few biographies of black leaders. The Negro is refused a hearing because he was poor and ignorant. The result is that most unfair caricatures of Negroes have been carefully preserved; but serious speeches, successful administration and upright character are almost universally ignored and forgotten." "We shall never have a science of history until we have in our colleges men who regard the truth as more important than the defense of the white race, and who will not deliberately encourage students to gather thesis material in order to support a prejudice or buttress a lie."

When Dr. DuBois appeared he gave to his people a sense of pride. The race had had scholars before, but not one of such distinction and influence. To younger men accordingly he became an inspiration and a challenge. In spite of the handicap, he had attained. Who knew but that they too could achieve?

29

HEROES OF THE WORLD WAR

WHEN THE UNITED STATES entered the war in Europe in April, 1917, the question of overwhelming importance to the Negro people was naturally that of their relation to the conflict. Their response to the draft call set a notable example of loyalty. At the outset the race faced a dilemma: If there were to be training camps for officers, and if the National Government would make no provision otherwise, did it wish to have a special camp for Negroes, such as would give approval to a policy of segregation, or did it wish to have no camp at all on such terms and thus fail to have any men of the race trained as officers? Discussion over the point was heated, but the camp was secured—Camp Dodge, near Des Moines, Iowa. Throughout the summer of 1917 the work of training went forward, the heart of a harassed and burdened people responding with more and more pride to the work of their men. On October 15, 625 young men became commissioned officers. More than 1,200 in all received commissions in the American army, and to the fighting forces of the United States the race furnished 368,000 men, of whom a little more than half saw service in Europe.

Negroes were in all branches of the military establishment, except that they were not formally and officially in aviation. For the handling of special questions relating to them Emmett J. Scott was appointed Assistant to the Secretary of War. Dr. Scott had spent a number of years with Booker T. Washington as secretary at Tuskegee Institute and in 1909 had served as one of the three members of a special commission appointed by President Taft for the investigation of Liberian affairs. Negro nurses were authorized by the War Department for work in base hospitals at six army camps, and women served also as canteen workers in France. Sixty Negro men served as chaplains, 350 as Y. M. C. A. secretaries, and others in special capacities. A contribution of exceptional value was that of Negro women in industry. Very largely also women maintained and promoted the food supply through agriculture at the same time that they released men for service at the front. Meanwhile the race invested millions of dollars in Liberty Bonds and War Savings stamps, and generously contributed to the Red Cross and other relief agencies. Every phase of life showed stimulus to activity.

In the summer of 1918 interest naturally centered upon the actual performance of Negro soldiers in France and upon the establishment of units of the Students' Army Training Corps in twenty institutions of learning. When these units were demobilized in December, 1918, provision was made in a number of the colleges for the formation of units of the Reserve Officers' Training Corps.

The remarkable record made by the Negro in the previous wars of the country was fully equaled by that in the World War. Negro soldiers fought with distinction in the Argonne Forest, at Château-Thierry, in Belleau Wood, in the St. Mihiel district, in the Champagne sector, at Vosges and Metz, winning often the highest praise from their com-

manders. Entire regiments were cited for exceptional valor and decorated with the Croix de Guerre—the 369th, the 371st, and the 372nd; while groups of officers and men of the 365th, the 366th, the 368th, the 370th, and the first battalion of the 367th were also decorated. At the close of the war the highest Negro officers in the army were Lieutenant Colonel Otis B. Duncan, commander of the third battalion of the 370th Regiment, formerly the Eighth Illinois, and the highest ranking Negro officer in the American Expeditionary Forces; Colonel Charles Young (retired), on special duty at Camp Grant in Illinois; Colonel Franklin A. Dennison, of the 370th Infantry; and Lieutenant Colonel Benjamin O. Davis, of the Ninth Cavalry.

The 369th Infantry, formerly the Fifteenth Regiment of the National Guard of New York, was the first unit of the Allied forces to reach the Rhine, going down as an advance guard of the French army of occupation. This organization was under shellfire for a hundred and ninety-one days, and it held one trench for ninety-one days without relief. The 370th was the first American regiment stationed in the St. Mihiel sector, and it was one of the three that occupied a sector at Verdun when a penetration there would have been disastrous to the Allied cause. It went direct from the training camp to the firing-line. General Vincenden said of the men of this regiment: "Fired by a noble ardor, they go at times even beyond the objectives given them by the higher command; they have always wished to be in the front line." General Coybet said of the 371st and the 372nd: "The most powerful defenses, the most strongly organized machine gun nests, the heaviest artillery barrages—nothing could stop them. These crack regiments overcame every obstacle with a most complete contempt for danger. They have shown us the way to victory."

Individual citations for gallantry in action were many. Only a few can be mentioned.

Henry Johnson and Needham Roberts, of the 369th, were the first men in the ranks in all the American Expeditionary Forces to receive the Croix de Guerre. The exploit in which they figured was so remarkable that Lincoln Eyre, staff correspondent of the New York *World*, described it as "The Battle of Henry Johnson." The two soldiers were on duty before day on May 14, 1918, when a raiding party of more than twenty Germans came against their post. The enemy, finding that they were discovered, fired a volley of grenades, wounding both men. Roberts, unable to rise, threw grenades out into the darkness. Johnson, formerly a red-cap porter at the New York Central Railroad Station in Albany, fired the three cartridges in his rifle, the last one into the breast of the German coming upon him. Although small of stature, he then swung his rifle around his head, bringing it down on the head of the next man advancing. When all other means failed, he brought his bolo knife into play; and he killed in all four of the enemy, wounding several others.

While the 368th Infantry was in the Argonne, John Baker, of Company I, volunteered one day to take a message to another part of his line. A shell struck his hand, tearing away part of it, but he went on his way without stopping. When he was asked why he did not have his wounds dressed before completing his task, he replied, "I thought the message might contain information that would save lives."

On another occasion it was necessary to send a runner from the same company across a field swept by fire. Edward Saunders responded to the call, but he had not gone far before a shell struck him down. As he fell he cried to his comrades, "Some one come get this message. I am

wounded." Lieutenant Robert L. Campbell dashed across the shell-swept field, picked up the wounded man, and carried him to safety. Both were cited for the Distinguished Service Cross, and Lieutenant Campbell, in addition, was recommended for a captaincy.

Under the same lieutenant, Robert L. Campbell, a few soldiers were moving one day over a road to the Château-Thierry sector. Suddenly their course was crossed by the firing of a German machine gun. They tried to locate it but could not. Lieutenant Campbell, who knew by the direction of the bullets that his party had not been seen by the Germans, ordered one of his men to crawl to some thick underbrush ahead and tie a rope to several stems, then to withdraw as far as possible and pull the rope, making the brush shake as though men were crawling through it. The ruse worked. Lieutenant Campbell then ordered three of his men to steal out and flank the machine gun on one side, while he and two others moved up and flanked it on the other. The Germans, their eyes fixed on the bush, poured a hail of bullets into it. At a signal those in the flanking party dashed up; with their hand grenades they killed four of the Germans and captured the remaining three, also the machine gun.

Two men of the 372nd Infantry, Corporal Clarence R. Van Alen, of Boston, and Sergeant Clifton Merrimon, of Cambridge, both received the triple decoration of the Croix de Guerre with palm, the Distinguished Service Cross, and the Medaille Militaire. Charles H. Williams says of them in *Sidelights on Negro Soldiers:* "On the morning of September 28, 1918, when his company was under a gruelling fire from hidden machine-gun nests, Corporal Van Alen, having determined the location of one of these, rushed it single-handed. He killed four of the operators and brought the other three as prisoners into the American lines, himself escaping with a few scratches. Later, on the same day and during the same engagement, he rushed out and captured single-handed a trench mortar battery that was inflicting severe losses upon the French lines. Corporal (afterwards Sergeant) Merrimon, near Bussy Farm on September 27, made an attack with hand grenades on an enemy machine-gun which was causing heavy losses to his platoon, and succeeded in killing the gunner and putting the gun out of commission. He then reorganized the remainder of the platoon, leading his men to their position south of Bussy Farm. Although gassed himself, he silenced the machine-gun single-handed."

30

Leaders in Religious Work

The church is that institution of the Negro people that has best given voice to their striving. It is also the one in which they have shown their best organization. Accordingly, from either the spiritual or the practical standpoint its work is of the highest importance.

In general the members of the race in the United States are strongly Protestant. If we speak in round terms we find that 3,250,000 are in the Baptist denomination, 650,000 in the African Methodist Episcopal, 500,000 in the African Methodist Episcopal Zion, 350,000 in the Methodist Episcopal, and 250,000 in the Colored Methodist Episcopal. There are 55,000 Episcopalians, 40,000 Presbyterians, 20,000 Congregationalists and 40,000 Disciples of Christ. There are nearly 200,000 Roman Catholics, and all other groups would total about the same number. It thus appears that the Baptists are greatly in the majority; they form in fact sixty per cent of the church membership. In other words we might say that six out of every ten Negroes who belong to the church are Baptists, and that nine out of ten are either Baptists or Methodists. It thus appears that anything affecting these two large groups touches the great host of the Negro people.

Since the Baptists and the Methodists have been so great in number, they have had more than others the problem of the education of the ministry. In a survey in North Carolina in 1930 it was found that ninety-six of the ninety-eight Negro Presbyterian ministers in the state were college men. The proportion was almost the same with the Episcopalians, and the Congregationalists were also well educated. Among the Baptists, however, the men of college or seminary training numbered less than ten per cent, and the Methodists were not a great deal better. Such figures seem to suggest that the more academic training a man has, the more effective he will be as a preacher; and that of course does not hold. That it does not hold may be seen from the experience of recent years when, under economic stress, many people went to new cults and to popular, even sensational, leaders in quest of spiritual peace. It may also be said that the Negro people, like others who are oppressed or struggling, are little helped by mere bookish philosophizing. When, however, there arises in any denomination a man who has both learning and spiritual power, he may be a genuine instrument for good. The Baptists and Methodists have many such men to-day.

It is important to distinguish among the different Methodist groups. The parent church in the country is that of John Wesley, the Methodist Episcopal; to this some Negroes have always belonged. In 1816, under the leadership of Richard Allen, some Negroes who had withdrawn formed the African Methodist Episcopal Church. These men represented congregations in or near Philadelphia. In doctrine and usage their organization was like that from which it sprang. In 1820, in New York, under the leadership of John Varick, another group of Negroes formed the

African Methodist Episcopal Zion Church. In polity this organization is slightly different from the A. M. E. Church. Laymen are in its conferences as well as ministers and elders, and there is no bar to the ordination of women. In 1844, because of increasing friction between the North and the South over slavery, there was a division in the main body of the Methodists, and the Methodist Episcopal Church, South, resulted. By this latter organization some work for the Negroes was done before the Civil War, the distinctively racial bodies not then being able to advance in the South. When the war was over and the way was clear for them, the Methodist Episcopal Church, South, observed a great defection of its Negro communicants to the A. M. E. and A. M. E. Z. churches, and thought it might be wise to establish its own special branch. Thus came into being in 1870 the Colored Methodist Episcopal Church. All along there were Negroes in the parent body, the Methodist Episcopal Church.

Much thought has been given to a possible union of all the Negro Methodist groups, but as yet they have not come together. In the spring of 1936 a special question affecting the Negro arose in the Methodist Episcopal Church. This organization was moving toward reunion with the Southern Methodists, and it had been proposed that Negro communicants be placed under a separate and distinct jurisdiction. The great majority of responsible Negroes opposed the plan, but the General Conference voted for segregation. To many who had hoped for the practical application of Christian principles this seemed like a backward step.

The Baptists are very democratic. The individual church is completely autonomous and each member has a voice. Therein lies the weakness as well as the strength of the denomination. Where the vote of the single member counts for so much it has been easy for church bodies to divide, and it is not easy to have coherence in enterprises of national scope. This accounts in turn for the fact that it is not so easy for Baptist leaders to be known as those in even some smaller groups. The editor of a reference book may ask for a list of Methodist bishops, but no list of prominent Baptists may so readily be had. All the same there have been some men who have risen to eminence. Only a few, a very few, can be mentioned.

In the early years of the republic Andrew Bryan, a slave in Savannah, Georgia, was converted by the preaching of George Liele, a Negro from Virginia who afterwards went to Jamaica. He too began to preach, and twice he was imprisoned and once publicly whipped; but he told his persecutors that he would "suffer death for the cause of Jesus Christ." At length he was permitted to go on with his work. He purchased his freedom and by 1791 had a church of two hundred members. It was later said of him that he was "clear in the grand doctrines of the Gospel, truly pious, and the instrument of doing more good among the poor slaves than all the learned doctors in America." Almost contemporary was Lott Cary (1780-1828), of Richmond, Virginia, a man of massive frame and strong personality. Born a slave, Cary worked for a number of years in a tobacco factory, leading an ungodly life. Converted in 1807, he made rapid advance in education and was licensed as a Baptist preacher. He purchased his own freedom and that of his children (his first wife having died), organized a missionary society, and then in 1821 himself went as a missionary to the new colony of Liberia, in whose interest he worked heroically until his death.

We have already referred to John Jasper. In the generation after the Civil War there was naturally more emphasis on formal training. Prominent in the decade after 1880 was William J. Simmons (1849-1890), a graduate of

Howard who had also studied at Rochester. This man had great inspirational power. After some early experience in politics in the South, he became a pastor in Louisville, and later a district secretary of the American Baptist Publication Society. In 1880 he became president of a school in Louisville operated by the Negro Baptists of Kentucky and later known as State University, now merged in the Municipal College. There were only thirteen pupils and the outlook was not promising, but immediately the situation improved. In addition Simmons was the organizer and the president of the American National Baptist Convention (founded 1886 and in 1895 merged in the National Baptist Convention), also president for four years of the National Negro Press Association, editor of the *American Baptist* and author of *Men of Mark* (1887), a notable collection of biographical sketches.

Edward M. Brawley (1851-1923) was born of free parents in Charleston, South Carolina, received part of his early training in Philadelphia, and in 1875 was graduated at Bucknell. In South Carolina he organized various associations and the State Baptist Convention, and assisted scores of young people in their effort to get an education. Early in his career he was president of Selma University in Alabama, later of Morris College in Sumter, South Carolina; and he held various pastorates, the last being that of White Rock Baptist Church, Durham, North Carolina. The possessor of an unusually logical mind, he was known for years as an outstanding scholar of his denomination, and especially excelled as a teacher of preachers and a writer of church and Sunday School literature. He edited and largely wrote *The Negro Baptist Pulpit* (1890).

Elias C. Morris (1855-1922) was born in North Georgia but went while still young to Stevenson, a little town in Alabama, where he grew up in the home of a brother-in-law, a minister, meanwhile working at the shoemaker's trade. Converted at nineteen, he felt a call to the ministry, and in 1879 became pastor of the Centennial Baptist Church in Helena, Arkansas, where he remained throughout his life. There his powers as an organizer soon came into play. He established and for two years edited the first religious paper published by the Negroes in the State, and in 1884 founded the Arkansas Baptist College, serving for years as chairman of the Board of Trustees. More and more Morris proved to have the ability and outlook of a states-man. He emphasized self-help and racial integrity and at the same time was discerning and prudent. Personally he was striking and handsome, of well proportioned figure and pleasing address. In 1895, when the American National Convention joined with the Foreign Mission Convention and the National Education Convention to form the Na-tional Baptist Convention of the United States of America, he became president and so remained until his death. A feature of the new organization was the National Baptist Publishing Board in Nashville. In this the leading spirit was R. H. Boyd, a man of genuine business ability. For some years there was steady progress but also increasing question as to whether the printing plant was owned by the Convention or by Boyd personally. This resulted in division in 1915, the Boyd group forming the National Baptist Convention, Unincorporated. The great majority of the Negro Baptists remained with Morris in the Na-tional Baptist Convention and they erected in Nashville a $600,000 building for their own Sunday School Publishing Board.

The successor of Dr. Morris is the Reverend Lacey Kirk Williams, who received his early training in Texas, and after service in Marshall, Dallas, and Fort Worth, became in 1916 pastor of Olivet Baptist Church in Chicago. Olivet has a membership of twelve thousand, with many social and cultural as well as religious auxiliaries, and a large staff of workers. It is understood to be the largest Protestant church organization in the world. Already while in Texas Dr. Williams had for twelve years been president of the Baptist Missionary and Educational Convention. After a year as president of the State Convention in Illinois, in 1922 he became president of the National Baptist Convention, and the work of the organization has steadily deepened and broadened under his direction. He is a member of the Interracial Commission in Chicago, in 1928 became vice-president of the Baptist World Alliance, and the next year received a Harmon Award for "outstanding work in the religious field."

Several men are eminent by reason of their long service in well known churches. In April, 1882, the Reverend Edward R. Carter, an alumnus and later trustee of Morehouse College, after early experience in Athens and Stone Mountain, Georgia, went to Friendship Baptist Church in Atlanta. In November of the same year the Reverend Walter H. Brooks, a graduate of Lincoln, after early work in Richmond and New Orleans, went to the Nineteenth Street Baptist Church in Washington. By the autumn of 1936 then, each of these stalwart figures had completed fifty-four years of service in a single church, and each was still strong and in active service. The record is one such as is seldom paralleled. The Reverend A. Clayton Powell, a graduate of Virginia Union who later studied in the Yale Divinity School, after early work in Philadelphia and fifteen years in New Haven, in 1908 entered upon his distinguished career as pastor of the Abyssinian Baptist Church in New York. The church is one with large property holdings and with all the problems of life in the great metropolis, but the work of the minister until his recent retirement was such as to reflect credit both upon himself and the cause he represented.

We have already spoken in other chapters of Richard Allen and Daniel A. Payne of the African Methodist Church. Two men, J. W. E. Bowen (1855-1933), of the Methodist Episcopal Church, and William S. Scarborough (1854-1926), who was affiliated with the African Methodists, were well known about the turn of the century for their scholarly interests. Dr. Bowen studied at New Orleans and Boston Universities, and received the degree of Doctor of Philosophy at the latter institution in 1887. He was devoted to Hebrew and Greek, Church History and Systematic Theology. After teaching at different institutions and holding various pastorates in the East, he entered in 1893 upon his notable career as a professor in Gammon Theological Seminary, where for a brief period after 1910 he was also president. Dr. Scarborough was graduated at Oberlin in 1875 and later had numerous degrees conferred upon him. In 1877 he became professor of Greek at Wilberforce and in 1908 president of the institution. He was a member of several learned societies, was the author of *First Lessons in Greek* and other works in classical philology, and also wrote many articles on Negro folk-lore and life. Three men of other branches of Methodism call for special and extended comment.

James Walker Hood (1831-1918) was born in Kennett Township, Chester County, Pennsylvania. He had only a few months of regular schooling, but while still a young man was impressed by the call to the ministry. In 1856, in New York, he was licensed to preach, and the next year, in New Haven, was received into the Quarterly Conference of the African Methodist Episcopal Zion Church. Appointed to Nova Scotia, he worked for thirteen months in a hotel to get money with which to go, and to provide for his family. Then in an unfriendly community he was still able to get a church with eleven members started. In 1863 he came to Bridgeport, Connecticut, and after six months was sent as a missionary to the freedmen within the lines in North Carolina. Then began his larger work. He was for eight years a minister in New Bern, Fayetteville, and Charlotte; in 1868 he became a member of the Reconstruction Constitutional Convention, and the next year Assistant Superintendent of Public Instruction, in which capacity he helped much in organizing public schools. On July 3, 1872, he was ordained bishop in the A. M. E. Z. Church, and for many years was the senior bishop. He was a delegate to the Ecumenical Conference in London in 1881, also to that in Washington in 1891, being the first Negro to preside over that body. Bishop Hood was the chairman of the Board of Trustees of Livingstone College from the founding of the institution until his death. For twenty-six years in his later life he served the Conference in the state of New York.

Joseph C. Price (1854-1893) won a singular reputation for eloquence and public spirit, and he did this without being in any sense a politician. He was born in Elizabeth City, North Carolina, and though his mother was free, his father was a slave and his early years were not promising. After the Civil War, however, he advanced rapidly. Having attended for some years an Episcopal school at his home, he taught for four years at Wilson. After a few months at Shaw University, where he made profession of faith, he entered Lincoln University in Pennsylvania. He took various prizes in public speaking and was valedictorian in 1879. As a delegate to the General Conference of the A. M. E. Z. Church in Montgomery in 1880, he made a strong impression by his oratorical gifts and his promise of distinguished service. It was in 1881, while he was on the way to London to attend the Ecumenical Conference, that Bishop Hood took up with him the matter of accepting the presidency of the proposed Livingstone College. When the Conference was adjourned he toured the British Isles and by his speaking raised ten thousand dollars for the cause. With this amount, and a thousand dollars contributed by the white merchants of Salisbury, the present site of the college was purchased. Within the next twelve years the work of Price was such that he was hailed as a new leader of the race. In order to give himself to his main task he declined the post of Minister to Liberia and refused to let his name be presented for the bishopric. His speaking was always simple and logical, but he had a resonant voice and superb presence, and some of the effects of his eloquence were astonishing. When he died, the Mayor and the City Council of Salisbury attended the service in a body.

Lucius Henry Holsey (*c*. 1845-1920) was the son of a slave woman in Georgia and her white master. He had no regular schooling in his early years, but, having received some instruction from a Southern bishop, was in 1868 licensed to preach. In 1870 he was a delegate to the first General Conference of the Colored Methodist Church, and three years later became bishop, being assigned to the Southwest. The work was new, and his quiet, logical method of speaking did not make a ready bid for popularity; but tall, simple, dignified, he held to his ideal of light and truth, often through great privation, and in the years that followed accomplished prodigious labors. For twenty years he was secretary of the College of Bishops of his church, for a long period also corresponding secretary, and commissioner of education as well. He raised the first money for Paine College in Augusta, and led in the founding of Lane College in Tennessee. In addition he edited the hymn-book and wrote the Manual of Discipline for his de-

nomination. In 1881 he too attended the Ecumenical Conference in London, and at many other great gatherings he was the representative of his church.

Reference has already been made to Absalom Jones as the first Negro rector in the Protestant Episcopal Church. In the third quarter of the last century James Theodore Holly (1829-1911) came into prominence. This worker was born in Washington, but within a few years his parents moved farther north and he received his elementary schooling. After some early experience as a journalist in Canada and as a teacher in Buffalo, he was in 1855 ordained as a deacon in the Protestant Episcopal Church, and the next year ordained as priest. At the time the question of emigration was agitating Negro men, and Holly combined this idea with missionary zeal by going to Hayti. Thenceforth he devoted himself to the welfare of his adopted country. On November 8, 1874, he was consecrated Bishop of Hayti in Grace Church, New York. Four years later, while in England as a member of the second Lambeth Conference, he preached in Westminster Abbey with great fervor and eloquence.

Alexander Crummell (1819-1898) led a life of singular trial with prejudice. He was born in New York City. After availing himself of the meagre school facilities there, he went with Henry Highland Garnet and another youth to the ill-fated abolitionist academy at Canaan, New Hampshire. The next year, at the age of seventeen, he went to Oneida Institute, Whitesboro, New York, also operated by the abolitionists, where he remained three years. He had difficulty in entering an Episcopal theological seminary, but finally studied in Boston and in 1844 was ordained priest in Philadelphia. After an unpleasant experience with Bishop Onderdonk of that city, he returned to New York and in 1847 went to England to solicit funds for a church he hoped to build. The trip marked the turning-point in his career. He talked with distinguished liberals and men of letters, and was assisted in going to Queen's College, Cambridge, where he was graduated in 1853. As his health was threatened and there was need of a warmer climate, he went to Africa, and for most of the next twenty years was in either Liberia or Sierra Leone, working with all the power of his being and speaking with the voice of an oracle. Returning to the United States in 1873, he was placed in charge of St. Mary's Mission in Washington. There he labored so effectively that he was soon able to erect St. Luke's Protestant Episcopal Church, where he spent nearly twenty-two years. Tall, erect, of noble bearing, Crummell was a marked man in any gathering. His life was above reproach, that of a scholar and a gentleman. He wrote numerous pamphlets and addresses, several of the best of the papers being brought together in *Africa and America* (1891).

In more recent years interest attaches to the Reverend George F. Bragg, of Baltimore, not only by reason of his long service as rector of the St. James Episcopal Church, but also because of his *History of the Afro-American Group of the Episcopal Church* (1922). Dr. Bragg has also written *Men of Maryland* (1914; revised 1925).

Prominent among the Presbyterians in the third quarter of the last century was Henry Highland Garnet (1815-1882), who was born in Maryland and, like Crummell, attended Oneida Institute, graduating in 1840. Shortly thereafter he was ordained to the ministry and founded a church in Troy, New York. From 1855 to 1864 he was at the Shiloh Presbyterian Church in New York, and later at the Fifteenth Street Presbyterian Church in Washington. However, it is not so much as a preacher as by reason of his public spirit that Garnet is remembered. As early as 1840

he delivered before the American Anti-Slavery Society an address in which he made it clear that the people of color were entitled to all the rights and immunities of American citizens. After the adoption of the Thirteenth Amendment he was invited to preach in the House of Representatives a sermon memorializing the victory of the Union arms and the abolition of slavery. A lifelong desire to see Africa was satisfied when at sixty-six years of age he was appointed Minister to Liberia. Friends had advised against his adventuring into a strange climate at his age, and he died within two months after reaching Monrovia. He was given a public funeral, Edward W. Blyden delivering the eulogy.

In more recent years distinction has attached to Francis James Grimké, who, born in Charleston, went with his brother, Archibald H. Grimké, to Lincoln University in Pennsylvania, and was graduated in 1870. In 1878 he was graduated also from the Princeton Theological Seminary. Ordained in this year, he became pastor of the Fifteenth Street Presbyterian Church in Washington, and there he served continuously for fifty years, except for four years (1885-1889) when he was in Jacksonville, Florida. Dr. Grimké soon became known throughout the country for his adherence to principle, his interest in education, and his insistence upon social justice. For a long period he was a trustee of Howard University, and even in his retirement has been alert to the great currents of thought. He has published more than forty pamphlets, among them being *The Negro and the Elective Franchise, Christianity and Race Prejudice,* and *The Paramount Importance of Right Living.*

Among the Congregationalists Lemuel Haynes (1753-1833) was the first man of color to be ordained. He served as pastor of several white congregations in New England, the first being in Torrington, Connecticut. For the last eleven years of his life he was in Granville, New York. Haynes was a man of unusual spiritual power and skillful in debate. For very recent years we have to note the career of the Reverend William N. DeBerry, who, having graduated at Fisk in 1896, received the degree of Bachelor of Divinity at Oberlin in 1899, then entered upon a pastorate of more than thirty years at St. John's Congregational Church in Springfield, Massachusetts. Dr. DeBerry has stressed the social idea in his ministry. In January, 1928, he received a first award from the Harmon Foundation of New York for "distinguished religious service," and in May of the same year the William Pyncheon Medal of the Springfield Publicity Club for "distinguished service as a citizen of Springfield."

31

Leaders in Education

Because a prime need of Negro colleges has been the enlargement of their physical resources, more prominence has attached to the administrator than to the teacher or scholar. Only within recent years have a few teachers risen to eminence. This was natural but not always fortunate; it emphasized the business rather than the art of education. At the same time there have been college presidents whose ability as well as their office made them genuine leaders.

One man of the older generation was James B. Dudley (1859-1925), president of the Agricultural and Technical College in Greensboro, North Carolina, for more than three decades. This leader was one of those who had to work with Southern politicians before the new day of educational advance; but he was a man of great heart and he especially encouraged Negro talent.

At the present time importance attaches to several executives in the so-called land-grant colleges. In 1862 Congress passed a bill presented by Senator Justin S. Morrill of Vermont and providing for a comprehensive system of scientific, technical, and practical higher education. This said that there would be grants of public lands to each state, these to be apportioned in a quantity equal to thirty thousand acres for each senator and representative according to the census of 1860. In 1890 there was a second act providing for a division of funds in states that separated the races. To-day, in accordance with this enactment, there are seventeen land-grant institutions for Negroes in the South. At first these had to reckon with the appeal of the older classical colleges, but within recent years enrollments have greatly increased. Presiding with success over the largest of the institutions are John M. Gandy, of the Virginia State College at Petersburg, John W. Davis, of the West Virginia State College at Institute, William J. Hale, of the Tennessee Agricultural and Industrial Teachers College at Nashville, and W. R. Banks, of the Prairie View State College, Prairie View, Texas. Among the alert presidents of schools other than the land-grant institutions are M. W. Dogan, of Wiley College, Marshall, Texas, H. Councill Trenholm, of the Alabama State Teachers College in Montgomery, and James E. Shepard, of the North Carolina College for Negroes in Durham.

Three men in recent years have perhaps more than others had touch with the larger life of the nation—Robert R. Moton, John Hope, and Mordecai W. Johnson.

ROBERT R. MOTON

Robert Russa Moton is a man who has approached the problems of his people not with resentment but with charity and a spirit of conciliation. He was born in Amelia County, Virginia, August 26, 1867, the son of Booker and Emily Moton. When he was three years old his parents went to the Vaughan plantation in Prince Edward County. There within the next few years he did the necessary chores, attending for a while a school that had been opened in the community, and later was for two years in a lumber camp. At the age of eighteen he was already larger than most men, with an aptness for public speaking, and some people in the community urged him to run for the state legislature. He would probably have gone if his mother had been willing to say he was twenty-one; but she refused to tell a lie, and the next year he went to Hampton.

It was found on examination that his early training was inadequate, but he was told that he could be given work with the privilege of attending night school. For twelve months he was in the saw-mill and then was admitted to the day school. Never did Hampton have a student who more clearly perceived its ideals. No matter how great the provocation in a given situation, he learned, one must still keep cool; no matter how grave the situation, one must still have faith. After four years, in 1890, he was graduated. Not yet quite twenty-three, of magnificent physique, of manly but gracious bearing, already he had impressed the institution by his wisdom and discretion.

Moton had plans for the law, perhaps even for a school at his home, but General Armstrong saw other need for his services, in the inner life of Hampton itself. He became assistant commandant and the next year succeeded to the post of commandant. The position was one to test his mettle, and also one of great responsibility, for the institution was then a meeting place of the races. The commandant was not only in charge of the battalion but of the discipline of all the men; and he had to deal not only with Negro students, some of whom came from Africa, but also with a number of Indians, and even young men from Hawaii, Armenia, and China. The faculty was one mainly of white people, from the South as well as the North; and General Armstrong died within a year, being succeeded by the chaplain, Hollis B. Frissell. How well Major Moton was to work in this situation and in this period of transition, only the years could show.

For one thing the campus could not hold him; he was too fine an example of Hampton training. He often spoke at meetings in the North, or directed a group of singers. He spoke also in the South, winning friends for the school or his people. In Virginia he led in the work of the Negro Organization Society. Meanwhile he experienced the joys and also the sorrows of home life. Elizabeth Hunt Harris, whom he married in 1905, died after little more than a year. In 1908 he married Jennie D. Booth, the companion of his larger labors and the mother of his five children.

No matter what might be the call from the outside, it was in Hampton itself that one would find the source of Major Moton's strength. He helped the young men who came to school over personal problems innumerable, and it was one of the sights of the section when the battalion lined up for formal inspection. All of his moral force crystallized in the Sunday evening service. Visitors came from far and near for the preliminary service of song. Sometimes he would lead in the noble chant so dear to General Armstrong:

> Hark! listen to the trumpeters,
>   They call for volunteers;
> On Zion's bright and flow'ry mount
>   Behold the officers.
>   They look like men, they look like men,
>   They look like men of war;
>   All arm'd and dress'd in uniform,
>   They look like men of war.

Again the song would be a spiritual of exalted feeling, like "Roll, Jordan, Roll," or one that was born of sorrow, like "Steal Away to Jesus." At still another time the leader might recall the words learned in his youth,

> I love you all,
>> Both bound and free;
> I love you if
>> You don't love me.

Quietly though he had worked, the attention of the country was more and more fixed upon Robert Russa Moton. When Booker T. Washington died in the autumn of 1915, he was elected as the man to succeed; and he gave to Tuskegee twenty years of exacting labor.

Dr. Washington had carried the school through the pioneer days and made it famous. He had also increased the yearly expense. It now remained to solidify the gains that had been made and to put the institution on a permanent basis. That meant an increased endowment. Accordingly, in 1925, when there was a national and a joint effort for Hampton and Tuskegee, for five million dollars to assure other large gifts, Dr. Moton gave of his best to the task. He succeeded in his attempt, but so lavishly did he spend himself and so great was the toll on his resources that it was necessary to take a long trip in the endeavor to regain his strength.

When the Commission on Interracial Coöperation was organized in Atlanta in 1918, Dr. Moton became one of the leading spirits; and both before and after the great effort for the endowment he made special trips through the South. He never avoided the hard places but sought them, and one of the most successful visits was to Mississippi. Typical was that to North Carolina in March, 1921. The invitation was extended by the State Department of Public Instruction, especially by N. C. Newbold, director of the Division of Negro Education. In the course of the week there were not less than twenty addresses. Three were in Chapel Hill, at the University; and Gerrard Hall was crowded with students, members of the faculty and their wives. In Raleigh there was a gathering of three thousand persons in the Auditorium, and a conference in the office of the Mayor. In Fayetteville the address was in the Academy of Music, in Wilmington in the largest theatre, and in Charlotte in the Auditorium; and most frequently the introduction in a city was by the Mayor. Everywhere Dr. Moton spoke frankly about delicate points in race relations, but so human was his presentation, and so searching were the stories he told, that the hearts of men were touched and his words were liberally applauded. The speaker disarmed many who were disposed to be unjust, and quite as much he strengthened those working to improve conditions. He also revealed himself more clearly to some of his own people who had objected to his published utterances.

It was in the course of the war that Negro criticism first became vocal. Against the black troops in France there was steady and insidious propaganda. Especially were there charges against the personal character of some. These reached the President and the Secretary of War, and Dr. Moton was asked to go to look into conditions. He found that of twelve serious charges only two had a reasonable basis. He also found both officers and men smarting under injustice, and very few in the mood for a message counseling patience.

It took two things to reveal to his own people the real stature of Robert R. Moton, and one of these affected the former soldiers themselves. When it was proposed to erect at Tuskegee a hospital for Negro veterans, President Harding assured the principal of the Institute that he would be consulted about the staff. Naturally the Negro people expected that this would be wholly or largely colored. While the hospital was being built, however, the white people in the town of Tuskegee determined that they would control it. There was to be a payroll of $65,000, and the institution could serve their social advantage. It was of course illegal in Alabama for a white nurse to attend a Negro man; but the law could be satisfied by having the white nurses receive full pay and Negro women on small pay to do the actual work. So well did the white people manage that the hospital opened under this arrangement. The Negroes of the country felt outraged; Dr. Moton protested to Washington; and there was appeal to the Veterans' Bureau. In turn the KuKlux Klan paraded about the grounds, and the situation became tense and critical.

All the while there was one man whose word the people of the town knew they needed. His endorsement, they felt, was indispensable. They called upon Robert R. Moton and asked him to sign an acceptance of the arrangement that had been made. He listened with patience to all they had to say. He himself was not sure that capable Negro physicians could be persuaded to leave their work and their homes to come to a Government hospital. At least, however, they should have the chance; some if not all of the places should be theirs. Beyond that he would not go.

The men from the town called and called again, and some of them were armed. They cajoled, they persuaded, they threatened, all to no avail. It was many men against one, but the one was not afraid. "Gentlemen," he said at length, "all my life I have believed in the Southern white man. I have believed that white and colored Southerners could work together. That has been the meaning of my life. Perhaps I was mistaken. And if I was mistaken, the best thing that can happen to me is to die."

He did not die, and he won his point. After the chief of the Veterans' Bureau had made a visit, the hospital was given a Negro staff throughout.

The other matter had to do with a book. After publishing in 1920 his autobiography, *Finding a Way Out*, Dr. Moton brought forth in 1929 a very different work, *What the Negro Thinks*, considering one after another matters in the life of his people that were felt but not always discussed. Some readers turned the pages with amazement. The book was a revelation; no one of any school of thought could have been more frank or straightforward.

Before he retired as head of Tuskegee in 1935 many other tasks came to Robert R. Moton, and many honors as well. In 1919 he became president of the National Negro Business League, and he is a trustee or director in about twenty educational or social agencies. Several degrees have been conferred upon him; among these are the Master of Arts from Harvard, and the Doctor of Laws from Virginia Union, Oberlin, Williams, and Howard. On April 22, 1930, before a distinguished company at the First Congregational Church in Washington, with the Honorable Ray Lyman Wilbur, Secretary of the Interior, making the presentation, he was given the Harmon Award of a gold medal and a thousand dollars for Distinguished Achievement in Race Relations. In 1932 he was awarded the Spingarn Medal.

JOHN HOPE

When in the decade after the Civil War different missionary agencies in the North approached the problem of educating the freedmen in the South, they acted independently, each covering the field as well as it could. The result was much duplication of effort; in such a center as Atlanta there were half a dozen colleges, while in other growing cities there was none at all. Not all of the institutions founded could be properly supported. Sooner or later there had to be reorganization. It is in connection with the

work of readjustment and coördination that John Hope
(1868-1936) will best be remembered.

This educator was born in Augusta, Georgia, the son of
James and Mary Frances Hope. After some years of elementary training, secured largely by his own efforts, he
entered Worcester Academy in Massachusetts in the
autumn of 1886. While he still had to work to support
himself, he was active in the life of the school, becoming
editor of the *Academy*, the student monthly. At graduation he was class historian and a commencement speaker.
He entered Brown University and received the bachelor's
degree in 1894, with the distinction of being class orator.
He married Lugenia D. Burns, of Chicago, December 29,
1897, and became the father of two sons. In 1907 Brown
conferred upon him the degree of Master of Arts, and
twelve years later elected him to Phi Beta Kappa "for
achievements since graduation." The degree of Doctor of
Laws was later conferred by several institutions—by Howard University in 1920, Bucknell in 1923, McMaster University, Toronto, in 1928, Bates College in 1932, and Brown
in 1935.

Entering the service of the American Baptist Home Mission Society after graduating from college, Mr. Hope
served for four years at Roger Williams University in
Nashville, and then in 1898 was transferred to Atlanta
Baptist College, now Morehouse, where he was professor of
Latin and Greek. He brought to the small denominational
institution the air of the Northern college at its best, and
interested the students accordingly. On the resignation of
Dr. George Sale in 1906 he became acting president, and
then, after a year, president of the college, being the first
man of Negro descent appointed to such office by any of
the great missionary boards.

In January, 1904, was founded in Atlanta a monthly magazine, *The Voice of the Negro,* which ran for three years. To the very first number Mr. Hope contributed an article, "Our Atlanta Schools," that is important in view of his later career. Already he showed that he was wrestling with the problem of the future of the institutions in sight of one another. He made the suggestion that the old Atlanta University be developed as a graduate school, and within the next few years assisted minor efforts at coöperation. Meanwhile his influence was widening; he became a member of several educational or social agencies, especially the Commission on Interracial Coöperation and the Georgia State Council of Work among Negro Boys. From July, 1918, to July, 1919, he directed Y. M. C. A. work among the Negro troops in France, and for several years was president of the Association for the Study of Negro Life and History. In 1929 he led in the organization of the new Atlanta University, becoming president. Morehouse College for men and Spelman College for young women, and later Clark University, a coeducational college, entered into the plan as affiliated institutions.

This new system radically altered the educational scene on the west side of Atlanta. A central administration building arose, and not far away new dormitories and a refectory. President Hope brought into the work prominent scholars, Dr. W. E. B. DuBois among them, and was a leading spirit in having the Federal Government erase a slum district of several acres in front of the colleges and erect instead scores of buildings carrying a modest rental. On the other hand, there were losses to offset the gains; thus Morehouse, an institution famous for years for its spirit and its emphasis on manly development, to some extent was submerged in the new order.

John Hope was a man with keen appreciation of literary

and artistic values. Writing to a friend from abroad he said, "The more I have wandered about England this summer, the more have I appreciated the advantages of a liberal education. My college Shakespeare has come back to me; once more I have heard Richard of Gloucester saying,

> Now is the winter of our discontent
> Made glorious summer by this sun of York.

And Venice—you wonder if it can be real; it all seems like a dream. Last evening as I was at dinner looking out over the water, the sun was setting. Gondolas glided about, and the sky was more blue than ever. I thought of the gentle Desdemona and Othello, who loved not wisely but too well. It was all an experience I can never forget."

Mr. Hope was also a stimulating force, but his influence was often critical and negative rather than directly inspirational. A man of wit, he could be witheringly cynical; a colleague once said that he had ability in showing every reason why a thing should *not* be done. At the same time, as has been shown, he could conceive and execute large designs. In committee and board meetings his approach was realistic; he would often mention a factor that was vital but that others had overlooked. More and more he was heard in high places, and his position at length was one of power. In 1929 he received the Harmon award in education, and in 1936, posthumously, the Spingarn Medal.

MORDECAI W. JOHNSON

Mordecai Wyatt Johnson was born in Paris, Tennessee, January 12, 1890, the son of the Reverend Wyatt Johnson and his wife, Carolyn Freeman before her marriage. The father was silent and stern, but of unbending rectitude; the mother was emotional, energetic, inspiring. Each, having had but limited opportunity in youth, desired the best training for the son. Young Johnson, after attending an elementary school at his home, went to Roger Williams in Nashville and Howe Institute in Memphis; then, while still of high school age, to the institution now known as Morehouse College. He threw himself into the activities of the school, athletic as well as religious, and rapidly developed his sense of moral and scholarly values. He especially excelled in debating. In 1911 he received the degree of Bachelor of Arts. As the leading student in his class, an unusually able class, he was the last of the speakers at commencement.

Johnson was immediately employed at Morehouse, first as a teacher of English, then of Economics and Sociology. In 1913 he received the bachelor's degree at the University of Chicago also. In the autumn of that year he entered the Rochester Theological Seminary. There his career was distinguished and his outlook steadily broadened; especially was he helped by Walter Rauschenbusch, author of *Christianity and the Social Crisis*. Throughout the three years at Rochester he was student pastor of the Second Baptist Church in Mumford. Johnson completed the course at the Seminary in 1916, and five years later, after writing the required thesis, the degree of Bachelor of Divinity also. In 1916 he was ordained to the Baptist ministry. On Christmas Day of this year he was married to Anna Ethelyn Gardner, a graduate of Spelman. After a year as student secretary of the Young Men's Christian Association, he entered in 1917 upon a notable period of service as pastor of the First Baptist Church in Charleston, West Virginia.

In that mountain state, working from the capital as a center, the young minister threw himself into every forward movement. He was active in the Negro Baptist Convention, was president of the branch of the National Association for the Advancement of Colored People, and also became, without respect to race, a defender of the miners of the state against capital. So constant was his application that his friends began to fear for his health, and he was at length persuaded to go away for a season of rest.

He did not rest: he went to the Harvard Divinity School; but in the peace of that scholarly retreat was refreshed and gained new strength. At the next commencement (1922) he received the degree of Master of the Science of Theology and represented the Graduate Schools on the program. He chose as his subject "The Faith of the American Negro."

That address was the most notable one given by a representative of the Negro people since the speech of Booker T. Washington in Atlanta in 1895. The time was one of friction and tension, and the war not yet four years in the distance. "We have," said the speaker, "the world's problem of race relationships here in crucible, and by strength of our American faith we have made some encouraging progress in its solution. If the fires of this faith are kept burning around that crucible, what comes out of it is able to place these United States in the spiritual leadership of all humanity. When the Negro cries with pain from his deep hurt and lays his petition for elemental justice before the nation, he is calling upon the American people to kindle anew about the crucible of race relationships the fires of American faith."

The speech made Mordecai W. Johnson a marked man. He might go back to West Virginia, but henceforth he belonged to the country. In the mountains he worked out a program of patience and non-resistance, and was in constant demand for addresses, sometimes on very important occasions. In 1926, when Howard needed a new president, he was asked to come to the helm.

The breath of the country was almost taken by the ap-

32

The Negro in the Professions

Two THINGS MORE than others seem to characterize what we know as a professional man. One is that he shall have a degree of learning and be master of the technique of his chosen field. The other is that he shall place above pecuniary reward the ideal of public service. A man then who is eminently scholarly and primarily devoted to the welfare of others, may be said to reflect credit on his profession. One in some other field may be similarly unselfish but is hardly able to accomplish such a large measure of good.

For decades and even centuries the ministry, the law, and medicine have been known as the basic professions. To them may be added that of the teacher, and even some lines of business; thus a banker has high opportunity to work for community welfare. When a man in any of these fields thinks first of personal gain, to that extent he lowers the standard. On the other hand, a member of a craft or trade may enter the higher sphere, as when a telephone employee is faithful through a flood or other danger. Nurses who toil long and late, or who are courageous in an epidemic, also may be said to have the professional ideal.

Chemistry building. By the close of the decade plans were under way for two new dormitories for men and a library building to cost $1,106,000. The same spirit of progress was manifest in the inner life of the university. There were notable additions to the faculty, increases in salaries, new funds for research, and large additions to the libraries. The Graduate School was organized and both the Law School and the College of Dentistry reorganized.

After hearing President Johnson speak at a meeting in Philadelphia a lady said: "Why did this man get under all defenses and so wring your heart that little else in the world seemed to matter? This is not the first time we have had our souls hung before us and the thin places and the smudges pointed out, but never before with such sincerity of comprehension of the struggle involved, with such sympathy for the weakness of the honest, striving soul. It is another demonstration of the compelling power of Love, which shells us out of our pitiful armor of evasion and leaves us sobbing, face to face with our stark selves."

Such has been the impression made by Mordecai W. Johnson. The world has given such honors as it could. Before he went to Howard that institution conferred the degree of Doctor of Divinity; and so did Gammon Theological Seminary later. He has served on numerous commissions and as president of the National Association of Teachers in Colored Schools. In 1929 he was awarded the Spingarn Medal.

THE NEGRO IN THE PROFESSIONS

TWO THINGS MORE than others seem to characterize what we know as a professional man. One is that he shall have a degree of learning and be master of the technique of his chosen field. The other is that he shall place above pecuniary reward the ideal of public service. A man then who is eminently scholarly and primarily devoted to the welfare of others, may be said to reflect credit on his profession. One in some other field may be similarly unselfish but is hardly able to accomplish such a large measure of good.

For decades and even centuries the ministry, the law, and medicine have been known as the basic professions. To them may be added that of the teacher, and even some lines of business; thus a banker has high opportunity to work for community welfare. When a man in any of these fields thinks first of personal gain, to that extent he lowers the standard. On the other hand, a member of a craft or trade may enter the higher sphere, as when a telephone employee is faithful through a flood or other danger. Nurses who toil long and late, or who are courageous in an epidemic, also may be said to have the professional ideal.

also became, without respect to race, a defender of the miners of the state against capital. So constant was his application that his friends began to fear for his health, and he was at length persuaded to go away for a season of rest.

He did not rest: he went to the Harvard Divinity School; but in the peace of that scholarly retreat was refreshed and gained new strength. At the next commencement (1922) he received the degree of Master of the Science of Theology and represented the Graduate Schools on the program. He chose as his subject "The Faith of the American Negro."

That address was the most notable one given by a representative of the Negro people since the speech of Booker T. Washington in Atlanta in 1895. The time was one of friction and tension, and the war not yet four years in the distance. "We have," said the speaker, "the world's problem of race relationships here in crucible, and by strength of our American faith we have made some encouraging progress in its solution. If the fires of this faith are kept burning around that crucible, what comes out of it is able to place these United States in the spiritual leadership of all humanity. When the Negro cries with pain from his deep hurt and lays his petition for elemental justice before the nation, he is calling upon the American people to kindle anew about the crucible of race relationships the fires of American faith."

The speech made Mordecai W. Johnson a marked man. He might go back to West Virginia, but henceforth he belonged to the country. In the mountains he worked out a program of patience and non-resistance, and was in constant demand for addresses, sometimes on very important occasions. In 1926, when Howard needed a new president, he was asked to come to the helm.

The breath of the country was almost taken by the appointment. There was no question about his brilliance; but he was only thirty-six, of limited academic experience, of experience in administration little or none: could he bear the weight imposed on him? When college formally opened in the autumn, the chapel was crowded. Long before noon every available seat was taken. Everyone wanted to hear the new prophet and leader.

The address was a call to duty, simple, sincere, reassuring. So far, said the president, only ten thousand Negro men and women had had collegiate training. Even at that moment there were but two to every thousand of the Negro people. A new era of achievement for the welfare of mankind was at hand. "It is quite possible," he said in conclusion, "that some of you will be creative contributors to this development and that some of you may be pioneers in it."

The work of President Johnson since that day is a marvel of achievement. With his spiritual interests he has been heard to regret that his administration has had to do so largely with things financial. However, he went to Howard at a time when the institution needed physical rebuilding. Within a decade more than $2,000,000 was secured from private philanthropy. Congressional appropriations increased from $218,000 in the first year to $1,760,000 in the fifth. A new building for the College of Medicine costing $500,000 was completed within a short time, and an endowment campaign for that college was closed. Important was the adoption of a twenty-year plan of development, this including a ten-year building program. This was jointly agreed upon by representatives of the Government and private boards. The first unit of the plan, three dormitories for women costing $770,000, was completed in 1931. There followed a new recitation building (Frederick Douglass Memorial Hall), a new power plant, and a large

In other chapters we have spoken of Negro ministers, teachers, and business men who became eminent by their earnest labors. We may now note a few of those spirits who have given of their best in medicine or the law.

In the early years of the last century James Derham, of New Orleans, became the first recognized Negro physician of whom we have record. Born in Philadelphia in 1762, as a boy he was in the service of a physician for whom he performed minor duties. Afterwards he was sold to one in New Orleans, and this man he also assisted. Two or three years later he won his freedom, and, having learned French and Spanish as well as English and also advanced in his chosen field, he commanded general respect by his learning and skill. About the middle of the century James Mc-Cune Smith, of New York, a graduate of the University of Glasgow, was prominent as the author of several scientific papers. He was a man of wide interests and universally held in high esteem. The first real impetus to bring Negroes in considerable numbers into the medical profession came from the American Colonization Society, through the efforts of which a number of intelligent young men were prepared privately in the South or publicly in the North for service in Liberia. John V. DeGrasse, of New York, after completing his course at Bowdoin in 1849, was admitted in 1854 as a member of the Massachusetts Medical Society. After the Civil War arose the School of Medicine at Howard University and the Meharry Medical College in Nashville. A. T. Augusta studied medicine at the University of Toronto and became the first Negro to hold a position as surgeon in the United States Army. Charles B. Purvis, a graduate of the Medical College at Western Reserve, also became a surgeon in the Army and was for a long time connected with Freedmen's Hospital in Washington. He did more than anyone else to develop the

School of Medicine at Howard in the early days. At the present time Negro physicians in the United States number nearly 6,000 and the dentists nearly 2,000.

Distinguished in the early years of the present century was Daniel Hale Williams (1858-1931). This physician was born in Hollidaysburg, Pennsylvania, but after the death of his father he removed to Rockford, Illinois, and later to Janesville, Wisconsin, where he was graduated from high school and also from Hare's Classical Academy. In 1883 he received the degree of Doctor of Medicine at Northwestern University; later he became a demonstrator in anatomy at that institution, and was also for four years a member of the Illinois State Board of Health. Having begun practice in Chicago in 1883, he became concerned about the fact that hospitals in the city refused to have men of Negro descent as internes and that training schools barred the way to Negro women as pupil nurses. Accordingly he began to interest others in his plan for a hospital where color would be no bar. From his effort resulted Provident Hospital, founded in 1891, with the first training school for Negro nurses in the United States. In 1893 Dr. Williams became famous by reason of a successful operation on the human heart. For five years thereafter he was surgeon-in-chief at Freedmen's Hospital in Washington. He reorganized the institution and established there too a training school for nurses. Having resigned in 1898, he returned to practice in Chicago, but soon became professor of clinical surgery at Meharry. For years he made annual visits to Nashville, holding a clinic for the benefit of a large number of students. He was attending surgeon at the Cook County Hospital from 1903 to 1909, was also an associate on the staff of St. Luke's Hospital in Chicago, and a charter member of the American College of Surgeons.

Solomon Carter Fuller (A.B., Livingstone, 1893; M.D., Boston University, 1897) began as interne at the Westborough (Massachusetts) State Hospital for the Insane; later he became pathologist there, serving until 1920. In the winter of 1904-5 he studied in Munich, Germany, and in· 1909 became a lecturer at the Boston University School of Medicine, retiring in 1935 as professor of Neurology. He has been a member of the leading psychiatric and neurological associations in the United States and has made numerous contributions to medical literature. Several of these have been studies of the patients admitted to the Westborough State Hospital.

Modern development in the field of medicine has been so rapid and is so much a matter of recent years that many of the most able men are just now well started on their careers.

William A. Hinton (S.B., Harvard; M.D., *ibid., cum laude*) has been chief of the Wassermann Laboratory of the Massachusetts Department of Public Health, pathologist and director of research in the Boston Dispensary, and instructor in Bacteriology in the Harvard Medical School. In 1936 he published through the Macmillan Company *Syphilis and its Treatment.* Dr. Hugh S. Cumming, former surgeon general of the United States, referred to the work of this investigator in an article in the *Journal of the American Medical Association* (June 8, 1935) as follows: "The Department suggests that physicians accept the Hinton Test as one of the most specific tests available, in that it is falsely positive with extreme rarity and detects syphilis as well as, if not more frequently than, any other test in use."

Julian H. Lewis (M.D., Ph.D., Chicago) is associate professor of Pathology at the University of Chicago and pathologist at Provident Hospital. For twenty years he has been engaged in research for the Otho Sprague Foundation, and has contributed to medical periodicals many articles on Immunity.

Theodore K. Lawless (M.S., M.D., Northwestern) is Elizabeth J. Ward Fellow in Dermatology at the Northwestern University School of Medicine. His time is devoted to teaching in the department of Dermatology and Syphilology and to research. He is also engaged in private practice as a specialist in skin diseases. His studies have carried him to the great medical centers of Europe as well as America, and his published articles have been of signal value to his profession.

Louis T. Wright (M.D., Harvard) is a police surgeon in the city of New York, a member of the staff of Harlem Hospital, and at present the only Negro member of the American College of Surgeons. Aside from general practice he has specialized more and more in injuries to the head, finding time with all his duties to write a considerable number of articles on the subject.

Hildrus A. Poindexter (M.D., Harvard; Ph.D., Columbia) is associate professor and head of the department of Bacteriology, Preventive Medicine, and Public Health in Howard University. He is a capable research worker, and, in addition to his duties and tasks at Howard, has engaged in research in Puerto Rico under the auspices of the School of Tropical Medicine of Puerto Rico, and conducted an intensive health survey in the state of Alabama. During the five years 1930-35 he made not less than twelve contributions to outstanding scientific journals in the United States, Puerto Rico, and Germany.

Arnold H. Maloney (M.D., Indiana; Ph.D., Wisconsin) is professor and head of the department of Pharmacology in Howard University. Within the last few years he has contributed about twenty articles to scientific periodicals in the United States and Belgium. He has the distinction of having discovered the antidotal action of Picrotoxin to poisoning by the Bartiturates, a group of sleep-producing drugs.

The first Negro formally admitted to the practice of law in the United States was Macon B. Allen, who passed the examination in Massachusetts in 1845. At least four other men were admitted to the bar in that state before 1865. In the years immediately after the war, when new opportunity was given to the Negro throughout the country, Robert B. Elliott and John Mercer Langston were especially distinguished. In addition to Blanche K. Bruce, of whom we have spoken, Judson W. Lyons, William T. Vernon, and James C. Napier have served as registers of the Treasury of the United States; and William H. Lewis (A.B., Amherst; LL.B., Harvard) was assistant attorney general of the United States from March 26, 1911, to April 1, 1913.

To-day the Negro lawyers in the United States number nearly fifteen hundred. Among them the position of Edward H. Morris is one of peculiar distinction. This man, born in Kentucky in 1860, received his early training in Chicago, and in 1879 entered upon the practice of law in that city. He has been successful in many important cases, showing special ability in criminal law. He has also served as attorney for the town of South Chicago and was for two terms a member of the Illinois House of Representatives.

Wendell Green (LL.B., Chicago) is also prominent among the criminal lawyers of Illinois. Living and working in Chicago, he has by his briefs gained in unusual degree the respect of others in his profession. Matthew W. Bullock (A.B., Dartmouth; LL.B., Harvard), after early experience as a teacher in Southern institutions, then as a Y. M. C. A. physical director in the war and Urban League secretary in

Boston, in 1921 concentrated on the work of his profession. In 1925 he was appointed special assistant attorney general for the state of Massachusetts, and a little later became a member of the State Board of Parole. He has impressed the public by his manly and honest approach to public questions and his lack of regard for the arts of the politician. Not a great deal has been published by members of the legal profession, but one must note by all means such articles as those on "Titles to Land by Adverse Possession" by William E. Taylor (A.B., LL.B., J.D., Iowa), dean of the School of Law at Howard, in the *Iowa Law Review* for March and May, 1935.

33

THE NEGRO IN LITERATURE

THE WRITING DONE by the Negro people in the United States before the Civil War has more social than literary interest.[1] Jupiter Hammon, whose first poem was published as early as 1761, was influenced by the current evangelical hymns; and Phillis Wheatley treated abstract themes after the manner of Pope. George Moses Horton, the slave poet of Chapel Hill, North Carolina, had a keen literary sense and a vein of humor, and in *The Hope of Liberty* (1829) and other booklets showed what he might have done with freedom and opportunity. Several writers of verse were on the scene just before the Civil War. One of them, James A. Whitfield, published in 1853 a very small book, *America, and Other Poems,* in which there are cries of protest; but as yet no poet seemed able to give to his feeling such form as was both beautiful and enduring. All either lacked the necessary training or were too much under the influence of the popular authors, Scott and Byron.

---

[1] For a more detailed treatment of the subject of this chapter and the next see the author's *The Negro Genius* (superseding *The Negro in Literature and Art*), Dodd, Mead & Co., New York, 1937.

The prose on the whole was better. One or two papers of the astronomer, Benjamin Banneker, the fiery *Appeal* of David Walker, some at least of the work of William Wells Brown, and, most of all, the speeches of Frederick Douglass and that orator's life story, *My Bondage and My Freedom,* showed not only strong and honest feeling but also, to some extent, a sense of style. All such effort of course has importance for the historian even if not always for the man of letters.

In the years between 1865 and 1890 two writers of verse were well known to the public, though neither reached the highest degree of success. Mrs. Frances E. W. Harper was the author of several booklets in the style of Felicia Dorothea Hemans, but, being a gifted lecturer, she was able to read her poems to advantage and thus was an inspiration to many. Albery A. Whitman, a Methodist minister, was a man of genius, with brilliant imagination and a sense of rhythm. In such a production as *The Rape of Florida,* a story concerned with the capture of the Seminoles and their removal to the West, he used the elaborate Spenserian stanza; but he lacked the discipline that would have brought his powers to genuine fulfilment. Once more the prose was better than the poetry, for nothing in the period surpassed the speech of Robert B. Elliott on the Civil Rights Bill, or some of the occasional addresses of John Mercer Langston.

The last decade of the century brought on the scene four men, each of whom had some unquestioned merit or excellence—Booker T. Washington, Paul Laurence Dunbar, W. E. Burghardt DuBois, and Charles W. Chesnutt. Aside from some more practical publications, Dr. Washington brought out several books that in beautiful English summed up his wisdom or experience—not only the autobiography *Up from Slavery* but also such works as *My Larger Educa-*

tion (1911) and *The Man Farthest Down* (1912). Dunbar, as we have seen, had a host of imitators, and such prose as that in *The Souls of Black Folk*, by Dr. DuBois, was a contribution to the literature not only of the Negro but of the nation as well.

Charles Waddell Chesnutt (June 20, 1858–November 15, 1932), hitherto mentioned only incidentally, became famous a few years before any of the other three men just named. He was a pioneer in the serious treatment of themes suggested by the color line. Born in Cleveland, Ohio, he began when sixteen years of age to teach in the public schools of North Carolina, and when twenty-three became principal of the State Normal School in Fayetteville. In 1883 he left the South, engaging for a short while in newspaper work in New York City, but going soon to Cleveland, where he worked as a stenographer and was admitted to the bar in 1887. Some of his early contributions to the *Atlantic Monthly* were so unusual and distinctive in quality that they called forth a special critical article in the magazine by William Dean Howells. Perhaps the most notable is "The Wife of his Youth," the story of a very fair colored man who, just before the Civil War, by the aid of his untutored Negro wife, made his way from slavery in Missouri to freedom in a Northern city, and who, after the years have brought success, culture, and social position, suddenly comes face to face with the woman to whom he was legally married. Chesnutt produced five books, aside from a brief life of Frederick Douglass and some uncollected stories. These include two collections of stories, *The Conjure Woman* and *The Wife of his Youth, and Other Stories of the Color-line*, and three novels, *The House behind the Cedars, The Marrow of Tradition*, and *The Colonel's Dream*. All of these books except the last were published by the Houghton Mifflin Company, of Boston.

The early decades of the new century brought into prominence two new writers, William Stanley Braithwaite and James Weldon Johnson. Mr. Braithwaite, after publishing two small books of original poetry, began to give most of his time to the making of anthologies of verse, especially the *Anthology of Magazine Verse*, issued each year from 1913 to 1929. By his work in this connection he came to have far-reaching influence, and he was the real leader in the revival of interest in poetry in the United States. The *Boston Evening Transcript* said in an editorial (November 30, 1915): "He has helped poetry to readers as well as to poets. One is guilty of no extravagance in saying that the poets we have—and they may take their place with their peers in any country—and the gathering deference we pay them, are created largely out of the stubborn, self-effacing enthusiasm of this one man. In a sense their distinction is his own. In a sense he has himself written their poetry." Something of the quality of Mr. Braithwaite's own verse may be seen from the lyric, "Sandy Star," which originally appeared in the *Atlantic* (July, 1909):

> No more from out the sunset,
>   No more across the foam,
> No more across the windy hills
>   Will Sandy Star come home.
>
> He went away to search it,
>   With a curse upon his tongue,
> And in his hands the staff of life
>   Made music as it swung.
>
> I wonder if he found it,
>   And knows the mystery now:
> Our Sandy Star who went away
>   With the secret on his brow.

James Weldon Johnson has had an interesting and varied career, as a teacher, as a writer for the stage, in the diplomatic service, and as secretary of the National Association for the Advancement of Colored People. He has produced numerous books in both verse and prose, some of the more notable being *Fifty Years, and Other Poems, God's Trombones: Seven Negro Sermons in Verse, The Book of American Negro Poetry* (edited), *Black Manhattan*, and an autobiography, *Along this Way;* and the race is especially indebted to him for the lyric, "Lift Ev'ry Voice and Sing," now widely known as the Negro National Anthem. One of his most noble poems is that praising the nameless makers of the Negro spirituals, beginning

> O black and unknown bards of long ago,
>   How came your lips to touch the sacred fire?
> How, in your darkness, did you come to know
>   The power and beauty of the minstrel's lyre?
> Who first from 'midst his bonds lifted his eyes?
>   Who first from out the still watch, lone and long,
> Feeling the ancient faith of prophets rise
>   Within his dark-kept soul, burst into song?

Meanwhile there were others who were making advance. To the credit of Alice Dunbar Nelson must be placed some beautiful lyrics; and Georgia Douglas Johnson has published three booklets of poems, many of them poignant or tender and some of exquisite finish. Much has been attempted in history and biography, but not all has been of the same degree of excellence. The *History of the Negro Race in America* (1883), by George W. Williams, represented the exploration of a new field and was the result of years of study. Though more than half a century has passed since the work appeared, much of it is still valuable.

Dr. Carter G. Woodson in 1916 began the quarterly publication of the *Journal of Negro History*, and among the best of his own books are *The Education of the Negro Prior to 1861* and *Negro Orators and their Orations* (edited).

With the World War a new note of racial consciousness came into the literature of the Negro. This was best represented by the work of Claude McKay, a poet who, born in Jamaica, came to the United States in 1912, studied for two years at the Kansas State University, was for a while associate editor of *The Liberator* and *The Masses*, and has since spent considerable time in Russia, Germany, and France. Mr. McKay has written several novels, but it is a book of poems, *Harlem Shadows* (1922), that best shows his range and power. In this will be found not only pieces that are rugged and stern but also many of superb craftsmanship and some of infinite tenderness. Here is the opening of "Flame-Heart," with its longing for old days in the West Indies:

> So much have I forgotten in ten years,
>   So much in ten brief years! I have forgot
> What time the purple apples come to juice,
>   And what month brings the shy forget-me-not.
> I have forgot the special, startling season
>   Of the pimento's flowering and fruiting,
> What time of year the ground doves brown the fields
>   And fill the noonday with their curious fluting.
> I have forgotten much, but still remember
> The poinsettia's red, blood-red in warm December.

The work in more dynamic vein, largely suggested by the race riots soon after the close of the World War, would be represented by such poems as "If We Must Die," "White Houses," and "The Lynching," the last of which we quote.

His spirit in smoke ascended to high heaven.
His father, by the cruelest way of pain,
Had bidden him to his bosom once again;
The awful sin remained still unforgiven.
All night a bright and solitary star
(Perchance the one that ever guided him,
Yet gave him up at last to Fate's wild whim)
Hung pitifully o'er the swinging char.
Day dawned, and soon the mixed crowds came to view
The ghastly body swaying in the sun:
The women thronged to look, but never a one
Showed sorrow in her eyes of steely blue;
And little lads, lynchers that were to be,
Danced round the dreadful thing in fiendish glee.

Two other poets who came into prominence in the decade after the war were Countee Cullen and Langston Hughes. Mr. Cullen in the early years of his career took several prizes in different contests. Although grounded in the traditional forms of writing, he too has shown racial consciousness, as in the books, *Color*, *Copper Sun*, *The Black Christ*, and *Caroling Dusk: An Anthology of Verse by Negro Poets*. His work is somewhat uneven in quality, but at its best shows a superb lyric sweep. Mr. Hughes has traveled much and seen life from many angles. His poems seek to be as free as possible in form, and they emphasize primitive passion, as in the first collection *The Weary Blues*. Even so, in some pieces, such as "The Negro Speaks of Rivers" and "Mother to Son," they sometimes rise to genuine nobility.

Two prose writers who showed unusual promise in the same period were Eric Walrond and Rudolph Fisher. Mr. Walrond is the author of *Tropic Death* (1926), a collection of ten stories or sketches dealing with the tragedy in the lives of the poorer people in the West Indies. The book

is not always a pleasant one, nor is it a perfect one. Some of
the stories are episodic, and at times even the diligent reader
may be puzzled; but such pieces as "Drought" and "Sub-
jection" leave no doubt as to the author's ability. Mr.
Fisher was a realistic writer with special interest in the short
story. "The City of Refuge," a story of life on the more
seamy side in New York, originally appeared in the
Atlantic Monthly; and a novel, *The Conjure Man Dies,* attracted considerable attention. The early death of this
writer cut short what bade fair to be a notable career.

One of the most remarkable things in the whole history
of American literature was the sudden change in the attitude of managers and publishers soon after the World
War toward the treatment of the Negro in the drama and
the novel. Twenty or thirty years before, when Charles
W. Chesnutt was doing his work, it was rare indeed for a
Negro to have anything in creative vein accepted in New
York. After the war, however, there was hardly a publisher who was not eager to have on his list a so-called
Negro book. Old modes of thought and conduct were in
the crucible; there was a demand for the new, even the
exotic; and the popular leader, Marcus Garvey, and James
Reese Europe, bandmaster with the 369th Infantry Regiment in the war, centered attention anew upon the black
man. In fiction white authors were quick to sense the new
temper, though their books were generally sordid and fa-
talistic in tone; and on the stage one could note such successes as *The Emperor Jones, In Abraham's Bosom,* and
The Green Pastures.

Among the Negro people there was almost feverish
activity in the drama, and sometimes success in the one-act
play, but in general enduring work in the full-length drama
yet remains to be done. In fiction there was *The Fire in
the Flint* (1925), by Walter F. White, followed the next

year by *Flight*. The first of these books, before it is through, grips the reader with a situation not only intense but powerful. In the main Jessie Fauset, author of *There is Confusion*, *Plum Bun*, and *The Chinaberry Tree*, and Nella Larsen (Mrs. Imes), author of *Quicksand* and *Passing*, have been concerned with the lot of the unusually attractive woman face to face with the ways of the world. Early in 1936 a new vein was struck by Arna Bontemps with *Black Thunder*, a story of Gabriel's insurrection in Virginia in 1800. Mr. Bontemps had already produced several excellent poems and a novel, *God Sends Sunday*, the brisk account of the checkered career of little Augie, a jockey "no bigger than a minute," who basks in the light of success until his "luck done change" and wanders to California to dream of his vanished glory. The new novel, though set in a distant day, was also close to the heart of the common folk, and it is alike distinguished in the sympathy of its character portrayal, and in the precision and elasticity of its prose.

To-day there are many currents and many writers of unusual gifts and promise. John F. Matheus, a professor in the West Virginia State College, has contributed to various periodicals stories of vigor and power. The conflict of temper is perhaps nowhere better illustrated than in the work of Sterling Brown, a professor at Howard University. Mr. Brown has been primarily interested in folk characters —the Negro of the railroad, the cotton-field, the chain-gang, as may be seen in the collection of his early work, *Southern Road* (1932); but he has also shown full acquaintance with conventional rhythms and in the noble "Salutamus," and other pieces as well, mastery of such a form as the sonnet.

34

MUSIC AND ART

WHEN WE CONSIDER the drama, music, and the fine arts, we come to that general field in which Negro achievement has been most distinguished. In music the contribution has been especially notable, and there have been many vocalists who have thrilled audiences by the fervor and brilliance of their singing.

In the creative drama much has been attempted but as yet nothing has been produced that can be said to approach greatness. With the acted drama, however, there is a different story; in spite of handicaps of all sorts, at least a few figures have risen to distinction. Even before the Civil War flourished Ira Frederick Aldridge (c. 1805-1867), an actor of superb physique and unusual power in the portrayal of passion. Aldridge spent much of his early life in Maryland. While still a young man he became acquainted with Edmund Kean, the famous English actor, who helped him to fit himself for the stage. Later he became best known for his work as Othello, and rose to his greatest triumphs on the continent of Europe. In more recent years one would note especially Charles Gilpin (c. 1872-1930), outstanding by reason of his work in *The Emperor Jones*, Richard B. Harrison (1864-1935), the very human "Lawd" of *The Green Pastures*, and Paul Robeson, just now at the height of his career as an actor and singer on the stage and for the screen. Prominent among the women was Rose McClendon (1884-1936), who excelled in the portrayal of old characters but concerning whom one may doubt if she ever had a part that did justice to her great talent.

Foremost on the roll of Negro composers is the name of a musician whose home was in England but who made three visits to the United States and in general did much to inspire workers in this country. Samuel Coleridge-Taylor (1875-1912) was born in London, the son of a physician who was a native of Sierra Leone, and an English mother. He attended the Royal College of Music. In November, 1898, he became world-famous by the production of the first part of his "Hiawatha" trilogy, *Hiawatha's Wedding Feast*. *The Death of Minnehaha* and *Hiawatha's Departure* followed within the next two years. Coleridge-Taylor also wrote a number of other cantatas for festivals, and many anthems. In 1904 he was appointed conductor of the Handel Society. In connection with Negro music one might note especially his symphonic pianoforte productions, *African Suite*, *African Romances* (with words by Dunbar), *Songs of Slavery*, and *African Dances*.

In the United States several composers have been active within recent years. The first to win high distinction was Harry T. Burleigh, who now has a place among the song-writers not only of America but of the world. Mr. Burleigh first came into prominence as a singer, a baritone. In May, 1936, he celebrated the close of forty-two years of service as a member of the choir of St. George's Episcopal Church, New York, and he has also served nearly as long at Temple Emanu-El, the synagogue on Fifth Avenue. His songs reveal both a sense of melody and great technical excellence. Among his stronger pieces are "Ethiopia Saluting the Colors," to words by Walt Whitman; "The Young Warrior," to words by James W. Johnson; and "The Soldier," a setting of Rupert Brooke's well known sonnet. A different division of Mr. Burleigh's work is that including his adaptations of Negro melodies, especially for choral work. In the field of popular music Will Marion Cook and J. Rosamond Johnson were especially successful with their songs for shows in the earlier years of the century. Mr. Johnson has recently issued *Rolling Along in Song* (1936). H. Lawrence Freeman, of New York, a director of church choirs and choral societies, now has to his credit not less than fourteen works in operatic vein, prominent titles being *Voodoo*, *Vendetta*, and *The Octoroon*. Clarence Cameron White has had wide experience as a concert violinist and as a teacher, chiefly at the West Virginia State College, Hampton Institute, and as the head of a studio in Boston. Aside from numerous smaller pieces he has written the opera, *Ouanga*, to the libretto by John F. Matheus based on the life of Dessalines, the Haytian patriot. R. Nathaniel Dett was graduated in music at Oberlin and later studied at Harvard, where within a year he won the Bowdoin essay prize with his paper, "The Emancipation of Negro Music," and the Francis Boott prize in composition. After teaching at two other institutions, he worked for a long period at Hampton, conducting the Hampton Institute Choir on its tours in the United States, Canada, and Europe. He has composed several suites for the piano, chiefly *Magnolia*, *Enchantment*, and *In the Bottoms;* his "Danse Juba" became very popular; and he excels in the writing of anthems. *The Chariot Jubilee*, a superb production, was written at the request of the Syracuse University chorus and its conductor. Among the most promising musicians who have appeared within the last few years are William Grant Still and William Levi Dawson. Mr. Still's *Afro-American Symphony* was rendered by the Rochester Symphony Orchestra in 1931 and has since been given in Europe. Mr. Dawson, director of the School of Music at Tuskegee Institute, is now well known for his *Negro Folk Symphony*, which was given most successful performances in 1934 by the Philadelphia Orchestra under the direction of Dr. Leopold Stokowski.

As for the singers, we find that even before the Civil War the race produced one of the first rank in Elizabeth Taylor Greenfield. This artist, born in Mississippi, was reared by a Quaker lady of Philadelphia. At her height she exhibited a voice of more than three octaves, and on a visit to England she delighted several highly critical audiences. The *Daily State Register*, of Albany, said after one of her concerts: "The compass of her marvelous voice embraces twenty-seven notes, reaching from the sonorous bass of a baritone to a few notes above even Jenny Lind's highest." About 1880 rose Madame Marie Selika, who appeared on many notable occasions, in Europe even more than in America. This brilliant soprano won the enthusiastic praise of critics in France and Germany. She could trill "like a feathered songster"; at the same time her voice was one of full rich quality, sweet and of extraordinary compass. Her rendering of the "Echo Song" was said to be "beyond any criticism, an artistic triumph." In the 1890's two other singers came into great prominence, Flora Batson and Sissieretta Jones. The first was a ballad singer, and sometimes the excitement she created amounted to a furore. She too had a voice of three octaves and sometimes after singing a selection as a soprano, would sing it again as a baritone. Madame Jones was a highly cultured singer; at the same time her voice had the plaintive quality that readily appeals to the heart of an audience. After a tour of the West Indies she was engaged as chief soloist for the Madison Square Garden Jubilee in April, 1892. Thereafter she was soloist at various expositions and she sang at the White House by invitation of President Harrison, and also before royalty in Europe. Within very recent years distinction has attached to Marian Anderson, a contralto, of Philadelphia. This singer first won notable success as soloist with the Philadelphia Philharmonic Symphony Society. In 1925, in a contest conducted by the New York Philharmonic Orchestra, she won over three hundred competitors, the prize being an appearance as soloist at one of the open-air concerts in Lewisohn Stadium. Since then she has steadily advanced, and some of her greatest triumphs have been in music-loving Sweden and Austria.

Of the men, Roland Hayes became internationally famous in the years just before the World War. The early life of this singer was one of hardship. While still a boy he worked in a factory in Chattanooga where paper weights were made. Sometimes he had to carry ladles brimming with melted ore, and often the liquid metal would fall and burn his feet. After a while came an opportunity to work with the Fisk Singers, and then to study with Arthur Hubbard in Boston. Later came concerts in Symphony Hall in Boston, and on May 31, 1920, the first of many recitals in London. Mr. Hayes appeared before King George V and Queen Mary, receiving a special token from the sovereign. In New York he has filled Carnegie Hall again and again. Audiences in Europe and America alike have been made to wonder at the spell cast by his voice. This is a tenor, not robust, but clear, smooth, and singularly sweet. Prominent among the baritones to-day is Jules (Julius) Bledsoe, a graduate of Bishop College, who first thought of medicine but was persuaded by friends to give serious attention to music. Mr. Bledsoe is a man of great versatility but excels in work calling for strength or nobility of utterance. His singing of the theme solo, "Ol' Man River," in *Show Boat* at the Ziegfeld Theatre in New York for two years brought him great popularity, but he has since appeared more than once as Amonasro in Verdi's *Aïda* and in general is interested in the highest development of his art.

Of many excellent pianists three at least have to-day a position of eminence. Hazel Harrison, after years of study in Germany, became distinguished in concert work. She has great technical facility and regularly gives prominence to Bach and Liszt on her programs. To hear her play "St. Franciscus Walking on the Waves" is to have an experience not easily forgotten. In 1936 she joined the faculty of the School of Music at Howard University. R. Augustus Lawson conducts at Hartford one of the leading studios in New England, and he has more than once been soloist at the concerts of the Hartford Philharmonic Orchestra. Roy W. Tibbs studied first at Fisk and Oberlin, later abroad, and is now a professor at Howard University. In April, 1934, he appeared in Washington as piano soloist with the Washington Symphony Orchestra directed by Hans Kindler. He is also giving increasing attention to the organ. Melville Charlton studied at the College of the City of New York, won a scholarship at the National Conservatory of Music, and in 1915, at the age of thirty-two, had advanced so far in his profession as to become an associate of the American Guild of Organists. After playing the organ at St. Philip's Episcopal Church in New York for some years, he accepted a similar position at the Religious School of Temple Emanu-El. There are to-day many capable violinists, but certainly one of the most brilliant is Louia Vaughn Jones, a graduate of the New England Conservatory in Boston, now an instructor at Howard University.

In painting and sculpture there has been surprising development within recent years, with more emphasis than before on racial themes. For some years the position of Henry Ossawa Tanner was almost one of lonely eminence. In 1891 this painter left Pennsylvania for study in Europe, and he has since lived in or near Paris. In 1897 his picture, "The Resurrection of Lazarus," awakened great enthusiasm. It was purchased by the French Government and now hangs in the Luxembourg. Since then there have been numerous other pictures on biblical subjects, and the artist has taken many prizes. In 1903 Meta Vaux Warrick (later Mrs. S. C. Fuller), also from Pennsylvania, began to exhibit at the Salon in Paris, exciting interest by the elemental and tragic character of her work. In the early piece, "The Wretched," are seven figures representing different forms of human anguish; but since it appeared there has been more emphasis on social subjects. In the second decade of the new century appeared another unusually capable painter, William Edouard Scott. This artist to some extent links the older and the newer tendencies. In 1912 his picture, "La Pauvre Voisine," shown at the Salon, was purchased by the Argentine Government; since then he has given much attention to mural work, receiving many important commissions. The number of artists who have been at work in recent years may be seen from the fact that a catalogue issued in 1935 by the Harmon Foundation, of New York, gave sketches of a hundred and nine painters or sculptors, with mention of several more. Archibald J. Motley, Jr., has had pictures in the exhibitions at the Art Institute of Chicago in practically every year since 1921. He has been represented in numerous other exhibitions; his "Blues" and "A Surprise in Store" were at the Century of Progress Exposition; and he has taken the Eisendrath Prize of the American-Scandinavian Foundation in Stockholm.

Aaron Douglas is prominent among those painters who strike the so-called African note in their work. Among his mural decorations are those for the Fisk University Library, the 135th Street Branch of the Young Men's Christian Association in New York, and the 135th Street Branch of the Public Library. Outstanding among recent sculptors is Richmond Barthé, another product of the Art Institute of Chicago. Mr. Barthé sold his "Blackberry Woman," "Comedian," and "African Dancer" to the Whitney Museum in New York; he exhibited at the Century of Progress Exposition in Chicago and the Texas Centennial in Dallas, and otherwise has won wide recognition.

A field of effort comparatively new is that of architecture. Prominent workers to-day are Paul R. Williams, of Los Angeles, Hilyard R. Robinson, head of the department at Howard University, and Albert I. Cassell, also of Washington. Mr. Williams has drawn plans for several fraternity and sorority houses in Los Angeles, as well as for the residences of a number of people of means, and has competed in open competition with distinction. Professor Robinson, who has studied and traveled extensively abroad, has recently been chief architect for a Federal housing project to cost over a million dollars. Mr. Cassell drew plans for a whole series of buildings at Howard University, these culminating in those for a library building to cost $1,106,000.

35

SCIENCE AND INVENTION

NEGROES HAVE LONG been interested in science and invention, but only within recent decades have they found full opportunity for the development of their talent. Before 1860 a situation that arose more than once took from them the credit for their work. If a slave devised something new, he was not permitted to take out a patent, for no slave could make a contract. At the same time his master could not take out a patent for him, for he could not make legal assignment. It is certain that Negroes, who did most of the mechanical work in the South before the Civil War, made more than one suggestion for the improvement of machinery, and it appears that to a slave on the plantation of Mrs. Nathanael Greene in Georgia belongs much of the credit for the invention of the cotton-gin.

Early in the present century a man of Negro descent, Henry E. Baker, was an examiner in the United States Patent Office in Washington. To him we are indebted for most of what we know about Negro inventors. Up to the present time Negroes have been granted very nearly 1,000 patents. The very first was granted to Henry Blair, of

Maryland, evidently a free Negro, who in 1834 took out a patent for a corn harvester. About 1884 Granville T. Woods, then in Cincinnati, began to have official record made of his inventions, and he continued his work without interruption until his death in New York in 1910. He made various improvements in telegraphy, these including a system of telegraphing from moving trains, also an electric railway and a phonograph. Several of his notable inventions were assigned to the General Electric Company, of New York, and the American Bell Telephone Company, of Boston. Elijah McCoy, of Detroit, who began his work about 1872, was granted fifty-seven patents, these relating chiefly to lubricating appliances for engines. He was a pioneer in the art of steadily supplying oil to machinery from a cup so as to render it unnecessary to stop a machine in order to oil it. Many of his inventions were long in use on the locomotives of the Canadian and Northwestern railroads and on the steamships of the Great Lakes. Jan E. Matzeliger, born in Dutch Guiana in 1852, came to the United States as a young man and served as a cobbler's apprentice, first in Philadelphia and then in Lynn, Massachusetts. He died in 1889 in his thirty-seventh year, but not before he had invented a machine for attaching soles to shoes, "the first appliance of its kind capable of performing all the steps required to hold a shoe on its last, grip and pull the leather down around the heel, guide and drive the nails into place, and then discharge the completed shoe from the machine." The patent for this invention was bought by the United Shoe Machinery Company, of Boston, and Matzeliger's invention thus formed the basis of an enterprise that consolidated forty subsidiary companies and that regularly gives employment to tens of thousands of people.

George W. Carver was born of slave parents on a farm near Diamond Grove, Missouri, about 1864. He lost his father in infancy, and was stolen and carried to Arkansas with his mother, who was never more heard of. Bought and returned to his home in Missouri, he studied in time to good effect an old blue-back speller, and later was graduated from high school and the Iowa State College of Agricultural and Mechanic Arts (B.S., 1894; M.S., 1896). Having become a member of the faculty at Iowa State, he was placed in charge of the greenhouse. There he was found by Booker T. Washington, who insisted on his going to Tuskegee, where he has been since 1896, chiefly as director of agricultural research. After patient experimenting Professor Carver has now brought forth not less than a hundred products from the sweet potato, nearly as many from the pecan, and at least a hundred and fifty from the peanut. Some of his demonstrations have attracted extraordinary attention. In 1923 he was awarded the Spingarn Medal.

Charles Henry Turner (1867-1923) (B.S., Cincinnati, 1891; M.S., *ibid.*, 1892; Ph.D., Chicago, 1907) was a neurologist and a pioneer in the field of Biology. He served as professer of Biology at Clark University in Atlanta from 1892 to 1905, and in his later years was a teacher at the Sumner High School in St. Louis. He made numerous contributions to scientific periodicals, these having to do largely with the life of bees and ants.

Ernest Everett Just (A.B., Dartmouth; Ph.D., Chicago) holds to-day in the field of Biology a place of unique distinction. After a brilliant career in college, this scientist began to teach at Howard, where since 1912 he has been professor of Zoology. He has brought a keen and highly trained mind to bear upon the problem of life, conducting research in fertilization, artificial parthenogenesis, and cell division. Dr. Just is the associate editor of *Physiological Zoology* (Chicago) and *The Biological Bulletin* (Woods

Hole, Massachusetts), and *The Journal of Morphology* (Philadelphia); he has served as vice-president of the American Society of Zoologists, and is an officer, fellow, or member of numerous other learned societies in Europe and America. In 1914 he became the first recipient of the Spingarn Medal.

In the fields of Chemistry and Physics there are to-day several promising scholars, some of whom have received the Doctor of Philosophy degree; but these men have so far been mainly devoted to theory and to the mastery of technique, so that they have not yet been able to give their studies the most direct application to life. Some are just now ready to enter the sphere of their larger achievement. One piece of work that could in no case be overlooked is the Ph.D. thesis presented in 1918 at the University of Michigan by Elmer S. Imes, who has since served as professor of Physics at Fisk University. This made a notable contribution to the discussion of infra-red absorption bands and receives highly commendatory attention in the authoritative reference work by Arnold Sommerfeld, *Atomic Structure and Spectral Lines*.

James A. Parsons, of Dayton, Ohio, even while a lad showed such ability in mathematics as to attract the attention of the family of his present employer, whom his father served as a butler. He studied electro-chemistry and electro-metallurgy at the Rensselaer Polytechnic Institute in Troy, New York, and after graduating did special work in aluminum bronze, contributing to the resources of the Aluminum Bronze Foundation. At the age of twenty-seven he became chief chemist and metallurgist of the Duriron Company, of Dayton, and his whole staff consists of Negroes, all chemical experts. In 1928 Mr. Parsons received from the Harmon Foundation a first award for his achievement in science.

Several men have now blazed a path in engineering and radio work. Archie A. Alexander, born in Ottumwa, Iowa, in 1888, attended high school in Des Moines, and in 1912 received the degree of Bachelor of Engineering from the University of Iowa. Later he took a special course in bridge designing at the University of London. For two years he was employed as a designing engineer for the Marsh Bridge Company of Des Moines. While thus engaged he formed a friendship with a white fellow worker, George F. Higbee, and the two decided to go into business together. Their firm was named Alexander and Higbee, and specialized in the construction of concrete and steel bridges. In 1925 Mr. Higbee was killed when struck by a steel beam while supervising the work on a bridge. Since then Mr. Alexander has been alone, and he has handled one large contract after another. One of the first was for a concrete conduit about a mile long between the heating plant of the University of Iowa and the main campus. Later came one for a power plant for the University costing half a million. Among his other tasks have been the construction of the sewer system in South Des Moines, this extending thirty-seven miles, the erection of the James River viaduct at Mitchell, South Dakota, and the building of the River bridge in Mt. Pleasant, Iowa, probably the largest highway bridge in the state.

36

THE NEGRO IN SPORT

NO MATTER WHAT the Negro may have done in religion or education, in science or art, or how well he may have achieved by serious effort, it is in the field of sport that he has made strongest appeal to the great American public. This is so for more than one reason. In the first place, there is something in human nature that finds interest in any kind of a contest. The rivalry is accentuated when two individuals face each other. Further, there is deeply engrained the feeling that in any test of ability there should be fair play. When, then, a Negro or any other man proves to be a good sportsman and enters a free competition, there is a disposition to give him his due.

In the field of pugilism, which has always made wide appeal, several Negroes have been champions. In fact it appears that the first champion the country had was a Negro slave, Tom Molineaux, of Richmond, Virginia, who was given his freedom when he won a great stake for his master. In 1810 Molineaux went to England and there in a long-drawn-out and grueling contest was defeated by the British champion, Tom Cribb. Peter Jackson was well

known as a contemporary of John L. Sullivan. George
Dixon was, with the exception of one year, either bantam-
weight or featherweight champion for the whole of the
decade 1890-1900; and Joe Gans was lightweight champion from 1902 to 1908. Joe Walcott was welterweight
champion from 1902 to 1904, when he was succeeded by
Dixie Kidd, who held his place until 1908. In 1908 Jack
Johnson, of Chicago, became heavyweight champion of
America, a position he was destined to hold for seven years.
In 1935 extraordinary attention began to center upon Joseph Louis Barrow, commonly known as Joe Louis, of Detroit, just twenty-one years of age, who had to his credit a
remarkable succession of victories, including those over two
former world champions, Primo Carnera and Max Baer, before he was defeated in the twelfth round by the German,
Max Schmeling, in June, 1936.

In professional baseball the Negro was proscribed,
though one or two men played on teams in the North in the
earlier years. In intercollegiate athletics, however, Harvard
about the turn of the century led in a liberal attitude, and
William C. Matthews of that institution was prominent in
baseball for two or three years about 1904. Within recent
years, in New England in general, there has been a change
of temper, and Negro athletes have turned more and more
to institutions in the West.

In football several men have won places on some of the
foremost teams in the country. William H. Lewis, at Harvard in the early 90's, proved to be one of the greatest of
centers; and Matthew W. Bullock, an end, was prominent
at Dartmouth a decade later. Since then at least three men
have won "All-American" distinction—Robert Marshall of
Minnesota, 1905, Fritz Pollard of Brown, 1916, and Paul
Robeson of Rutgers, 1918. Several others have been hardly
less distinguished. In 1935 Ozie Simmons, of the University

of Iowa, a half-back, attracted attention by his elusive running; and the next year Homer Harris, also of Iowa, was
elected captain of his team.

About the turn of the century Major Taylor was a champion bicycle rider. A year or two later John B. Taylor, of
the University of Pennsylvania, became the first Negro
runner to break intercollegiate records, and also the first to
represent America in the Olympic games. In the Yale-
Pennsylvania meet in 1904 he established a new record for
the 440-yard dash, and three years later, at Soldiers' Field,
Harvard University, lowered his own mark to 48⅘ seconds. By the time he went to London to the Olympic
games of 1908, however, his health was failing, and he died
soon after.

A few years later Binga Dismond, of Howard and Chicago, Sol Butler, of Drake, and Howard P. Drew, of
Southern California, were destined to win national and even
international honors in track work. Drew broke numerous
records as a runner, and Butler was the winner in the broad
jump at the Inter-Allied Games in the Pershing Stadium in
Paris. In 1921, in a meet in which Harvard, Yale, Cambridge, and Oxford were represented, Edwin O. Gourdin,
of Harvard, made a distance of 25 feet 3 inches in the running broad jump. Four years later, in the National Collegiate Track and Field Championship meet in Chicago,
DeHart Hubbard, of the University of Michigan, made in
the same event a mark of 25 feet 10⅞ inches. At the
Olympic games in Paris in 1924 Gourdin, Hubbard, and R.
Earl Johnson, of the Thompson Steel Works in Pittsburgh,
were on the team that represented the United States; and
Hubbard, in spite of a strained tendon that caused great
pain, excelled in the running broad jump, thus becoming
the first Negro to win an Olympic championship.

Up to 1932, however, many hopes were still unfulfilled.

Again and again a man had given promise, and then faded out of the picture. Now there was a change. As the tenth Olympiad, in Los Angeles, approached, scores of Negro athletes entered the preliminary meets in different sections of the country. Eighteen withstood the tests and reached the final tryouts at Stanford University in July. At the close of the trials four had won places on the American team. These were Eddie Tolan, formerly of the University of Michigan, Ralph Metcalfe, of Marquette University, Edward L. Gordon, of the University of Iowa, and Cornelius C. Johnson, of the Los Angeles High School. Gordon won the championship in the broad jump with a leap of 25 feet ¾ inch, and Johnson was in a tie with three other men for first place in the high jump.

There was special interest in the 100-meter and 200-meter runs. More people attended on the days of these events than at any other time, and there was great excitement over the outcome. In the 100-meter final, Yoshioka of Japan was away first and led for the first twenty meters. Tolan then took command of the situation, but near the goal Metcalfe redoubled his speed and the two men were so close at the finish that the judges had to see the moving pictures of the race before they could finally give a decision in favor of Tolan. In the 200-meter event Tolan ran the best race of his career, winning in 21.2 seconds for a new Olympic and a new world record. The crowd applauded thunderously. He had won for his people and his country two Olympic championships.

The record made by Negro athletes in 1932 was continued and even surpassed at the eleventh Olympiad in Berlin in August, 1936. Negro performers were the sensation of the meet, especially in the opening days, and they rapidly captured first places to bring victory to the United States. There was something ironical in their success in a

country officially hostile to non-Aryans. Jesse Owens, of
Cleveland and Ohio State University, won the 100-meter
and the 200-meter races, Archie Williams, of California,
the 400-meter, and John Woodruff, of the University of
Pittsburgh, the 800-meter race. In addition, Cornelius
Johnson, of California, took the high jump at a new Olympic level of 6 feet 7 15/16 inches, Owens won the broad
jump, and Owens and Ralph Metcalfe were respectively
the first and second runners on the victorious relay team.
Metcalfe was second in the 100-meter race, and others who
won points in the different events by being near first place
were David Albritton, Matthew Robinson, and James
LuValle.

The outstanding performer of the Olympiad was Jesse
Owens, who by his individual achievements and work in
the relay won four gold medals, with souvenir oaktrees.
Five times he surpassed the Olympic broad jump record,
winning the championship with a leap of 26 feet 5 21/64
inches. His feat in breaking the record for 200-meters, in
the face of a cold wind and on a rain-soaked track, was
especially astonishing to the spectators. Running without
apparent effort, he finished in 20.7 seconds, seven-tenths of
a second faster than any previous victor in the event in
Olympic history. On his return to the United States he
was given an ovation. In Cleveland Mayor Harold H. Bur-
ton and Lieutenant-Governor Harold G. Mosier rode with
him to the Auditorium, where four thousand persons were
assembled. He received a $500 gold stop-watch with an
engraved scroll carrying resolutions of the City Council,
and there were other tokens of personal esteem. Three
days later he received similar honors from the state of Ohio
in Columbus. At the close of the year, in a poll conducted
by writers for the Associated Press, he was easily given
place as the foremost American athlete in 1936.

37

The Negro Woman in American Life

In the history of the United States no more heroic work has been done than that performed by the Negro woman. The great responsibilities of life have naturally drifted to the men; but in thousands of homes it is the mother who chiefly bears the burden, and the story of love and patience and sacrifice is unending. Even before emancipation a strong character made herself felt in more than one community, and to-day in social service and education, business and the professions, literature and art alike, the Negro woman is making her way and reflecting credit upon the people she represents.

It was but natural that those should first be known who were interested in the struggle for freedom. Notable were Sojourner Truth and Harriet Tubman. It was impossible for anyone to carry on the tradition of such distinctive characters as these, and more recent years have brought forward women who realized the value of training and culture. The general force of the social emphasis has led those who were concerned with community improvement to come together for greater effectiveness; and thus we have had developing in almost all of our cities and towns clubs

working for the good of the race, whether the immediate
aim was literary culture, an orphanage, an old folks' home,
or the protection of working girls. All such work received
impetus from the founding in 1896 of the National Association of Colored Women's Clubs, among whose achievements has been the purchase of the home of Frederick
Douglass at Anacostia, in the District of Columbia.

One of the pioneers in club work in the generation
after the Civil War was Mrs. Josephine St. Pierre Ruffin, of
Boston, a woman of unusual culture and breadth of experi-
ence. The terrific increase in lynching in the decade
1890-1900 brought into prominence Ida B. Wells (Mrs.
Ferdinand L. Barnett), an outspoken leader in the agitation
against the crime and the organizer of numerous clubs.
Prominent in the early years of the present century were
Margaret Murray Washington (1865-1925), Lucy Smith
Thurman (1849-1918), Mary B. Talbert (1862-1923), and
Mary Church Terrell, all four of whom served at one time
or another as president of the National Association. Mrs.
Washington gave valiant assistance to her husband, Booker
T. Washington, both at Tuskegee and on the public plat-
form. Mrs. Thurman began with interest in temperance.
A woman of commanding presence and great inspirational
power, she had the eloquence of a genuine orator. Mrs.
Talbert was especially active at the time of the World War.
For four years she was president of the National Association, and she was the leading spirit in the effort for the purchase of the Douglass home. For her general achievement,
this including her war work, she was in 1922 awarded the
Spingarn Medal. Mrs. Terrell, whose husband, Robert H.
Terrell, a Harvard graduate, was for years a municipal
judge in Washington, is herself a graduate of Oberlin and a
public speaker distinguished for grace and poise. She was
the first president of the National Association, was twice

reëlected, and at the International Congress of Women held in Berlin in 1904 won general admiration by delivering one speech in German and another in equally good French. A well known correspondent said: "This achievement on the part of a colored woman, added to a fine appearance and the eloquence of her words, carried the audience by storm and she had to respond three times to the encores before they were satisfied. It was more than a personal triumph; it was a triumph for her race."

In the professions, especially medicine and law, and in scholarship as well, the Negro woman has made rapid advance within recent years. Before 1920 there was in the South very little provision for high school work for Negroes in public school systems; but since then secondary institutions have multiplied, and the larger number of students going to college has naturally increased the number of those anticipating graduate or professional work. In 1921 the degree of Doctor of Philosophy was for the first time awarded at representative universities to women of Negro descent, and in that year there were three successful candidates—Eva B. Dykes, in English, at Radcliffe; Sadie T. Mossell, in Economics, at Pennsylvania; and Georgiana R. Simpson, in German, at Chicago. In 1926 Otelia Cromwell received the degree in English at Yale, and since then still others have won it. Dr. Mossell is now Mrs. Raymond P. Alexander, wife of a prominent lawyer in Philadelphia, and she herself has also taken a degree in law at Pennsylvania. Dr. Dykes and Dr. Simpson are now teaching at Howard University, and Dr. Cromwell at the Miner Teachers College in Washington. In the meantime, although in the North at least they sometimes faced various difficulties, Negro women have graduated from schools of medicine; and they are now beginning to be accustomed to courts of law. Mrs. Ruth Whitehead Whaley, a graduate of the Law School of Fordham University, set a precedent when she appeared to plead before the New York Court of Appeals; and Mrs. Violette N. Anderson was admitted to practice before the Supreme Court of the United States after it was shown that she had practiced for more than three years before the Supreme Court of Illinois.

In the public schools the great majority of the teachers is composed of women. This means that the women are considerably more than half of the sixty thousand Negroes now engaged in educational work in the United States. In the chapter that follows, attention will be invited to a few of those whose pioneer effort entitles them to high recognition. Just now we must not fail to note Elizabeth C. Wright, who founded the Voorhees Normal and Industrial School at Denmark, South Carolina; Cornelia Bowen, who founded Mt. Meigs Institute, Mt. Meigs, Alabama; Nannie H. Burroughs, of the National Training School for Women and Girls in Washington; and, for very recent years, Arenia C. Mallory, who is in the Delta section of Mississippi. One of the most important developments in education within the last few decades has been the appointment of a number of young women as supervisors in county schools under the terms of the will of Anna T. Jeanes, a Quaker lady of Philadelphia who, shortly before her death in 1907, set aside a million dollars for the improvement of Negro rural schools in the South. Representative of those who have worked under such auspices is Virginia E. Randolph, of Hanover County, Virginia, who in 1927 received from the Harmon Foundation a first award in Education, for her original plan of adapting school programs to the needs of Negroes in the rural districts of the Southern states.

Ruth Anna Fisher, a graduate of Oberlin College, after a period of study at the London School of Economics and some time spent in collecting manuscript material for

American historians, entered upon the work for which she has become distinguished, that in connection with the Manuscript Division of the Library of Congress. Dr. J. F. Jameson, chief of the Division, said some time ago: "The work in which Miss Ruth Anna Fisher is engaged is the supervision and conduct of all the work which the Library of Congress is now carrying out in London for the securing, on a very large scale, of photographic reproductions of manuscripts relating to American history which are to be found in the archives and libraries of that city. She has been engaged in that work since September, 1927. . . . Having seen Miss Fisher at work in London in the conduct of this enterprise, I take pleasure in saying that she has not only managed it with extraordinary ability and greatly to the satisfaction of the Librarian of Congress, but also that she has manifestly made herself very distinctly *persona grata* to the authorities of the British Museum and to all those assistants who have worked under her direction."

In church work and missions one has only to look about him to see what the Negro woman is accomplishing. We all know the extent to which women have had to bear the burden not only of the regular activities but also of the numerous "rallies" that still unfortunately seem necessary in our churches. They have also assisted nobly in the work of more secular relief and welfare agencies.

In the realm of business the Negro woman has stood side by side with her husband in the rise to higher things. In almost every instance in which a man has prospered, investigation will show that his advance was largely due to the faith, the patience, and the untiring industry of his wife. Booker T. Washington liked to refer to Mrs. Junius G. Groves, wife of a grower of potatoes in Edwardsville, Kansas. Mrs. Groves helped her husband when he had hardly a dollar, and she lived to see him gather in one year

hundreds of thousands of bushels of white potatoes, sur-
passing all other growers in the world. Dr. Washington
also told about Mrs. E. C. Berry, wife of a hotel-keeper of
Athens, Ohio. At night, after the guests were asleep, she
would press their garments, adding buttons and repairing
rents; and thus it was that she and her husband came to have
the leading hotel in the city, one with fifty rooms and
favored by commercial travelers.

To-day there are hundreds of women who are thus
assisting their husbands. One is Mrs. P. B. Young, wife of
the editor of the Norfolk *Journal and Guide*. Several
women on their own initiative have become engaged in
large enterprises. The next chapter speaks of the work of
the late Maggie L. Walker, of Richmond. Outstanding in
their field, that of the manufacture of toilet preparations,
have been the Madam C. J. Walker Manufacturing Company, with headquarters in Indianapolis, and Poro College,
in St. Louis, founded by Mrs. A. M. Malone.

Of special importance is the contribution of the Negro
woman to the industrial life of the country. According to
the census of 1910, 1,047,146, or 52 per cent of those at
work, were either farmers or farm laborers; and 28 per
cent more were either cooks or washer-women. In other
words, 80 per cent were doing some of the hardest and
most necessary work in our home and industrial life.
Within the next ten years, by reason of the war and migration, there was a notable shift. In 1920 the number of
farm workers had fallen to 612,261; and whereas ten years
before there was just one woman listed as running an elevator, the number was now 3,073. Those employed in iron,
steel, and other metal industries rose from 349 to 2,208;
and those in textile industries from 2,234 to 7,257. The
changes wrought in a few years by the demands of
the war were remarkable. Mary E. Jackson, writing at the

time in the *Crisis,* said: "Indiana reports Negro women in glass works; in Ohio they are found on the night shifts of glass works; they have gone into the pottery works in Virginia; wood-working plants and lumber yards have called for their help in Tennessee." She quoted a social worker of Cleveland, who said further: "We find them on power sewing-machines, making caps, waists, bags, and mops; we find them doing pressing and various hand operations in these same shops. They are employed in knitting factories as winders, in a number of laundries on mangles of every type, and in sorting and marking. They are in paper box factories doing both hand and machine work, in button factories on the button machines, in packing houses packing meat, in railroad yards wiping and cleaning engines, and doing sorting in railroad shops. One of our workers recently found two colored girls on a knotting machine in a bed spring factory, putting the knots in the wire springs." All along of course the Negro woman had found some opportunity in meat packing plants like those in Chicago.

In a large way there was service even beyond that in such lines as these. When Negro men were called away to training camps, or to France, and when some of their sisters found employment in the industries of the North, tens of thousands of Negro women still remained in the cotton-fields of the South; and cotton was now needed more than ever. If the country was to hold its own, it was for them and their children to raise the usual crop; and they did it, even in the face of harsh and uncertain conditions, all in the hope that the future might hold a better day for those who were dear to them. The burden of the World War thus in the last analysis rested on the back of the hard-working Negro woman of the South, and it is not too much to say that in a time of peril she helped to sustain the country and win the war.

38

MAGGIE L. WALKER AND HER ENTERPRISE

ON THE AFTERNOON of Sunday, November 30, 1924, there was a host of people assembled in the City Auditorium in Richmond, Virginia. The weather was chill and threatening; but as early as one o'clock they began to come, and two hours later the throng was unprecedented. Visitors had come from other cities; civic leaders and ministers gave the support of their presence; and the Governor of the Commonwealth, E. Lee Trinkle, added his word of praise, saying, "If the State of Virginia had done no more in fifty years with the funds spent on the education of the Negroes than educate Mrs. Walker, the State would have been amply repaid for its outlay and efforts."

Who was the woman who was thus so signally honored? Maggie Lena Mitchell was born in Richmond July 15, 1867, and died December 15, 1934. Her mother, early left a widow, lived in an alley and worked hard at the washtub to support the children in her care. Maggie, with a radiant disposition, helped in any way she could, and in 1883, when not quite sixteen years of age, was duly graduated from high school. Already serious far beyond her age, she became a teacher, but, being drawn to business, left the schoolroom to take a course in this field, and in 1889 became the executive secretary of the Independent Order of St. Luke. Ten years later she became the secretary-treasurer of the organization, a position which she held for thirty-five years. Meanwhile, in 1890, she was married to Armstead Walker, and in course of time became the mother of two sons.

The original idea behind the Order of St. Luke was that of many similar organizations, by small weekly dues to assist a man or woman to provide against sickness in old age and for funeral expenses. There had been many such orders or societies in the South; Virginia seemed to have more than her share; and sometimes they had not been very well managed. The history of St. Luke was to be different. Thanks to the initiative and energy of a consecrated woman, it was to set a new standard and show what at least was possible in all such enterprises.

When Mrs. Walker began her work with the organization, she received as her salary only eight dollars a month, and for this sum she was expected to collect dues, verify cases of illness and death, keep the books, and pay out all claims as they were due. She looked not at the reward, however, but at the opportunity; and she had vision. If the Order could help a thousand persons, why not ten thousand, a hundred thousand? And why should it think only of sickness and death? Why should it not train the people to save and invest their money, to own their homes, and to win their way to independence? Why should it not also teach the children thrift, letting them learn the value of their pennies, and telling them to avoid extravagance or waste?

With such an aim, and with her genius, Maggie L. Walker had the energy of a dozen women, and all who

Maggie L. Walker

came into her presence felt the inspiration of her character. She seemed to think in big terms, and lived in a realm above things little or mean. Eminently religious, she appealed to the solid, church-going element in the city, and helped in ways innumerable. When she took charge of the Order, it had 3,408 members, but no reserve fund and no home property. At the time of the testimonial in 1924, it had 100,000 members, a building costing $100,000, an emergency fund of $70,000, and a newspaper, the *St. Luke Herald*. Fifty-five clerks were employed in the home office; there were 145 field workers; and 15,000 children were enrolled in the thrift clubs.

As the organization grew and the volume of its business increased, the need of a bank was felt. Accordingly in 1902 Mrs. Walker brought before her council the plan of the St. Luke Penny Savings Bank. Though this bore the name of the order, it was legally to be separate. She was able to convince her hearers, and became the president of the new enterprise. As with insurance, she had to learn the business from the ground up as well as she could; but again her faith and initiative told, and the institution became in time the St. Luke Bank and Trust Company, a depository for gas and water accounts in Richmond, and for city taxes.

"When any of our girls are advanced to making as much as fifty dollars a month," said Mrs. Walker, "we begin to persuade them to buy a home. As soon as they save enough for the first payment, the bank will help them out. There is a woman in the office here who came to us eighteen years ago. She did odd jobs of cleaning, and we paid her a dollar a week, which she was glad to get. But we encouraged her to fit herself for better things. She studied, took a business course at night school, and has worked her way up until now she is our head bookkeeper, with a salary of one hundred and fifty dollars a month. She owns a nice home, well furnished and fully paid for, and has money in the bank.

"Then there was that one-legged little bootblack at Second and Clary Streets. He joined our Order. He had a rented chair out on the sidewalk in the weather. We helped him save, and when he had fifty dollars, we helped him rent a little place with three chairs. That was seven years ago. Now he has a place of his own with twelve chairs. He has bought a home for his mother—paid $1,900 for it—and has it furnished and free of debt. And his bank account never falls below five hundred dollars.

"Numbers of our children have bank accounts of from one hundred to four hundred dollars. They sell papers, cut grass, do chores, run errands, work in stores Saturdays. We teach them to save with the definite purpose of wise use of the money. We do a great deal of the same kind of work with the grown people. Our bank lends money for home-building at six per cent, and we tide the deserving ones over times of trouble. Six hundred and forty-five homes have been entirely paid for through our bank's help."

This same spirit went over into community and interracial work. When Mrs. Janie Porter Barrett, another noble spirit, was founding the home for delinquent Negro girls at Peake, eighteen miles from Richmond, and needed money to pay for the tract of a hundred and forty acres, Mrs. Walker organized a Council of Women with fourteen hundred members, and thus raised the first five thousand dollars necessary for the purchase of the farm. Later she contributed liberally of her own means according as the home had need.

From this service for the unfortunate developed community work in Richmond. "The white women began it," said Mrs. Walker. "You know what some of them have done here—women who stand at the top socially and who

are leaders in the church and the club life of the city and
state. They had done fine community work for white people, and at length they went to our preachers and asked
them to invite their leading women to a conference. As a
result we began some forms of community work. Then
a philanthropist who gave the white women a house for a
working girls' home said that if we colored women would
show our interest in social work among our people by raising a thousand dollars for it, he would give us the use of a
large house, and if we made good, he would deed it to a
board of white and colored women.

"You know we had to make good after that. We raised
the thousand dollars, and we have kept right on. The
house has been deeded now to our bi-racial board. The
white women don't work for us,—they work with us; and
they've helped us to connect up with every charitable organization in the city. We have four paid workers, and the
Community House is just such a center of influence as we
have needed all these years."

Meanwhile Mrs. Walker's influence was widening. A
tall, large woman with clear kindly eyes and a firm mouth,
she was a marked figure in any assemblage. She became
president of the state branch of the National Association
of Colored Women, and served on numerous other boards
and councils. All the while she was working not for a day
or a year but the large future. It was her desire to have
the Order of St. Luke and the bank on such a basis that they
could still move steadily forward when she was gone. Most
admirably did she succeed in her endeavor.

Let no one think that she did not have her trials and sorrows. With all of her generosity there were those who
were envious or jealous, and even in the Order itself she
more than once had to face intrigue. Then suddenly came
the hardest blow of all, one under which any heart, how-

ever brave, would have quailed. Her husband, mistaken for a burglar, was shot by one of his sons. Dark days followed, but for the mother it was the breaking of sunlight when the young man was exonerated in court. Later she had a fall, one from which she never recovered; still she gave of her best, never faltering. Thus it was that she became one of the noblest of Negro Builders.

39

WOMEN WHO HAVE LED IN EDUCATION

IN A FORMER chapter our thought was upon the general contribution of the Negro woman to American life. In no field has that contribution been more far-reaching than in education. Among those whose work has been most distinctive have been Fanny Jackson Coppin, Maria L. Baldwin, Lucy Laney, Charlotte Hawkins Brown, Mary McLeod Bethune, and Maudelle Brown Bousfield.

FANNY JACKSON COPPIN

In the book, *Reminiscences of School Life, and Hints on Teaching*, which appeared in 1913, is the dedication: "This book is inscribed to my beloved aunt, Sarah Orr Clark, who, working at six dollars a month, saved one hundred and twenty-five dollars and bought my freedom."

The woman who wrote those words was born a slave in the District of Columbia about the year 1836. Liberated through the self-sacrifice of the aunt of whom she spoke, she was sent while still young to another aunt living in New Bedford, Massachusetts, and then to a relative in Newport, Rhode Island, in order that she might go to school. In the

latter city, when she was fourteen years of age, she entered
the service of George H. Calvert, a great-grandson of the
Lord Baltimore who settled Maryland. Mr. Calvert was a
man of culture, and his wife, who had no children of her
own, took interest in the girl in her care, looking out for
her health, teaching her to sew, and giving her opportunity
to advance in her studies.

Thus Fanny Jackson prepared to enter the Rhode Island
State Normal School, then in Bristol. There her heart and
mind were awakened as never before to the fascination and
joy of teaching. Some day, she said to herself, she would
use the talents that God had given her in the education of
her people. With this thought in mind, she resolved, on the
completion of her normal course, to enter Oberlin College.
The aunt to whom she owed her freedom still helped her,
and Bishop Daniel A. Payne saw that she was given a
scholarship of nine dollars a year, a sum that meant considerably more then than now.

It was in 1860 that Fanny Jackson entered Oberlin, and
there she spent five and a half years. The Christian at-
mosphere of the college, and the years spent in the homes
of two of the professors, made an impression she could
never forget. Young women were not generally supposed
to pursue the course emphasizing Greek and Mathematics,
but she took those subjects and also French, which was not
then in the regular curriculum. She never rose to recite, she
said, without feeling that the honor of the whole African
race was on her shoulders. Fortunately she was most often
able to give a good account of herself.

Those were the years of the Civil War. Freedmen
poured into Ohio from the South, and some settled in the
township of Oberlin. Moved by their need, Miss Jackson,
in her last year in college, formed a class for them, and she
was deeply touched by the efforts of old men to read and

spell; but already she rejoiced that, in some measure at least, she had entered upon the chosen work of her life and had definitely begun to serve her people.

It was the custom at Oberlin to employ forty juniors and seniors to teach the preparatory classes. Fanny Jackson was informed that she would be given a class but that, if there was any rebellion on the part of the pupils, the faculty would not be disposed to force the matter. Already, however, she was more mature than the average young woman in college, and she had the advantage of her normal training. While there was some surprise when she entered the classroom, there was no objection, and the number of those enrolled increased so much that the class had to be divided, the teacher being given both sections.

The next year came a request from a Friends' school in Philadelphia for a young colored woman who could teach the classics and mathematics. The answer given from Oberlin was, "We have the woman, but you must wait a year for her." In the autumn of 1865 accordingly, having completed her course and served as class poet, Fanny Jackson began her work in Philadelphia, at what was then the Institute for Colored Youth and is now the Cheyney Training School for Teachers. She had been there only four years when changes made it necessary for her to assume the duties of the principalship. More and more also she realized that the Negro people in the city needed not only training in the classics but also acquaintance with the trades and industries. She recalled that such was the original purpose of the Institute for Colored Youth, and she was greatly impressed by the exhibits from foreign trade schools at the Centennial Exposition in 1876. It grieved her to think that the only place in the great city where a Negro boy could learn a trade was in the House of Refuge or the penitentiary. Accordingly it now became the great purpose of her life to see that people were enlightened as to the advantages of industrial education. In the pursuance of her plan she spoke before any gathering that would hear her, not only in Philadelphia but elsewhere; and she was greatly encouraged when a Negro man, Walter P. Hall, gave her on one occasion twenty-five dollars. At last her hope was realized, and bricklaying, plastering, carpentry, shoemaking, printing, and tailoring were established for the boys; dressmaking and millinery for the girls; and for both boys and girls stenography, typewriting, and cooking.

Meanwhile, in 1881, Fanny M. Jackson was married to the Reverend Levi J. Coppin, of the African Methodist Episcopal Church. She remained at the Institute for nineteen years more, until she had served for a total of thirty-five years; and her influence steadily widened. In 1888 she went to England to attend the Missionary Congress as a representative of the Sarah Allen Mission. So eloquently did she speak that the Duke of Somerset rose to give her special commendation. At a political meeting in Philadelphia the mayor was so deeply moved by her words that he appointed her a member of the Board of City Examiners for clerical officers.

In 1900 the Reverend Mr. Coppin became a bishop in his church and was assigned to South Africa. He preceded his wife to Cape Town, but she came later and gave him valiant assistance, especially in the work with the women. In her travels she went as far as Bulawayo, more than thirteen hundred miles from Cape Town. There the shadow of the future fell, for, as she learned later, the Government had native spies present. It took some time for everyone to be convinced that the purpose of the effort was purely missionary and not political. However, Mrs. Coppin kept her faith. "The Kingdom of God," she said, "does not proceed in its conquests by the employment of carnal weapons and right can afford to be patient because it is bound to win in the end." She died in Philadelphia, January 21, 1913.

MARIA L. BALDWIN

Maria Louise Baldwin was born in Cambridge, Massachusetts, September 13, 1856, the daughter of Peter L. and Mary E. Baldwin. She attended the Allston Grammar School, the Cambridge High School, and the training school for teachers in the city. Not finding an opening in Massachusetts, she went to Maryland for two years; but the agitation of Negro leaders at length won an appointment in Cambridge. She entered upon her service at the Agassiz School in the autumn of 1882, and seven years later became principal. In 1915 the old school building was torn down and a new one erected; and in the autumn of 1916 the position of the principal was raised to that of "master," one seldom held by a woman at the time. Maria L. Baldwin now directed the work of twelve teachers, all white, and she had in her care five hundred children, many of them from the families of Harvard professors. On the night of January 9, 1922, while addressing at the Copley-Plaza in Boston the council of the Robert Gould Shaw House Association, an organization that ministered to the Negroes of the city, she collapsed and in a few minutes was gone.

The shock to those present was overwhelming. The Reverend Dr. Alexander Mann, rector of Trinity Church and president of the council, adjourned the meeting; and three days later there were tributes of high regard in the service at the Arlington Street Church.

Such are the facts; but they give little idea of the culture of Maria L. Baldwin, of her high conception of her profession, or her concern for her own people. She was alert to all the movements and tendencies in the teaching world; was a member of the Twentieth Century Club of Boston, served a term as president of the Boston Ethical Society, and was for years president of the League of Women for Community Service, a distinctively racial organization. To one who entered upon the work of the ministry she said, "Good, but I will not grant that even that is more sacred than the work of the teacher." About a year after her death there was unveiled at the Agassiz School a tablet to her memory. This was the gift of the class of 1922, the last she taught, and the ceremony was under the auspices of the Agassiz Parent-Teachers Association. The room was dedicated as Baldwin Hall, and the inscription on the tablet recalled her as "inspiring teacher, wise and beloved master of this school."

It was in dealing with problems of discipline that some of Miss Baldwin's greatest successes were won. She sought to enlist a child's coöperation and to lead him to make the right decision for himself. One day while a teacher was out of the room something happened, and within a few minutes an uncomfortable little boy was sitting in the principal's office. Just then the superintendent of schools came in. "Mr. Fitzgerald," said the principal, "we are sorry you are here to-day. Please don't ask us why"; and it could be observed that the boy was trying hard to keep out of sight. "When you come in next week," continued Miss Baldwin, "we shall have all nice boys and girls." When the superintendent was gone the boy came up and said, "You won't let Mr. Fitzgerald know I was that little boy, will you, if I promise never to do it again?"

One of the school officials, speaking of her career, said: "From the first day I saw her I realized that she was a rare character. I was then serving on the Cambridge School Board and she was teaching in one of the lower grades in the Agassiz School, which was in my care. Her poise and dignity, her calmness and beautiful voice struck me at once, and I felt that her mere presence must be a valuable lesson to all the children. Several parents told me their children realized this and always spoke of her in admiration and affection. . . . When the principal of the school was changed the superintendent told me it would be my duty to appoint a new principal. 'Why,' I said, 'you know as well as I do there is only one suitable person, Miss Baldwin.' 'I think so too,' he said, 'but I was not sure about the color.' 'It is not a question of color,' I said; 'it is a question of the best.' She took the place and for forty years filled it with gentleness and capability, and in all those years, with all the changes that come in city governments, I am not aware that there was any dissatisfaction or any suggestion of change."

LUCY LANEY

The development of high school education for Negro youth in the South is a matter of comparatively recent years. For a long time if a Negro boy or girl wished to go beyond the elementary grades, it was necessary to go to an institution maintained by private, often religious, agencies. It was this situation that called into being such a school as Haines Institute in Augusta, Georgia.

Lucy Craft Laney, the founder of Haines, was born in Macon, Georgia, April 13, 1854, the seventh of the ten children of David and Louisa Laney. The father was a man of initiative. Born a slave in South Carolina, he learned the carpenter's trade, accumulated money for the purchase of his freedom, and, fifteen years before the Civil War, went to Macon, where he was employed by a number of masters to teach his trade to their slaves. Interested in religion, he studied hard, and in course of time was formally ordained as a minister in the Presbyterian Church. His wife was first a slave in the prominent family of the Campbells, being the maid of a daughter in the home; but David Laney purchased her freedom also and thus assured freedom to his children.

While very young Lucy spent many hours in the home where her mother was working, and Miss Campbell, noting her interest in reading, selected books for her and otherwise directed her education. For her secondary training she went to the Lewis High School, later the Ballard Normal; then she became one of a group selected by the American Missionary Association to form a class at the old Atlanta University. There, after a brilliant career as a student, she was graduated in 1873 as one of the four members in the first class.

For ten years after she left college Miss Laney taught in the public schools of Macon, Milledgeville, Augusta, and Savannah. While in this last city for the second time, she was persuaded by a representative of the Presbyterian Board of Missions to return to Augusta, in view of the need there; and thenceforth that city was her home.

First she rented the lecture room of the Christ Presbyterian Church, and her idea seems to have been to have a nursery and day school for girls. Boys came also, however; they could not be turned away; and some of the children who came in time were so young that they hardly knew any mother except herself.

It was in 1883 that the school was thus opened. Three years later, on January 6, 1886, it received from the state of Georgia a charter. Meanwhile it had become necessary to seek other quarters, as there was complaint in the neighborhood by reason of the noise made by the children while at play. Moreover the enrollment, 75 at the close of the first year, at the end of the second year had increased to 234. A frame building on Gwinnett Street was rented, but this was soon overcrowded. The school then moved to lower Calhoun Street, where there was a two-story frame structure with a barn in the rear. Here it remained for some time, passing through its most critical period. There was no money, and debts were accumulating; a fire came, then a flood, and finally typhoid fever, which took away Miss Freeman, the founder's first assistant. The tale of disaster would have daunted any heart except the stoutest.

On the advice of a minister in Augusta, Miss Laney went in 1887 to Minneapolis to present her cause to the General Assembly of the Presbyterian Church. As she encountered jealousy on the part of others who had matters to present, she did not immediately press her suit, but simply stated the needs of the school, saying that some day all would hear from it, and asking for her fare back home.

The trip was more successful than at first appeared. The Board did not immediately help financially, but after some months began to pay salaries in whole or in part and otherwise to help with maintenance. In Minneapolis also Miss Laney met her first influential friend, Mrs. Haines, who persuaded others to help and in general so inspired the hard-working principal that the school was named for her. It was moved from Calhoun Street to the present site on Gwinnett, and within the next three decades grew from one teacher and five pupils to more than thirty teachers, nine hundred students, and three brick buildings, besides a number of frame structures.

There was never anything showy about Lucy Laney or her work. She never cared to be in the public eye, and would move about the school in the simplest garb, with a little shawl thrown over her shoulders. Her emphasis was on scholarship and character, and to her the possibilities of a human being were infinite. Moreover she had a keen sense of social need. When a hospital was burned in Augusta, she placed the school buildings at the disposal of the officials. She also opened the first kindergarten in the city, conducted institutes for teachers, and made the singing in Sunday schools brighter and better. When she died, October 23, 1933, the *Augusta Chronicle* said: "Lucy Laney was great because she loved people. She believed that all God's children had wings, though some of the wings are weak and have never been tried. She could see in the most backward that divine personality which she endeavored to coax into flame."

CHARLOTTE HAWKINS BROWN

One day in October, 1901, a young Negro woman got off the train at McLeansburg, North Carolina, roamed for some hours through the desolate country, found at length an old tumble-down shack, and then announced to the people in the vicinity that she was going to have there a school. To-day, if one will go to Sedalia, on the national highway, ten miles east of Greensboro, he will find an institution with stately modern buildings, well-kept grounds, and a general air of progress, all being a monument to the initiative of the founder, and her ability to get others to coöperate with her.

The school, now a junior college, is the Palmer Memorial Institute, named for Alice Freeman Palmer, wife of George Herbert Palmer, for years a professor at Harvard, and herself a distinguished educator.

The young woman who started the work was Charlotte Hawkins, known after her marriage in 1911 as Charlotte Hawkins Brown. She was born in Henderson, North Carolina, but in her early years was taken by her people to Massachusetts, and, after attending public schools in Cambridge, was in 1901 graduated from the State Normal School in Salem. She decided not to remain in the North but to cast in her lot with her people in the South, and conceived the idea of a "farm-life" school, one that would be a genuine cultural center, intimately connected with the life of the people for miles around.

With such an aim the young teacher began to work, organizing her school out of the remnants of a church congregation. Some friends in Cambridge sent barrels of goods, and the next summer she appeared at the resorts in Massachusetts, giving readings from Dunbar and having a few students with her to sing spirituals. Thus it was that she raised her first hundred dollars. One of those interested at the beginning was Mrs. Palmer; but that noble spirit soon passed, and then some of her friends resolved to assist in the work. A Sedalia Club was organized in Boston; the board of trustees began work in 1903; a local Congregational minister gave fifteen acres of land; and some New York people who had a hunting lodge near by also began to help. Then came two great boons. Mr. and Mrs. C. S. Guthrie, of New York, undertook to finance the school for a year, and a large farm was purchased by Miss Helen Kimball, of Brookline. Part of the land was given to the school outright, and part was sold for homes of the patrons in the community. It was a red-letter day in the history of the school when three ladies from Boston and Brookline, representing the Sedalia Club, came for a visit. One was Mrs. Charles Talmage, a sister of Mrs. Palmer. Later Professor George Herbert Palmer came also.

On a cold night in December, 1917, there was a disastrous fire, but in the end this opened the way to larger things. Edward Wharton, a prominent banker of Greensboro, chairman of the board of trustees, helped to organize a meeting; the principal of the school spoke; and in the evening she returned to her work with a thousand dollars in cash and pledges to the amount of ten thousand—all a token of the interest of Southern friends. Julius Rosenwald began to make contributions for maintenance, and in 1920 Alice Freeman Palmer Hall was erected at a cost of a hundred and fifty thousand dollars.

Meanwhile the principal herself was making her impress on the state and the country. She bristled with energy, was effective in public address, and somehow inspired confidence with her audacity. One year she was away completing the work for a college degree at Wellesley; and she studied also in the Harvard Summer School, at Simmons College, and Chicago. She became president of the North Carolina Federation of Colored Women's Clubs, and was a leading spirit in the movement for a home for delinquent Negro girls. Livingstone, Wilberforce, and the North Carolina College for Negroes conferred upon her honorary degrees.

To-day the school is known far and near for its alertness and precision. It has come a long way from the beginning, and the equipment is beyond anything dreamed of at first; but the spirit is still the same, that of helpfulness and good cheer—the spirit of the founder and teacher, Charlotte Hawkins Brown.

MARY MCLEOD BETHUNE

Mary McLeod was born on a little cotton and rice farm about three miles from Mayesville, South Carolina, the daughter of Samuel and Patsy McLeod. She attended a little mission school in Mayesville, and was converted at the age of twelve. Later she was graduated at Scotia Seminary, Concord, North Carolina, and then went to the Moody Bible Institute in Chicago. In the years of her schooling she received assistance from a scholarship given by Miss Mary Chrisman, a dressmaker of Denver, Colorado; and she was deeply impressed by the fact that the help came from a working woman. Some day she intended to justify that earnest woman's faith.

Having left Chicago, Miss McLeod taught for a while with Miss Lucy Laney at Haines Institute. She then taught for two years in Sumter, South Carolina, where she was married to Albert Bethune. After a brief stay in Savannah, where her son was born, she went to Palatka, Florida, to work in a mission school. There she remained five years— five hard years of praying, of waiting, and hope deferred; but through them all the lonely worker never lost her faith either in herself or God. She gained further experience, sang in the churches of the town, broadened her acquaintance in the state, assisted any forward movement she could; and all the while she knew that the great task was yet to come.

By the autumn of 1904 the call was definite. Going over to Daytona on the East Coast, with five little girls by her side and only a dollar and a half in capital, in a rented cabin, Mrs. Bethune began to work. The site was that of an old dumping ground. By means of concerts and festivals the first payment of five dollars was made, and with their own hands the teacher and pupils cleared away much of the rubbish. In 1905 the board of trustees was organized, some of the members being men of means who spent their winters in Florida; and a charter was taken out for the Daytona Normal and Industrial Institute for Negro Girls. Two years later Faith Hall, a four-story frame house, forty by fifty feet, was "prayed up, sung up, and talked up." In March, 1918, a spacious auditorium was dedicated, and among those who spoke on the occasion were the Governor of Florida and the Vice-President of the United States. Other blessings followed, and in 1923 the school was taken under the auspices of the Board of Education for Negroes of the Methodist Episcopal Church, Cookman Institute being merged with it. Henceforth the name was Bethune-Cookman College. By 1935 there were on the grounds fourteen buildings worth much more than half a million dollars.

From the first the girls were trained in the virtues of the home, in thrift and cleanliness and self-help. "We notice strawberries are selling at fifty and sixty cents a quart," said a visitor, "and you have a splendid patch. Do you use them for your students or sell them?" "We never eat a quart when we can get fifty cents for them," was the reply. Yet for one interested in education few pictures could be more beautiful than that of the dining-room on a morning in midterm.

One of the most touching pieces of extension work was that begun in 1912 for the children in a turpentine camp not far away. There has also been effort in behalf of the boys and young men. In Florida, hotel life, a shifting tourist population, and a climate of unusual seductiveness, have all left their impress. In town after town one finds not a single center of wholesome recreation. Accordingly in Daytona, in 1913, on a lot near the school campus, one of the trustees, Mr. George S. Doane, erected a neat, commodious building to be used as a general reading-room and home for the Young Men's Christian Association.

Meanwhile the president of the institution was becoming a national figure. With a glowing personality, a pleasing voice, and a sense of humor, she has been one of the most popular speakers on the public platform. It has fallen to her to appear before many distinguished audiences and on many notable occasions, one of the most important being a great patriotic meeting in the Belasco Theatre in Washington in December, 1917. Naturally many institutions have honored her with their degrees.

Mrs. Bethune served from 1924 until 1928 as the presi-

MARY McLEOD BETHUNE

dent of the National Association of Colored Women's
Clubs. She has also served as president of the Florida State
Federation of Colored Women and the Southeastern
Federation, of the Florida State Teachers Association, and
of the National Association of Teachers in Colored Schools.
She led in establishing the home for delinquent Negro girls
in Ocala, and is a member and director of the Commission
on Interracial Co-operation, a member of the International
Council of the Women of the World, and of several other
boards. Recently she has led in organizing the National
Council of Negro Women, the aim of which is to bring
together all the national bodies that Negro women have
formed. In 1936 she became director of Negro Affairs
in the National Youth Administration, with headquarters
in Washington. For her general achievement she was in
1935 awarded the Spingarn Medal.

MAUDELLE BROWN BOUSFIELD

The first woman of Negro descent to become dean of
girls in a high school in Chicago, and the first to be appointed to a principalship in that city, was Mrs. Maudelle
Brown Bousfield.

Maudelle Brown was born in St. Louis, Missouri. Her
father, Charles H. Brown, was for more than fifty years a
teacher, chiefly in St. Louis; her mother, Arrena L. Tanner
before her marriage, was a cousin of Henry O. Tanner,
the painter. The life of the family was one of high thinking
but also plain living, for the father's salary was not large
and there were several children to be educated. The
daughter Maudelle helped whenever she could by increasing the load of her studies. After completing her preparatory work in St. Louis, she entered the University of
Illinois, where the precision of her scholarship and a rare
human quality in her personality won the good will of both

teachers and students. In 1906, after three years of work, she received the Bachelor of Arts degree. Later she received the Master of Arts degree at the University of Chicago and was graduated at the Mendelssohn Conservatory of Music.

In the earlier years of her career Miss Brown was a teacher of mathematics in high schools in Baltimore and St. Louis. In 1914 she was married to Dr. Midian O. Bousfield, of Chicago, and the care needed by a little daughter kept her close to her home for eight years. In 1922 she returned to the classroom as a teacher at the Wendell Phillips High School. The enthusiasm she created for a subject often avoided by young people directed attention to the personal element in her teaching and her ability to enlist the coöperation of students for their own mental discipline. In 1926, when the school needed a dean of girls, Mrs. Bousfield was appointed to the position, and now her tact, ready sympathy, and social insight found full play. She had to adjust the personal problems and supervise the extracurricular activities not only of Negro students, many of whom were but recently from the South, but also of those of other races, some with widely different heritage and background. In 1928 she became principal of the Keith School, and in 1931 of the Stephen A. Douglas School.

Mrs. Bousfield came into prominence just as the country was entering upon some of the most critical years in its economic history. She has had to be alert to innumerable situations arising in the life of her students and of the great city in which she has been called to labor. At the same time she is active in educational and musical organizations. There is nothing spectacular about her work, but instead, emphasis on fundamental virtues. She has shown, even in a crowded profession, that if one has diligence, culture, and social vision, all things are possible.

40

American Ideals and the Negro

High over the portal of the new Supreme Court building in Washington is the motto, EQUAL JUSTICE UNDER LAW. The Declaration of Independence says: "We hold these truths to be self-evident: That all men are created equal; that they are endowed by their Creator with certain inalienable rights; that among these are life, liberty, and the pursuit of happiness." The Fifteenth Amendment to the Constitution of the United States reads: "The right of citizens of the United States to vote shall not be denied or abridged by the United States, or by any State, on account of race, color, or previous condition of servitude."

As regards the Negro these provisions have been singularly violated. Three things more than others have affected his citizenship. The first is the series of disfranchising acts in the Southern states. In 1915 the Supreme Court of the United States made a notable decision as to the law in Oklahoma, reaffirming the validity of the Fifteenth Amendment; but the real barriers to voting have not yet been removed. The second matter is that of the crime of lynching. Not all the victims of mobs have been Negroes, but most of them have been black men, and it is the Negro people who have been most affected. It has been made possible for Federal officials to deal with kidnapping; yet even in the most flagrant instances of lynching, and when state lines have been crossed, the National Government has refused to interfere. The third matter is that of segregation, and this includes every other—all the injustice in court, the unequal traveling facilities, and the inadequate provision for paving and lighting streets and for education.

Important as is proscription, and far-reaching as it is in the daily life of the Negro people, there is one matter to them of even more consequence, and that is lynching. The reason is that this crime is an outrage not only to a human being but to humanity itself. With it men lose the gains of centuries and relapse in a moment to savagery. The Federal Government insists that it is the problem of the individual state, but that the states have failed to handle the situation is obvious. Even in the present enlightened age, in the years 1930-1935, nearly one hundred persons in the United States died at the hands of mobs.

Fortunately there is basis for hope. The Southern press is far more united in opposing the evil than it was thirty years ago. The Commission on Interracial Coöperation and the Association of Southern Women for the Prevention of Lynching have both worked and are working effectively. One must remember that with this as with any social evil there are underlying forces with which we have to reckon. To understand the background against which a lynching occurs, we must take account of the narrow and thwarted lives of the people in small towns and rural communities—their scanty reward for their labor, their lack of opportunity for culture, and their provincial outlook. It was this phase of the matter that led the editor of the *Chat-*

tanooga News to say (May 6, 1936): "We must learn that cornpone and sorghum, as a diet, do not nurture aesthetic souls. Hookworm and malaria do not produce culture. Share-cropping and tenant farming, the form of slavery which we exchanged for chattel slavery, does not make sensitive, cultured citizens of its victims." The share-croppers in Arkansas, we were shown, have an average income of $212 a family a year. This figure includes an advance for "furnishing"—for cornmeal, flour, and pork, charged at the highest prices and at a high rate of interest. The average in cash, when such debts are cleared, is $50. These are the people who toil month after month, year after year, with an outlook more and more hopeless. When for weeks they have been denied wholesome recreation or amusement, and their rage one day seeks an outlet, their hatred turns upon the nearest defenseless object at hand, often a Negro unjustly accused; and a lynching is the result.

The welfare of the Negro is thus bound up with that of all the handicapped or struggling people in the United States. It is as true to-day as when Booker T. Washington spoke, that "one of the most vital questions that touch our American life is how to bring the strong, wealthy, and learned into helpful contact with the poorest, most ignorant, and humble, and at the same time make the one appreciate the vitalizing, strengthening influence of the other."

As for the Negro people themselves, they can only take advantage of every opportunity that is offered. The foregoing pages have told of some of those who have succeeded in spite of difficulty. Elliott spoke for his people in Congress, Dunbar wrote poems that have lived, and Henson went with Peary to the Pole. More recently young Negroes have brought to their country Olympic crowns.

This, however, is not the whole story. Daily, in an obscure village, there is a brave or generous deed; sometimes an humble man in a moment becomes a hero.

In the summer of 1935, in the city of Washington, lived Sterling Calhoun, thirty-two years of age. He had a wife and three children, and food was often scarce in his little home. One day, while fishing in the Anacostia River, he heard Mary Kerns, a white girl of fourteen, calling for help. She was trying to rescue her younger brother, who had waded into deep water. Calhoun tore off his shoes, shouted to a boy in a rowboat, and swam toward the two children. Before he could reach the girl, she disappeared; then he too sank in the stream, when the rowboat was but fifteen yards away. That was all, but not all for the city of Washington. The sacrifice impressed the capital profoundly. Two newspapers and a chain of theatres accepted contributions for Calhoun's family. He himself received honor in burial; later the Carnegie Hero Fund Commission took note of the deed.

What this man did could be multiplied many times. Hundreds of helping hands, white and black, have reached across the color line. Thousands of Negro men have died for their country in battle. In view of the record, their people hope for fair dealing, especially in the courts. Less than this they should not expect; more than this they do not want. In the words of Joseph B. Foraker, "They ask no favors because they are Negroes, but only justice because they are men."

BIBLIOGRAPHICAL NOTES

I. GENERAL REFERENCES

Biographical Directory of the American Congress, 1774-1927.
Washington, United States Government Printing Office,
1928.
Dictionary of American Biography. 20 vols. New York,
Charles Scribner's Sons, 1928-1936.
Early Negro American Writers. Edited with biographical and
critical introductions by Benjamin Brawley. Chapel Hill,
The University of North Carolina Press, 1935.
Homespun Heroines. Compiled and edited by Hallie Q.
Brown. Xenia, Ohio, The Aldine Publishing Company, 1926.
In Spite of Handicaps. By Ralph W. Bullock, with Foreword
by Channing H. Tobias. New York, Association Press, 1927.
In the Vanguard of a Race. By L. H. Hammond. New York,
Council of Women for Home Missions, 1922.
Masterpieces of Negro Eloquence. Edited by Alice Dunbar
Nelson. New York, The Bookery Publishing Company,
1914.
Men of Mark. By William J. Simmons. Cleveland, George
M. Rewell and Company, 1887, 1891.
Men of Maryland. By George F. Bragg. Baltimore, Church
Advocate Press, 1914, 1925.
National Cyclopedia of the Colored Race, The. Edited by

Clement Richardson. Montgomery, The National Publishing Company, 1919.

Negro Author, The. By Vernon Loggins. New York, Columbia Press, 1931.

Negro Genius, The, a new appraisal of the achievement of the American Negro in literature and the fine arts. By Benjamin Brawley. New York, Dodd, Mead & Company, 1937.

Negro in American History, The. By John W. Cromwell. Washington, The American Negro Academy, 1914.

Negro Orators and Their Orations. Edited by Carter G. Woodson. Washington, The Associated Publishers, 1926.

Negro Year Book, The. Edited by Monroe N. Work. Eighth Edition, 1931-32. Tuskegee, Ala., Tuskegee Institute, 1931.

Portraits in Color. By Mary White Ovington. New York, The Viking Press, 1927.

Twentieth Century Negro Literature. Edited by D. W. Culp. Naperville, Ill., J. L. Nichols & Company, 1902.

Who's Who in America. Vol. I (1899-1900)—Vol. XVIII (1934-1935). Chicago, The A. N. Marquis Company, 1899-1934.

Who's Who in Colored America, 1928-1929. New York, 1929; *1930-31-32,* Brooklyn, 1933.

Who's Who in the Colored Race. Chicago, 1915.

II. SPECIAL REFERENCES FOR DIFFERENT SECTIONS

SECTIONS 1 AND 2, AFRICA AND THE SLAVE TRADE

The story of the *Zong* has been told more than once, but note Frank J. Klingberg: *The Anti-Slavery Movement in England* (New Haven, Yale University Press, 1926), p. 59; and for both it and the story of Amboe Robin John, see John R. Spears: *The American Slave-Trade* (New York, Charles Scribner's Sons, 1900).

SECTION 3, CRISPUS ATTUCKS

See article in *Dictionary of American Biography;* also *A Memorial of Crispus Attucks, Samuel Maverick, James Caldwell,*

Samuel Gray, and Patrick Carr, Printed by Order of the City Council (Boston, 1889); and, most important of all, the exhaustive study by John Fiske in *Unpublished Orations* (Boston, The Bibliophile Society, 1909).

SECTION 4, PHILLIS WHEATLEY

For full bibliographical study see Benjamin Brawley: *The Negro in Literature and Art* (New York, Dodd, Mead & Company, 1929), pp. 219-21; and *idem, Early Negro American Writers* (Chapel Hill, U. of N. C. Press, 1935), pp. 34-36; also C. F. Heartman: *Phillis Wheatley, A Critical Attempt and a Bibliography of Her Writings* (New York, 1915).

SECTION 5, BENJAMIN BANNEKER

See Brawley: *Early Negro American Writers*, pp. 77-79, for review of the extensive literature.

SECTION 6, RICHARD ALLEN

Note biography by Charles H. Wesley: *Richard Allen, Apostle of Freedom* (Washington, Associated Publishers, 1935); also Brawley: *Early Negro American Writers*, pp. 87-95.

SECTION 7, PAUL CUFFE

See *Memoir of Capt. Paul Cuffe* (York, Eng., 1812); Peter Williams: *Discourse Delivered on the Death of Capt. Paul Cuffe* (1817); and H. N. Sherwood: "Paul Cuffe," *Journal of Negro History*, VIII (April, 1923), 153-232.

SECTION 8, INSURRECTIONISTS

For full study of the literature see the author's *Social History of the American Negro* (New York, Macmillan, 1921), pp. 405-7. Especially note the following original sources. For Denmark Vesey, see Lionel H. Kennedy and Thomas Parker: *An Official Report of the Trials of Sundry Negroes* (Charleston, 1822); and *An Account of the Late Intended Insurrection among a portion of the Blacks of this City*, published by the Authority of the Corporation of Charleston (Charleston, 1822). For Nat Turner, see *The Confessions of Nat Turner* (1831); and *Horrid Massacre: Authentic and Impartial Narrative of the Tragical Scene which was witnessed in Southampton County on Monday the 22nd of August last* (New York, 1831).

SECTION 9, JOHN CHAVIS

Many articles have been written; one of the best is Stephen B. Weeks: "John Chavis: Antebellum Negro Preacher and Teacher," *Southern Workman*, XLIII (February, 1914), 101-6. All evidence is reviewed in Edgar W. Knight: "Notes on John Chavis," *North Carolina Historical Review*, VII (July, 1930), 326-45. There is also a book by G. C. Shaw: *John Chavis, 1763-1838*, but this is hardly in best form and adds little to what is contained in articles previously published.

SECTION 10, THE AMISTAD CASE

See *Argument of John Quincy Adams before the Supreme Court of the United States* (in the case of the United States, Appellants, vs. Cinque, and others, Africans, captured in the schooner *Amistad*, by Lieut. Gedney) delivered on the 24th of February and 1st of March, 1841 (New York, 1841); also *Africans Taken in the "Amistad."* Document No. 185 of the 1st session of the 26th Congress, containing the correspondence in relation to the captured Africans (New York, Reprinted by Anti-Slavery Depository, 1840).

SECTION 11, FREDERICK DOUGLASS

There is now considerable Douglass literature, but the speeches of the orator are as yet uncollected. For list of references, and special selections, see Brawley: *Early Negro American Writers*, pp. 175-215. Several speeches are in Carter G. Woodson: *Negro Orators and Their Orations*.

SECTION 12, HARRIET TUBMAN

See Sarah H. Bradford: *Harriet, the Moses of Her People* (New York, 1886, 1901); and Hallie Q. Brown: *Homespun Heroines*, pp. 55-68.

SECTION 13, SOJOURNER TRUTH

See Olive Gilbert: *Narrative of Sojourner Truth* (Boston, 1875; Battle Creek, 1884); also Arthur Huff Fauset's article in *Enquirer and Evening News* (Battle Creek, Mich.), Sunday, November 26, 1933. Mr. Fauset has a biography forthcoming.

SECTION 14, JOHN JASPER

See news article "Rev. John Jasper Died Yesterday," in *The Times* (Richmond, Va.), Sunday, March 31, 1901, and editorial in the same issue; also article "Jasper's Body Lies in State," in the issue for Thursday, April 4, 1901, the day of the funeral; and William E. Hatcher: *John Jasper: The Unmatched Negro Philosopher and Preacher* (New York, Fleming H. Revell, 1908).

SECTION 15, MARTIN R. DELANY

Aside from Delany's own works cited in text and the list in Vernon Loggins: *The Negro Author* (New York, Columbia University Press, 1931), note Frank A. Rollin (Frances E. Rollin Whipper): *Life and Public Services of Martin R. Delany* (1883).

SECTION 16, DANIEL A. PAYNE

See bibliographical study and poems in Brawley: *Early Negro American Writers*, pp. 147-59; also note Josephus R. Coan: *Daniel Alexander Payne: Christian Educator* (Philadelphia, A. M. E. Book Concern, 1935). The author has a brief biography of Payne forthcoming through the University of North Carolina Press.

Sections 17 and 18, Fifty-fourth Massachusetts and Fort Wagner

The literature is now considerable, but note especially Luis F. Emilio: *History of the Fifty-fourth Regiment of Massachusetts Volunteer Infantry* (publisher's title "A Brave Black Regiment") (Boston, 1891); Norwood P. Hallowell: *The Negro as a Soldier in the War of the Rebellion* (Boston, 1897); Henry Greenleaf Pearson: *The Life of John A. Andrew.* 2 vols. (Boston, Houghton Mifflin Company, 1904); Thomas Wentworth Higginson: *Harvard Memorial Biographies* (Cambridge, 1867), II, 172-98, this being sketch of Robert Gould Shaw contributed by his mother, Sarah B. Shaw; also *Memorial, R G S* (Cambridge, 1864); and *Exercises of the Dedication of the Monument to Colonel Robert Gould Shaw and the Fifty-fourth Regiment, May 31, 1897* (Boston, 1897).

Section 19, The Negro in Congress

See *Biographical Directory of the American Congress;* William J. Simmons: *Men of Mark.* For Revels, see *Dictionary of American Biography;* also Alrutheus A. Taylor: "Negro Congressmen a Generation Later," *Journal of Negro History*, VII (April, 1922), 127-71.

Section 20, Blanche K. Bruce

See *Biographical Directory of the American Congress;* Simmons: *Men of Mark;* the *Evening Star* (Washington), March 17, 1898; John W. Cromwell: *The Negro in American History;* G. David Houston: "A Negro Senator," *Journal of Negro History*, VII (July, 1922), No. 3; and Carter G. Woodson: sketch of Blanche K. Bruce in *Dictionary of American Biography*.

Section 21, Robert B. Elliott

See *Biographical Directory of the American Congress;* Simmons: *Men of Mark* (quoting eulogy by D. Augustus Straker);

D. Augustus Straker: *A Trip to the Windward Islands* (Detroit, 1896), pp. 65-67; and Cromwell: *The Negro in American History*. Straker, a law partner of Elliott in South Carolina, is important as settling the disputed point as to place of birth.

SECTION 22, JOHN M. LANGSTON

See *Biographical Directory of the American Congress;* the *Evening Star* (Washington), November 16, 1897; Cromwell, *The Negro in American History;* sketch in *Dictionary of American Biography;* and especially Langston's own books, *Freedom and Citizenship* (with Introductory Sketch by Rev. J. E. Rankin) (Washington, 1883), and *From the Virginia Plantation to the National Capitol* (Hartford, 1894).

SECTION 23, BOOKER T. WASHINGTON

See autobiography *Up from Slavery* (New York, Doubleday, 1901); *Selected Speeches*, edited by E. Davidson Washington (Garden City, Doubleday, 1932); the various references in Loggins: *The Negro Author;* W. E. B. DuBois: *The Souls of Black Folk* (Chicago, McClurg, 1903), pp. 41-59; and Charles S. Johnson: "The Social Philosophy of Booker T. Washington," *Opportunity*, April, 1928.

SECTION 24, PAUL LAURENCE DUNBAR

A recent biography, *Paul Laurence Dunbar: Poet of His People*, by Benjamin Brawley (Chapel Hill, U. of N. C. Press, 1936), endeavors in an Appendix to cover all available literature.

SECTION 25, CHARLES YOUNG

A Biography of Colonel Charles Young prepared by Abraham Chew (Washington, 1923), is a pamphlet including brief life sketch, official record, addresses, clippings, program of service at Arlington, and account in the *Evening Star* (Washington), June 1, 1923.

SECTION 26, MATTHEW A. HENSON

See Matthew A. Henson: *A Negro Explorer at the North Pole*, with a Foreword by Robert E. Peary and an Introduction by Booker T. Washington (New York, Stokes, 1912); also Robert E. Peary: *The North Pole* (New York, Stokes, 1910); and Matthew A. Henson, "The Negro at the North Pole," *World's Work*, XIX (April, 1910), 12825-37, this being splendidly illustrated; article in *Literary Digest*, XLIV (March 16, 1912), 551, this being a full review of Henson's book; and article in *Liberty Magazine*, July 17, 1926.

SECTION 27, JOHN MERRICK

Note R. McCants Andrews: *John Merrick: A Biographical Sketch* (Durham, 1926); but much in the chapter is based on first-hand information.

SECTION 28, W. E. BURGHARDT DuBois

Note that *The Souls of Black Folk* contains several chapters in subjective vein, and that *Darkwater* (New York, Harcourt, 1920), has as its first chapter "The Shadow of Years," an autobiographical sketch. See also Mary White Ovington: *Portraits in Color*, and Benjamin Brawley: *The Negro Genius*.

SECTION 29, HEROES OF THE WORLD WAR

See Emmett J. Scott: *The American Negro in the World War* (Chicago, 1919); Charles H. Williams: *Sidelights on Negro Soldiers* (Boston, 1923); Arthur W. Little: *From Harlem to the Rhine* (New York, Covici-Friede, 1936); and Monroe N. Work, ed.: *The Negro Year Book, 1931-32*, pp. 331-33.

SECTION 30, LEADERS IN RELIGIOUS WORK

Information is widely scattered, but ordinary reference books will help to some extent. Articles on Cary, Holly, Holsey, and Hood in *Dictionary of American Biography* were written by the author of the present work. For Crummell, see Brawley: *Early Negro American Writers* and special chapter in DuBois: *The Souls of Black Folk*. For both Garnet and Crummell, see Cromwell: *The Negro in American History*. For Holly, Hood, Simmons, and Crummell, see Loggins: *The Negro Author*. In general, note Carter G. Woodson: *The Negro Church* (Washington, 1921); George F. Bragg: *Men of Maryland*, and *History of the Afro-American Group of the Episcopal Church* (Baltimore, 1922); and Miles Mark Fisher: *A Short History of the Baptist Denomination* (Nashville, Sunday School Publishing Board, 1933). Fisher has a biography of Lott Cary forthcoming. See also Willis N. Huggins: "The Catholic Church and the Negro," *Opportunity*, September, 1932.

SECTION 31, LEADERS IN EDUCATION

Sketches of Hope and Johnson are written from first-hand information, but note that Johnson's speech, "The Faith of the American Negro," is in *Crisis*, August, 1922, and in Woodson: *Negro Orators and Their Orations*. Sketches of Hope are in Ralph W. Bullock: *In Spite of Handicaps*, and in Charles S. Johnson: *A Preface to Racial Understanding* (New York, Friendship Press, 1936). Sketches of Johnson are in Bullock: *In Spite of Handicaps* and in Mary White Ovington: *Portraits in Color;* note also Anne Biddle Stirling: "Mordecai Johnson: An Impression," *Opportunity*, March, 1927. For Moton note autobiography, *Finding a Way Out* (New York, Doubleday, 1920); sketches in Ovington: *Portraits in Color* and in L. H. Hammond: *In the Vanguard of a Race;* and numerous articles in *Southern Workman*, especially N. C. Newbold: "Dr. Moton in North Carolina," *Southern Workman*, June, 1921; Robert R. Moton: "A New Business Program," *Southern Workman*, October, 1922; Benjamin F. Hubert: "Robert R. Moton as I Know Him," *Southern Workman*, July, 1923; and G. Lake Imes: "The Harmon Award for Doctor Moton," *Southern Workman*, June, 1930.

SECTION 32, THE NEGRO IN THE PROFESSIONS

The advance of the Negro in Medicine is so largely a matter of recent years that comprehensive study of the subject is yet to be made. Any review at the moment must be largely original. As to Law, note Fitzhugh Lee Styles: *Negroes and the Law* (Boston, Christopher Publishing House, 1936).

SECTION 33, THE NEGRO IN LITERATURE

See, by the author of the present work, *The Negro Genius* and *Early Negro American Writers*. Also note Alain Locke, ed.: *The New Negro* (New York, A. & C. Boni, 1925); Elizabeth Lay Green: *The Negro in Contemporary American Literature* (Chapel Hill, U. of N. C. Press, 1928), being study outlines and bibliographies; *The Book of American Negro Poetry*, chosen and edited with an essay on the Negro's creative genius by James Weldon Johnson (New York, Harcourt, Brace & Company, 1922, 1931); Robert T. Kerlin: *Negro Poets and Their Poems* (Washington, Associated Publishers, 1923); *An Anthology of Verse by American Negroes*, edited by Newman Ivey White and Walter Clinton Jackson, with an Introduction by James Hardy Dillard (Durham, Duke University Press, 1924); Countee Cullen, ed.: *Caroling Dusk* (New York, Harper, 1927); *Readings from Negro Authors*, with a bibliography of Negro literature by Otelia Cromwell, Lorenzo Dow Turner, and Eva B. Dykes (New York, Harcourt, Brace & Company, 1931).

SECTION 34, MUSIC AND ART

As to music, note Brawley: *The Negro Genius;* James M. Trotter: *Music and Some Highly Musical People* (Boston, 1878); and Maud Cuney Hare: *Negro Musicians and Their Music* (Washington, Associated Publishers, 1936). As to painters and sculptors, all students of the subject have reason to be grateful for the series of pamphlets and catalogues issued by the Harmon Foundation, 140 Nassau St., New York, especially

Negro Artists: An Illustrated Review of Their Achievements (1935).

SECTION 35, SCIENCE AND INVENTION

For Just, see ordinary reference books and the sketch in Mary White Ovington: *Portraits in Color*. For Parsons, see *Opportunity*, February, 1928, p. 46. All later accounts of Negro inventors are based on the work of Henry E. Baker, who was for years an employee of the United States Patent Office and who issued through the Crisis Publishing Company a pamphlet, *The Colored Inventor*, and contributed "The Negro in the Field of Invention" to the *Journal of Negro History*, II, No. 1 (January, 1917).

SECTION 36, THE NEGRO IN SPORT

Note especially Charles H. Williams: "Negro Athletes in the Tenth Olympiad," *Southern Workman*, November, 1932, and "Negro Athletes in the Eleventh Olympiad," *Southern Workman*, February, 1937; Elmer A. Carter, "The Negro in College Athletics," *Opportunity*, July, 1933; and Roy Wilkins: "Negro Stars on Big Grid Teams," *Crisis*, December, 1936.

SECTION 37, THE NEGRO WOMAN IN AMERICAN LIFE

The chapter is indebted to some extent to the author's little book, *Women of Achievement* (1919). Note also on various points, the recent issues of Monroe N. Work: *The Negro Year Book*.

SECTION 38, MAGGIE L. WALKER

See *Maggie Lena Walker*, "A Testimonial of Love" (Richmond, Va., The St. Luke's Press, 1925); Wendell P. Dabney: "Maggie L. Walker: A Tribute to a Friend," *Opportunity*, July, 1935; also sketches in Mary White Ovington: *Portraits in Color*, and in L. H. Hammond: *In the Vanguard of a Race*, the author being indebted to the last for the quotation from Mrs. Walker.

Section 39, Women in Education

For Fanny Jackson Coppin, see that teacher's *Reminiscences of School Life, and Hints on Teaching* (Philadelphia, A. M. E. Book Concern, 1913); and Cromwell: *The Negro in American History*, pp. 213-18. For Maria L. Baldwin, see Hallie Q. Brown: *Homespun Heroines*, pp. 182-83; and *Boston Evening Transcript*, January 10, 1922 (account of death) and January 12, 1922 (funeral service and letter from Francis G. Peabody). For Lucy Laney, note news item in *Augusta Chronicle*, October 24, 1933, and editorial in *Augusta Chronicle*, October 25, 1933; also Mary Jackson McCrorey: "Lucy Laney," *Crisis*, June, 1934; sketch in Mary White Ovington: *Portraits in Color;* and sketch by A. C. Griggs in *Journal of Negro History*, XIX (January, 1934), 97-102. For Charlotte Hawkins Brown, see *Who's Who in Colored America;* Anna S. L. Brown: "Alice Freeman Palmer Memorial Institute," *Opportunity*, August, 1923; and sketch in Charles S. Johnson: *A Preface to Racial Understanding* (New York, Friendship Press, 1936), pp. 113-21. For Mary McLeod Bethune, see *Who's Who in Colored America;* also chapter in Brawley: *Women of Achievement;* and "Mrs. Bethune: Spingarn Medalist," *Crisis*, July, 1936. For Maudelle Brown Bousfield, see *Who's Who in Colored America;* and Charles S. Johnson: *A Preface to Racial Understanding*, pp. 131-34.

INDEX